GENERALS AT WAR

MAJOR-GENERAL SIR FRANCIS DE GUINGAND, K.B.E., C.B., D.S.O.

SAPERE
BOOKS

GENERALS AT WAR

Published by Sapere Books.
24 Trafalgar Road, Ilkley, LS29 8HH
United Kingdom

saperebooks.com

ISBN: 978-0-85495-175-8.

To
MARYLOU

TABLE OF CONTENTS

FOREWORD

Operation Victory was written very soon after the war ended and published while I was still a serving soldier. This imposed limitations on what I could say; there was much I would have liked to include, but I had to use discretion, one reason being that the book had to be approved by the War Office. However much water has flowed under the bridge since those days and material that had to be discarded then can now be used. In view of the manifold books that have appeared on the last war, I feel that what I have to say now can perhaps throw an entirely different light on subjects that I hope will prove of more than ordinary interest to the reader.

Criticism there has been in abundance and my book does state very candidly my own views on many famous — and not so famous — people, but I maintain that criticism if not governed by malice or self-interest should surely be voiced and I hope the public will appreciate that what I have to say cannot be so accused.

The connecting link in this book is the war and in considerable measure that fascinating character, my old wartime chief, Field-Marshal Montgomery. The intimate stories, told I believe for the first time, may well throw fresh light upon his true make-up, and show him as an entirely different person to the image held by so many at present. Field-Marshal Wavell, Eisenhower, Auchinleck and that controversial character, General 'Chink' Dorman-Smith, are dealt with at length. I don't expect every reader to agree with my comments but at least these comments are made with sincerity.

It is well known that old soldiers enjoy reminiscing about the past, too often, I'm afraid, at the expense of their suffering listeners. I hope, however, that this collection of both serious and light-hearted episodes will bring back treasured memories to many of my old comrades and remind them of those days we spent together.

War is a grim business, but in spite of it we had a lot of laughs. Keeping a sense of humour was an essential quality to help one stand the strain of years of war.

F. W. DE G.

PART ONE: WAVELL — A CRITICAL REASSESSMENT

INTRODUCTION

Like so many great soldiers and statesmen, Wavell created intense loyalties among his immediate entourage, who had an unswerving admiration for his skill as a strategist. Certainly at the beginning of the war Wavell's reputation in the army was already considerable. He had written a famous study of Allenby's highly mobile invasion of Palestine during the First World War, and in the early 1930s he had commanded the experimental motorized infantry brigade in manoeuvres on Salisbury Plain. When the French collapsed in June 1940, Wavell was Commander-in-Chief, Middle East — a job second only in importance to that of Chief of the Imperial General Staff. Would he justify his pre-war reputation?

By the close of that terrible year 1940 he seemed to the public in Great Britain like another Marlborough — a soldier whose flashing victories against Graziani in Libya and the Duke of Aosta in Italian East Africa proved that the British too could produce *blitzkriegs*. Despite the loss of Greece and Crete and Rommel's first successes in the Western Desert, and despite the disaster of Singapore while he was Supreme Commander of the A.D.B.A.,[1] Wavell has never lost his colossal 1940 reputation. He is perhaps the only great British soldier of the Second World War never to have his legend questioned by post-war criticism.

And yet was the Wavell of the war years really so marvellous a commander-in-chief? How far was the debacle in Greece due to his wrong judgement and advice, and how far to the political

---

[1] The Allied Commander in South-East Asia.

pressures? How far was our first defeat at Rommel's hands avoidable?

During Wavell's period of command in the Middle East I was a staff officer at G.H.Q., Cairo, a member of the Inter-service Joint Planning Staff. I, therefore, saw at close quarters how the vital decisions of the Mediterranean campaign in 1940-41 were reached, and the part Wavell played in them.

First-hand experience and post-war study convince me that the Wavell of the war years did not justify his vast reputation; that the time has come for a sober and balanced reassessment. This I now attempt.

CHAPTER ONE: THE DECISION TO INTERVENE IN GREECE

A few years ago I was in Southern Rhodesia, staying in the Salisbury Club, and happened to wander upstairs to the library to spend a relaxed half-hour or so. Glancing around the rows of books, I chanced to see one by General Collins entitled *Lord Wavell*. As I had never seen it before, I drew it from the shelf, settled down in a comfortable chair and started to scan its pages. Before long I came across the following passage which concerned the evacuation of the ill-fated expedition to Greece:

> The actual plan of evacuation produced an almost more difficult problem. The value of having sent on a staff officer to study from the outset just such an operation now made all the difference. Luckily, too, he had done a sterling piece of work and so good was it that it brought the officer's name to notice. He was Major de Guingand, later as a major-general to become Chief of Staff to Field-Marshal Viscount Montgomery. The only part of his plan which did not work was the suggested movement on a broad front to the Corinth Canal, over which the troops were to be ferried in caiques to be collected locally. Unfortunately, these were not forthcoming.
>
> (Page 385)

I was rather startled by what I read, because it was not factually correct. I then proceeded to read the other pages which dealt with this particular episode in the war, and I became more than ever disturbed. About two hours later I rose rather stiffly from my chair, more than somewhat bewildered, for I realized that the reader of this book would undoubtedly be left with the impression that Wavell was a truly great Commander. On reflection, it dawned on me that this was, in point of fact, the opinion held by the majority of our people, many of whom looked upon him as an almost legendary figure. This chance selection of a book to pass a few hours was the cause of this present study.

It was early in December 1940 that I left, to my great delight, the Staff College at Haifa, where I had been a 'teacher', to take up the appointment of G.1 on the Middle East Joint Planning Staff. Although this meant working mainly in Cairo, visits to various sectors of activity were not infrequent, and in any case it meant being nearer to the hub of things.

It was only a matter of days before the Western Desert Force attacked the Italian Army in its positions around Sidi Barrani. It was from this very campaign that Wavell gained so much prestige that he was able to survive a long list of defeats, disasters and unsound decisions which would have submerged any other British Commander.

For those who have forgotten these early days of the last great war, I shall describe briefly the situation in the Middle East and Africa at the time I arrived in Cairo, i.e. in December 1940. The Italians, under General Graziani, having crossed the Egyptian border, had halted about Sidi Barrani, and had constructed armed camps which were wired and dug-in. These stretched in an arc which ran south and then south-westwards. Sidi Barrani was described to the people of Italy, on their home radio news, as a modern town with its trams still running! It was, in fact, just a collection of mud huts in the desert. In the Sudan in early July the Italians had also advanced upon Kassala. Somaliland was being threatened and Wavell decided to accept the risk and keep a small garrison in the Colony.

General Collins in his account does his best to defend this decision, but nevertheless concludes, 'No one can get the right answer every time, and in this case and in the light of after events, it might have been better to have withdrawn.' By the end of August the Colony had to be abandoned; while most of the troops were evacuated to Aden, all transport and a great deal of equipment had to be left behind, and these we could ill afford to lose.

About the end of August 1940 Wavell asked General Platt, who was commanding in the Sudan, for 'an appreciation as to ways and means of invading Eritrea'. Later on in October he began to think of some offensive action against the Italians in the area of Sidi Barrani. Plans were made for arming the Abyssinians, in order that guerrilla operations could be carried out against the Italians garrisoned in this Colony, and Wingate was the man selected for this useful task. In November General Cunningham arrived in Nairobi to command the forces that were to drive the Italians out of the Negus' country. In addition there was a host of other problems that cropped up in Wavell's sphere of responsibility, such as the Italian invasion of Greece; the question of Turkey's attitude; and political problems in Egypt and elsewhere. There is no doubt that his task was fantastically difficult and his hands were very full.

We know now that Graziani's army was militarily worth little, and that Cunningham in East Africa was to have nothing much more difficult than a long car journey to get to Addis Ababa. However at the time neither Wavell nor any other commander knew this; Graziani had done well in Abyssinia before the war, and Fascism was supposed to have toughened up the Italian Army. Indeed the Italians fought very bravely against Platt at Keren in Eritrea; we were lucky the other Italian armies were not so good. Wavell's Middle East forces were only a fraction of the enemy's in number, and short of all kinds of equipment. The great Middle East base in Egypt — workshops, dumps, camps — that Auchinleck and Alexander enjoyed had only just been begun by Wavell. Sidi Barrani, Nairobi and the Sudan were separated by hundreds of miles of bad or non-existent communications. Wavell had to juggle his small strategic reserve between these theatres. No later Commander-in-Chief in the Middle East had so many problems and so few resources.

The Command set-up in the desert at that time must be understood. General Dick O'Connor, a most able soldier, was commanding the Western Desert Force. Behind him sat General 'Jumbo' Wilson whose official appointment was G.O.C.-in-C. B.T.E., and behind him again was the Commander-in-Chief — Wavell. In so far as the attack on the Italians was concerned, however, O'Connor corresponded to Montgomery, and Wavell to Alexander, in terms of the Battle of El Alamein. It was Wavell who directed that the operation should take place and approved the plans, and G.H.Q. Middle East was heavily involved on the administrative and equipment side. But it was O'Connor, assisted where necessary by Wilson and his Headquarters, who planned and carried out the attack. It is very doubtful, however, whether B.T.E.'s role on this occasion was really necessary. It was O'Connor's plan of a single stroke against the Italian centre that was carried out in preference to Wavell's own original idea of twin attacks on the Italian flanks.

Wavell's strategy was to neutralize Graziani's threat to Egypt by a major raid that would badly damage the Italians, after which a large part of the striking force, the 4th Indian Division, would be sent to Platt for use against Eritrea. In terms of space and time and sparse resources, this was clever strategy.

However, Wavell never foresaw the enormous possibilities of a great victory in the desert — the chances of utterly destroying the Italians in North Africa.

To start with, Wavell had never anticipated that the first operation at Sidi Barrani would be so successful, and it is almost true to say that the later successes of the Western Desert Force were achieved *against* C.-in-C. Middle East's intentions and advice. General Collins writes quite frankly about all this in his book. He quotes an extract from a cypher cable sent by Wavell to London on the eve of the battle, in which the C.-in-C. described it as 'nothing more than a major raid'. I can substantiate this narrow conception of the possibilities from personal knowledge. After two weeks or more of tremendous successes, Wavell was taking Admiral Cunningham (C.-in-C., Med.), around the War Room in G.H.Q., Cairo, and several of us were following in their wake. During a pause Wavell turned to the Naval C.-in-C. and said, 'You know, I never thought it would ever go like this.' This is, however, a good illustration of Wavell's basic honesty. Then I remember the papers that the Joint Planning Staff hastily wrote on possible future phases of the campaign. Our B.G.S. Operations, Jock Whiteley, used to come along to our office and discuss the next appreciation to be made. There were papers on the problems of the capture of Bardia, then Tobruk, Derna and finally Benghazi. Wavell's reception of these papers, or even their objects, was cool, to say the least, but O'Connor through his forceful leadership usually made up Wavell's mind for him by producing a *fait accompli*, and more often than not had started on the next phase before the J.P.S. had completed its studies! It seems as though Wavell was reluctant to be drawn deep into the Libyan campaign because of his other projects in Italian East Africa. Yet with the clear opportunity of a colossal victory on the Mediterranean shore, opening up an eventual route to Sicily and Italy, Wavell was surely both rigid and ill-judged in keeping to his original three-point strategy.

When O'Connor was forming up for the attack against Bardia, 'Wavell took a somewhat serious view of this advance...' And this prompted him to make his first visit to the victorious Desert Force — *nearly three weeks* after the commencement of the attack. It seems strange that Wavell should have sat back in Cairo for so long, if he had really been the 'directing brain *throughout*', as General Collins put it in his book.

Alexander was always coming up to the Eighth Army to see whether he could be of any help and to discuss plans with Montgomery. However, it must be acknowledged that the area of the Middle East Command was much greater under Wavell, and he may have felt it necessary to remain at the centre of things, in Cairo.

The victories in the desert were of course spectacular, despite the fact that they were earned at the expense of the Italians whose morale was low — the people were not really enthusiastic about Hitler's war — and whose arms and equipment were terribly inadequate, but the heartening news was just the tonic required by the British public, who had been made to swallow a series of unpleasant pills since the end of the 'phoney' war. There had been Dunkirk and the initial Italian successes in Somaliland, the Sudan and the Western Desert; there had also been the heavy air attacks against Britain and our losses at sea. It was not surprising, therefore, that Wavell was acclaimed the victor, for the other commanders responsible were virtually unknown to the people. It was this tremendous store of prestige, and the reputation gained from the Italian defeats, that stood him in such good stead during the coming months of failure and disaster. Whereas any other general would have passed into oblivion, Wavell was saved this fate and was spared for tasks far removed from the tangled arena of the Middle East.

I now come to the Greek episode, which proved such a disaster and which very nearly put paid to our whole position in the Middle East.

When writing my account of the Greek disaster,[2] shortly after the end of the war, I felt very bitter about the way the politicians had forced the intervention issue when the odds were so heavily loaded against success. In particular, I criticized Anthony Eden, at that time Secretary of State for War; for he took part in the vital negotiations that were held in Athens in February 1941. As the years pass by one is often able to assess the lessons of history more fairly, and I now hold the very definite conviction that the main blame must be placed upon Wavell because he failed to stand up to political pressure when he should have done. Of one thing I am certain, there would never have been an expedition to Greece, had Alexander, Montgomery or Slim been in Wavell's place during that critical phase of the war. Wavell gave it as his professional opinion that the project had every hope of success, and, therefore, Eden cannot really be blamed for acting on this advice. But to this day I cannot see any sound military reason for Wavell acting as he did, and, what is more, the disaster might have been far worse had not certain officers acted contrary to his orders.

There are three passages in General Collins's book which give the reader the impression that Wavell had, in the early stages, contemplated the probability of evacuation, and had

---

[2] *Operation Victory.*

specifically given the Joint Planning Staff the task of preparing plans in case such an operation ever became necessary. They also suggest that he took me over with him on one of his visits to Greece, in order that, in the event of evacuation being decided on, no time would be lost in putting the plan into effect. I shall quote the extracts in question after describing the facts as I know them, and show how misleading these statements were. For it was virtually *against* Wavell's orders, and in spite of his opposition, that the vital studies and preparations for the inevitable move out of Greece were available when required.

During the winter of 1940-41, it became reasonably clear that Germany was making preparations to invade and occupy Greece. By our treaty of alliance we were in honour bound to go to her help, if she asked for assistance. General Metaxas, the Prime Minister, was, however, a realist, and he made it quite clear early on that unless our help could be in sufficient strength to be effective, then he did not want it. In January 1941, having assessed all the circumstances, he formally declined this British offer of assistance. But Metaxas died at the end of January, and a change in the Greek attitude then became apparent. The new Prime Minister and General Papagos, the Commander-in-Chief, who had achieved such success against the Italians in Albania, once again raised the question of possible British aid to Greece, in view of the impending German attack. This change of heart was no doubt partly due to the spectacular victories which the British had gained in Cyrenaica. But the fundamental and governing factors of this whole problem were: first, had we adequate resources available for the task, and secondly, would they arrive at the right place in time. It was really as simple as all that. And it is in his assessment of the *military* problems involved that I consider Wavell failed so badly.

I would not deny that it is the Commander-in-Chief who has to make the final decision, for it is he who must shoulder the responsibility. But he should, as a matter of course, consult his staff and not cast aside their advice too lightly. It is my recollection that the advice Wavell received was almost unanimously against this expedition. I know the anxiety and almost amazement that was shared by the Intelligence and Operations branches of the Staff; while the Navy and Air Force were equally apprehensive regarding any decision in favour of sending an expeditionary force to Greece. I would go so far as to claim that any young staff officer of average intelligence would, without any hesitation, have reached the conclusion that the project was in every way an unsound military operation. Brigadier Shearer, Director of Military Intelligence M.E., wrote a very able and forthright paper showing the enormous dangers involved, but it came back from Wavell with the following written in his own hand across the top:

'"War is an option of difficulties" — Wolfe A.P.W.!'

The J.P.S. was busy working out plans for a further advance to Tripoli and we viewed a diversion of our limited resources to Greece as missing the chance of cleaning up the whole of North Africa, as well as the probability of a satisfactory link-up with the French. After the war, General Dick O'Connor confirmed this opinion in a letter he wrote to me. He held the view, at the time he was commanding the Western Desert Force, that the capture of Tripoli was then a feasible operation, provided of course that he was not denuded of his resources.

But Wavell appeared to be unmoved by this solid body of opinion. He had received a telegram from the Prime Minister saying that the capture of Benghazi 'confirms our previous directive, namely that your major effort must now be to aid Greece and/or Turkey. This rules out any serious effort against Tripoli…'

It seems clear that henceforward Wavell thought it was his duty to carry out this directive and try to make it work. Was this the conduct of a great general? His earlier opinion, as expressed to London, had been that our intervention could not save the Greeks from the German Army, while we had a fair chance of taking Tripoli. Surely a commander as fine as Wavell is supposed to have been, would have firmly told the Prime Minister that if he wished to proceed with the Greek expedition against his advice, he would resign his command. Or had Wavell changed his mind about the feasibility? As it was, after the arrival of Eden, the Secretary of State for War, and Dill, the C.I.G.S., events moved along the road to ultimate crisis.

As I have already described in *Operation Victory*, I was detailed to accompany Eden, Dill and Wavell to Greece for the momentous meeting with the Greek King, George, and his cabinet, which resulted in the British offer of help being accepted. But before recounting Wavell's part in this decision, I think it would be a suitable moment to set out briefly the principal pros and cons affecting the problem, as most of us saw it at that time.

CONS

(a) The resources available in the Middle East were already so meagre that there was a great danger that if so large a portion of our forces was sent to Greece, it might well be found impossible to fulfil our other commitments, such as the security of the M.E. base.

(b) The chance of capturing Tripoli and joining up with the French at a very favourable moment was thrown aside.

(c) An examination of the 'relative strengths' factor proved *beyond all doubt* that Germany would have a tremendous advantage over the Allies in Greece. The following were relevant points:

(i) The German air power was numerically and technically far superior to anything we could muster. The effect of the dive-bomber was not fully appreciated in high places at that time.

(ii) One of our armoured divisions had no tanks, and the other was weak, ill-armed and inexperienced.

(iii) The provision of another Headquarters with the necessary staff and signals was one of great difficulty.

(iv) The numerous routes of advance and the communications available to the enemy were so much more favourable than those available to us, that they would be able to beat us with ease in any race for the battle front.

(d) The communications available to us in Greece were terribly poor: indifferent roads and a narrow gauge railway. Once Salonika fell, which was an agreed certainty, they were totally inadequate for supplying both the Greek Army and our own expeditionary force.

(e) Our lines of communication from Egypt were highly vulnerable to submarine and air attack, and the Navy was already hard put to it in respect of shipping.

(f) The state of the Greek Army, both in respect of morale and equipment, was lamentable. The price paid for their victories over the Italians was there for all to see. I was left in no doubt of this myself after talking to Greek officers, visiting the army hospitals in Athens, and after a tour of the Albanian front. Colonel Salisbury-Jones,[3] who was serving in the British Mission, had an extremely clear appreciation of the general situation, and I believe the fact that he stuck to his guns

---

[3] Now Major-General Sir Guy Salisbury-Jones.

regarding the inadvisability of sending forces to Greece, unless certain conditions were fulfilled, did not help him in his subsequent military career. He was, however, an intelligent realist. Eventually he was appointed our Military attaché in Paris, where he served with distinction and later was appointed Marshal of the Diplomatic Corps in London.

PROS

(a) It has been held as justification in some quarters that we had to go to Greece because of our treaty obligation, but the whole issue rested upon our ability to defend Greece against a German invasion. The Greeks, as I shall explain, were never more than lukewarm.

(b) There were some who hoped that our intervention in Greece might bolster up Yugoslav resistance to a German advance. This was a very bad and ill-founded conclusion, for the knowledge of German strength and their ruthless methods gave scant reason for expecting major results in this direction.

(c) The possibility that our aid to Greece might bring Turkey in on our side was another point put forward. There was no evidence to support this view. Success was the only thing that would impress neutrals: any other approach was merely wishful-thinking.

(d) Some protagonists of the Greek adventure have claimed that it delayed Germany's attack upon Russia. Could there ever be such a specious argument? Russia was then Germany's ally, so how could this factor have ever been taken into account by us at the time? In any case, I hold that the end of the rains was the deciding factor as to the date Germany invaded Russia, and only nine divisions were employed in Greece, compared with the 150 used initially in the offensive against Russia. Also, it was Hitler's interference, more than anything else, that was responsible for Germany's failure to capture Moscow in 1941. For it will be remembered that he insisted on the withdrawal of divisions opposite Moscow for use in his thrust on the southern front, that finally met disaster in the area of the Caucasus.

I think it is important for the record that I describe the conference that I attended in the King's Palace at Tatoi, just outside Athens, on 22nd February, 1941. It began about 10 in the evening and went on till the small hours. In the vast and ornate conference room we sat round a long table. King George of the Hellenes, an Edwardian kind of monarch, not very knowledgeable but clearly the boss, sat at the top with the Greek premier on one side, and on the other General Papagos, Greek C.-in-C., hero of the Albanian victories against the Italians, but now looking tired and anxious. He knew how near collapse his brave army was. Below Papagos sat Eden and Wavell.

King George, pro-British, was prepared to accept British aid if a sound case could be made. Papagos was dubious; Eden, on the other hand, 'sold' the proposition with all the enthusiasm at his command. Being then only a junior staff officer, I was not present at the whole of the meeting; nevertheless, I was sitting at the table when the question of our ability to help Greece was under discussion.

The following is what I wrote in *Operation Victory*:

Rather frightened, I sat down and put my massive file on the table. It contained details regarding the force we proposed to send: the number of men, guns, and tanks, as well as a great deal of other things.

I think it was Eden who stressed and enumerated the 'formidable' resources which we were prepared to send over. It sounded pretty good, but if a real expert had carried out a more detailed investigation, I doubt whether those present would have been so satisfied. Totals of men and guns are generally impressive… In the aircraft flying over I had been asked to produce a list showing totals of items we were proposing to send. My first manpower figures excluded such categories as pioneers, and in the gun totals I only produced artillery pieces. This was nothing like good enough for one of Mr. Eden's party who was preparing the brief. He asked that the figures should be swelled with what to my mind were doubtful values. I felt that this was hardly a fair do, and bordering upon dishonesty. I don't know, however, whether figures meant very much to the Greeks by the time they were produced.

Our assistance was to be sent over in three echelons, the initial contribution in fighting troops being one infantry division, an armoured brigade group and some extra artillery. Naturally a large number of Base and L. of C. units would have to precede this contribution. Two contingents were to arrive, each consisting — so far as I can remember — of a division and something extra. But the process was a slow one owing to shipping and port capacity.

As far as I could gather, there seemed to be general acceptance of the British offer of help, but the plan was still being considered. Discussion went on as to where the Germans should be held, and naturally Salonika's part in such a plan was stressed. Papagos explained that the troops holding the static defences in Western Thrace and Macedonia possessed no mobility and therefore were unsuitable for fighting a withdrawal from their far-flung positions. It was generally accepted that the holding of Salonika was not a practicable proposition and that the Aliakmon Line was the right answer under the circumstances. The political disadvantages and dangers of giving up so much Greek territory were mentioned. As far as I understood the discussion, it appeared that the Greeks agreed that the troops holding these isolated positions should be withdrawn as early as possible. This would prevent their being cut off, and at the same time, provide much needed reinforcements to man the defensive line decided upon.

The Greeks referred frequently to the question of Turkey and Yugoslavia. The danger of a German advance through the latter was brought up on many occasions. If either or both these countries came in against Germany, the whole outlook would be vastly improved.

And so the Aliakmon Line was decided upon as the strategic plan in the event of our sending our expeditionary force to Greece. There were further discussions as to the weight of the German attack when it came. The number of divisions required to hold the Aliakmon Line was also brought up — nine was, I think, the planning figure. To me, sitting there with the facts in front of me, the prospect of producing the requirements from Greek and British resources looked rather remote. My impression was that Papagos looked none too happy. He had a lot on his hands already.

I was now asked to leave the room, and I left the assembly endeavouring to draft the signal that was to be sent to London, which, of course, would include the agreement for us to send forces to Greece.

What I did not include in the above account was the mention of Wavell giving his considered view as to the chances of success. When the time came for an expression of opinion on the military prospects, and the chances of success of British intervention, Eden turned to General Wavell and asked him to say his piece. It was a tense moment and you could have heard a pin drop as Wavell climbed to his feet and prepared himself for his reply. I remember almost praying that he would voice some doubt as to the outcome, and when he had completed his exposé I felt a hot wave of anger surge over me, for I failed to understand how it was possible for an experienced soldier to say the things he did say. In a low and subdued voice Wavell told the negotiators that it was his considered view that the assistance being offered held out every chance of permitting the Allies to withstand a German advance into Greece. He explained the need to base our defence on the Aliakmon Line, and stressed the impossibility of staging our main line of defence in Macedonia, covering the important part of Salonika. He stated that the resources we were offering should prove adequate for the task. It was all very general and completely ignored the salient factors that had a bearing on the problem and which, when added up could not, by any stretch of the imagination, support the conclusions which he was voicing to the King of the Hellenes and his Cabinet. I can remember to this day the intense feeling of sadness which replaced that of anger as I left the meeting. It was crystal-clear to me that the reward for the Greeks' gallant and successful fight against Mussolini's armies was to be misery and disaster. This assessment of the military probabilities by so distinguished and famous a soldier as Wavell had removed many of the doubts that previously had existed only too clearly in the minds of the Greeks. But the die was now cast.

How far had Wavell been influenced by Eden's enthusiasm and pressure, as Foreign Secretary and personal emissary of the Prime Minister, who had so far been so insistent on aiding the Greeks? Was Wavell 'subdued' in the Conference because he was arguing a bad case out of loyalty to his political chiefs? *This* would be as damaging an indictment as the alternative — that his *military* judgement was quite unsound.

I remember after the Conference Eden entered the ante-room where I was and preened himself before the chimney-piece on how well he had swayed the meeting. His entourage assisted at this melancholy exhibition of vanity, and a rather fulsome signal was composed for dispatch to Churchill.

I was secretary of the Commander-in-Chief's Committee in Cairo as one of my jobs, and I well remember the rather different Eden who attended a hastily convened meeting after Rommel, taking advantage of our denuded forces in Cyrenaica, had driven us back to Tobruk and beyond. Here is how I described this meeting in *Operation Victory*:

> That afternoon a meeting took place at which the Commander-in-Chief, Eden and Dill were present. The atmosphere was certainly tense. The subject was Tobruk. I noticed Eden's fingers drumming on the table; he looked nervous and a very different person to the Eden at the Palace in Athens. After the problem had been discussed from each service point of view, Wavell was asked to give his views. I admired him tremendously at that moment. He had a very heavy load to carry but he looked calm and collected, and said that in his view we must hold Tobruk, and that he considered that this was possible. One could feel the sense of relief that this decision produced, and the other Commanders-in-Chief agreed, and it was decided to send Air-Marshal Tedder and myself up the next day to Tobruk to report on the situation and to discuss possible reinforcements.

Despite the results of this conference, however, another chance presented itself to withdraw from the Greek commitment with honour, but Wavell remained firm in his conviction and the opportunity passed by. This is how it occurred:

On 23rd February Wavell instructed me to carry out a reconnaissance of the Aliakmon position as well as an examination of other matters affecting our participation in holding up a German invasion. Disguised as a journalist and wearing plain clothes, I spent an extremely interesting and exciting few days with a number of Greek officers. We were briefed by Papagos himself before we proceeded on our mission. As one day followed another my views hardened, instead of the reverse which I had hoped might be the case. Arriving back in Athens late one evening on the termination of my mission, I had just dropped off to sleep when I was rung up and told that General Arthur Smith wanted to see me at once downstairs. I hurried off to see Wavell's Chief of General Staff. I shall now quote once more from *Operation Victory*.

> I turned in at about 11 p.m., but was rung up at 1 a.m. to hear that General Smith wished to see me downstairs. I slipped on some clothes and found him in his room. He told me that complications had set in and that I must fly back early that morning to Cairo and report matters to General Wavell. He then proceeded to dictate to me a memorandum setting out the salient difficulties that had emerged. Apparently Papagos was not happy with the military situation; he was a realist, and as the time drew near, he must have had grave doubts as to the soundness of the plan. I think there were about four major issues which worried him.
>
> First, was the prospect of fighting the Germans without any assistance from the Turks and Yugoslavs. Then, there was the question of the withdrawal of troops from North-Eastern Greece. This movement had not started, and Papagos was worried at the effect such a move would have upon the Army's morale and upon Greek public opinion. The time factor was another problem. Could this withdrawal take place before the Germans attacked? And would sufficient British forces arrive before that critical moment arose? Finally, there appeared to be some divergence of views as to whether, under the circumstances, the Aliakmon Line was in fact the best line to hold. Here indeed was a crisis, and I remember a significant sentence towards the end of General Smith's clear account which ran something like this:
>
> 'From the strictly military point of view this would provide us with the opportunity of withdrawing from what appears now to be an unsound venture.'

I took this to mean that the Greeks did not consider our help could save them.

On arriving back in Cairo, however, I found that Wavell had already left for Greece, and so I was unable to deliver the message.

It is interesting to read Churchill's account of this particular crisis.[4]

On 5th March Eden sent a message to the British Prime Minister from Athens giving a very forthright account of the dangers of this new situation and the effects of Papagos's changed views. *Inter alia*, he said, '...The hard fact remains that our forces, including Dominion contingents, will be engaged in an operation more hazardous than it seemed a week ago...'

This message, showed that Eden's views had somewhat altered. This, as well as further time for reflection, produced a far more apprehensive view at home. 'A marked change now came over our views in London. The Chiefs of Staff recorded the various factors developing against sending an army to Greece.'

The Chiefs of Staff then enumerated the various factors which 'were developing unfavourably against our Balkan policy'. These can be tabulated as under:

(a) The depression of Papagos, the Greek C.-in-C.

(b) The failure of the Greeks to withdraw their troops to the line which had been agreed should be held, if Yugoslavia did not come in on our side.

(c) It had been arranged that thirty-five Greek battalions were to help hold this line, but now only twenty-three, at the maximum, would be available; and these newly formed and untried, as well as lacking in artillery.

---

[4] *The Second World War*, Vol. III, Winston Churchill.

(d) The expectation of the withdrawal of several Greek divisions from the Albanian front when the Germans attacked was nullified for, 'General Papagos now says that this cannot be done, as they are exhausted and outnumbered.'

(e) There were also other adverse elements affecting our own situation:

(i) Because Rhodes had not been captured, a considerable portion of our air effort would now have to be employed in air operations against the island in order to ensure that our lines of communication to Greece received the maximum degree of protection.

(ii) The Suez Canal had been completely blocked by mines and it was not expected that clearance would be effected before 11th March. This blockage had produced a situation where all the ships carrying motor transport were north of the Canal and all the personnel ships south of it.

(f) Finally, the Chiefs of Staff estimated that the Germans could concentrate two divisions on the Aliakmon Line by 15th March, and three more by the 22nd. Against this, however, the best we could hope for would be to have one armoured division and one New Zealand brigade against the first two German divisions.

The Chiefs of Staff concluded by stating, 'The hazards of the enterprise have considerably increased.' And most significantly they added that they did not feel they could, as yet, question the military advice of those on the spot, who described the position as not by any means hopeless. In brief, they relied mainly on Wavell's *military* judgement.

Churchill, although sitting in London, saw the red light, and on 6th March sent this realistic message to Eden who was now back in Cairo.

The situation has indeed changed for the worse. Chiefs of Staff have presented serious commentary, which follows in my next. Failure of Papagos to act as agreed with you on 22nd February, obvious difficulty of his extricating his army from contact in Albania, and time-table of our possible movements furnished by Wavell, together with other adverse factors recited by Chiefs of Staff, e.g. postponement of Rhodes and closing of Canal — make it difficult for Cabinet to believe that we now have any power to avert fate of Greece unless Turkey and/or Yugoslavia come in, which seems most improbable. We have done our best to promote Balkan combination against Germany. We must be careful not to urge Greece against her better judgement into a hopeless resistance alone when we have only handfuls of troops which can reach scene in time. Grave Imperial issues are raised by committing New Zealand and Australian troops to an enterprise, which, as you say, has become even more hazardous. We are bound to lay before Dominion Governments your and Chief of Staff appreciation. Cannot forecast their assent to operation. We do not see any reason for expecting success, except that of course we attach great weight to opinions of Dill and Wavell.

We must liberate Greeks from feeling bound to reject a German ultimatum. If on their own they resolve to fight, we must, to some extent share their ordeal. But rapid German advance will probably prevent any appreciable British Imperial forces from being engaged.

Loss of Greece and the Balkans, by no means a major catastrophe for us, provided Turkey remains honest neutral. We could take Rhodes and consider plans for 'Influx' (descent on Sicily) or Tripoli. We are advised from many quarters that our ignominious ejection from Greece would do us more harm in Spain and Vichy than the fact of submission of Balkans, which with our scanty forces alone we have never been expected to prevent.

I send you this to prepare your mind for what, in the absence of facts very different from those now before us, will probably be expressed in Cabinet decision tomorrow.[5]

On the same day, Sir Michael Palairet, our Minister in Athens, who was full of Foreign Office optimism, waded in to stress the disastrous political effects if we withdrew from our commitments. He made a great point of the views of the King. I am sure that far too much importance was attached to the King's opinion — the problem was now primarily a military one, and it was only natural that the Greek King was by that time prepared to snatch at any straw.

Eden rightly consulted the three Commanders-in-Chief, and they expressed the view that despite 'the heavy commitments and grave risks', the previous decisions made in Athens should stand. As the whole feasibility of the campaign depended on whether the army could or could not carry out successfully its role with the Greek Army of holding the German invasion, Wavell's voice was predominant. And in his reply, Churchill says, 'I am deeply impressed with the steadfast attitude maintained by you and your military advisers, Dill, Wavell and, I presume, Wilson...'

This stresses that he recognized that the Army view was paramount and, as Wavell was C.-in-C. of the Middle East, no decision could have been taken without his agreement. At the end of his message there appears the following significant passage: '...so far you have given us few facts or reasons on their authority which can be presented to those Dominions as justifying the operation on any grounds but *noblesse oblige*. A precise military appreciation is indispensable.' It is almost unbelievable that this major course of policy had been accepted without a clear-cut military appreciation to prove its feasibility. Is anything more needed, therefore, to prove that political considerations were originally absolutely paramount,

---

[5] *The Second World War*, Vol. III, Winston Churchill: page 90.

and that the stark military factors had received insufficient attention?

Eden sent another long signal on 7th March, giving reasons for his continued support of the policy of intervention. One cannot disagree with most of what he said on the effect if Greece were allowed to fall under Germany's control. But here again the chances of military success were lightly passed over, and it is obvious that Eden, as well as everyone else involved, accepted without question Wavell's viewpoint on the military prospects of success. How different things might have been if he had told Eden and the P.M., 'I consider that there is little chance of successful intervention in Greece. Even if we land our forces, it will almost certainly end in an evacuation.' And that is the conclusion that he must have come to had he really studied the full military aspects of the situation.

If further proof is required to show how confident Wavell was as to the prospect of the coming operation, it is in his attitude to the preparation of plans for an evacuation.

On my return to Cairo from the reconnaissance in Greece I gave my colleagues in the J.P.S. an account of my adventures and of the prospects as I saw them. I was, however, preaching to the converted, for I found a general air of gloom and incomprehension in J.P.S. and other staff circles. We held a meeting to review the decision to go to Greece in the light of the latest information and from the military point of view it just didn't make sense. An evacuation, with worse consequences than Dunkirk, seemed to us to be inevitable. We even began to think that something was being kept from us, although this was unlikely as the J.P.S. had as a matter of course access to all the most secret and confidential signals and communications. As Brigadier Malaby, the Operations Staff Officer whom Dill had brought out with him, was still in

Cairo, we decided to ask him to meet us so that we could obtain some light on this difficult problem. A meeting was arranged but it did nothing to allay our fears. We had prepared a number of specific questions, but the answers we received were entirely unsatisfactory. Here are one or two examples:

'How were we to get sufficient forces to the Aliakmon position in time?'

'How did he expect us to deal with the weight of air and armour that we must expect to be thrown against us?'

'In view of the losses and hardships sustained by the Greek Army and the acute munition problems that existed, how could we rely on them for a sustained effort?'

'How was it possible for the Greek and British Commonwealth forces to be maintained after Salonika fell, in view of the poor communications?'

And so it went on; each direct and straightforward question was left unanswered.

I came back from the meeting feeling extremely worried, for it seemed to me that there was a very grave risk of losing our whole position in the Middle East as well as suffering a major disaster in Greece. I also felt extremely critical of our Commander-in-Chief. I then convened a meeting at our level of the J.P.S. and suggested that we should be shirking our responsibilities if we did not start to examine the problem of evacuation, and this, I must add, was before any of our forces had landed! And so we got down to work, for there was an immense amount to be done, such as the ear-marking and the collection of the necessary shipping; the examination of the various beaches for evacuating the troops; the selection of staging ports in Crete, in order to obtain a quick turn-round; the study of various routes for withdrawal; the problems of withdrawing our air forces, and their eventual moves from the mainland of Greece; the selection of other airstrips and plans for air support during the critical phase of evacuation; the organization and collection of beach parties together with the necessary signal equipment; the disposal of warlike stores, dumps, etc.; what was to happen to the Greek Army; and a host of other difficult matters that had to be considered.

A few days after we had started to busy ourselves with the 'Evacuation of Greece' planning paper, I was sent for by General Arthur Smith. I duly reported at his office and the interview went something like this:

> 'I hear that the J.P.S. are working on a paper dealing with the possible evacuation from Greece — is that correct?'
> 'Yes, we are, sir,' I replied.
> 'Well, the C.-in-C. is very annoyed about it, and I'm afraid you will have to stop.'

I then explained how we saw the situation, and that as planners we were responsible for studying probable developments. But that was not the end of the business. I realized that the C.G.S. did not feel very happy about it, for at my interview with him in Athens he had shown how worried he was about the whole project.

I reported back to my colleagues and, luckily, the Naval and Air representatives took exception to this ruling, as they considered that Wavell had no jurisdiction over their activities. So I returned to the attack and explained this new point to General Smith. In the end he gave authority for us to proceed, but told me that 'on pain of death' we must keep what we were doing entirely to ourselves, with which instruction I, of course, agreed. I left him, I remember, feeling very uncomfortable about the whole matter.

Days passed by and the Expeditionary Force began to arrive in Greece and the reports of German preparations became clearer and no less worrying. Of the lack of confidence felt by Wilson, the Commander of the Expeditionary Force which was to sail to Greece, the following story told to me by his then B.G.S., Sandy Galloway, gives an illustration.

Wilson, accompanied by Galloway, was flown to Greece in advance of the landings of any troops in order to reconnoitre and prepare plans for the coming campaign. When visiting Athens they attended a conference with Sir Charles Palairet, the British Minister accredited to Greece.

At this conference His Majesty's representative spoke with great enthusiasm about the outlook. He used such terms as 'the turn of the tide' and 'this great moment when the Allies will return to Europe'. When the discussions were over, Jumbo Wilson said good-bye, and as he went down the marble steps of the Legation, turned to Sandy and said, 'Well, I don't know about all that, but I have already ordered maps of the Peloponnese!' — i.e. the region south of the Corinth Canal, a long way from the Aliakmon Line!

Eventually, on 16th April, the invasion started, and by the 24th Greece was forced to surrender and the inevitable evacuation commenced. The whole campaign had proceeded exactly as any average soldier who had studied the facts would have predicted.

When things began to look pretty desperate, the J.P.S. felt the time had come to make some of our plans and researches available to those on the spot, and so at one of our meetings it was decided that I should go over with that object in view. We foresaw, however, the difficulty of overcoming Wavell's opposition and so Commodore Bill Norman and our Senior Air Force member saw their respective Commanders-in-Chief, in order to obtain their authority to set things in motion. The necessary permission was granted and it was decided that on this occasion I should act for the other two services.

I went up to see the C.G.S. and he was obviously embarrassed by my proposal but he could not, of course, refuse to let me go in my inter-service capacity. On the other hand, he made it perfectly clear that I must make no contact with any Army Officer and restrict my talks entirely to the Navy and the R.A.F.

Hearing that a Sunderland flying-boat was leaving the Nile early next morning, I got authority for a passage and reported at about 5 a.m. armed with a case of 'Most Secret' and highly inflammatory documents.

It was a cold and dull morning, and I was waiting for the launch to take me off, when I sensed a certain amount of excitement behind me, and looking round was rather shaken to see Wavell getting out of his car. I did my best to fade into the background, but he had spotted me and called out, 'De Guingand, what are you doing here?' I walked over, feeling rather like a small boy who had been caught stealing apples in a neighbour's orchard.

'I am going to Greece on behalf of the Joint Planning Staff,' I replied and added quickly, 'I am representing the other two Commanders-in-Chief.'

Then in no uncertain terms I was told how unfavourably he viewed my activities and also my proposed visit to Greece. 'But I suppose I can't stop you,' he added. 'And I must give you a direct order that in no circumstances whatever will you disclose or discuss with any Army Officers the papers you have been preparing in the J.P.S.'

Anxious and rather crestfallen I acknowledged the rebuke, but I was also intensely worried because Wavell appeared still not to have seen the writing on the wall, which was there to be read in bolder letters than ever before. I certainly felt very resentful. When my turn came to go aboard, I crept in rather like a fugitive and made for the tail of the machine, where I found somewhere to sit away from the V.I.P.s cabin. When I judged that we were somewhere near Crete, I decided that I must have a peep at this great island which was to be used as a stepping-stone in our evacuation plans. The crew allowed me into the observation deck, and it was not long before the western end of Crete was visible far below, looking beautiful and serene with the unbelievably blue waters of the Mediterranean lapping its shores. I picked out the various landmarks and my thoughts went back to the days of study spent over our maps. I also wondered what role this island was destined to play in the days to come. Would it be spared the misery of enemy occupation, and remain within the orbit of Allied control?

Finally, we came within sight of Athens and the great port of Piraeus and, after circling round, made a perfect landing on the smooth water; we then taxied to our mooring buoy, a launch came alongside and Wavell and his party left for the landing-stage. I felt I had better let them get well clear — otherwise the C.-in-C. might change his mind!

I spent that day and the next morning discussing plans at the Naval and Air Force Headquarters. D'Albiac was the A.O.C., but I cannot recall the name of the Naval officer with whom the discussions took place. Wigglesworth of the R.A.F. had come over with me, and he got down to brass tacks with the Air Force Staff.

It was late the next morning, as I was sitting in the S.N.O.'s office at Piraeus, that a phone call came through for me from

Athens. I was handed the telephone and to my great surprise it was the Commander-in-Chief on the other end.

> 'Is that you, de Guingand?'
> I replied that it was.
> 'I want to see you early this afternoon at the Hotel Grand Bretagne in Athens. Come along at three o'clock.'
> 'Very good, sir,' I replied, and then rang off.

Wavell had been to see General Wilson, who was commanding the forces in Greece, so I thought it possible that the C.-in-C. had at last revised his views on the situation.

I borrowed a car and set off for Athens after a hasty lunch. I arrived at the hotel at the appointed hour and asked where I could find General Wavell. An A.D.C. appeared and I was taken to a room on one of the upstairs floors. He knocked at the door and, in answer to the call, I walked in to find the Commander-in-Chief standing by the window. He turned round and said,

'Oh, there you are, Freddie.'

This form of address rather startled me for I had never been called by my Christian name before by Wavell. Obviously the atmosphere had improved considerably since last we had spoken! Then he went on roughly as follows:

> 'I have just returned from General Wilson's Headquarters, and I'm afraid things are not too good. The enemy is very strong and his air force is causing us a lot of trouble. The Greek Army on our left is in difficulties and we shall have trouble in withdrawing. It now looks as if we shall have to consider evacuation. You and the J.P.S. have been busy working out plans for such an eventuality, have you not?'

I replied that this was the case and that I had many of the papers with me and had discussed some of the problems already with the Navy and R.A.F.

> 'Very good,' he went on. 'You now have my authority to discuss this matter with Brigadier Brunskill[6] and of course with General Wilson if you see him.' He stressed: 'But with no one else.'

I nearly sighed audibly with relief at this change of outlook. I remember, however, feeling very sorry for Wavell at that moment. He looked tired and depressed and there was no doubt that he was shouldering a very heavy load, for the operation of which he had approved and which he, as the highest military authority in the Middle East, had considered would have a reasonable chance of success, was now on the brink of failure — in fact there was the possibility of disaster ahead.

I now quote the passages from General Collins's book, to which I referred earlier on in this story:

> Pages 374-5: Wavell's second visit to Greece had brought home to him the immense difficulties, tactical and administrative under which 'W' Force was labouring and how little it was likely to accomplish now that the Yugoslav Army had proved a broken reed and the whole Greek scheme of defence was giving way. It was for this reason, that as soon as he got back to Cairo, after consulting his co-Commanders-in-Chief, he instructed the Joint Planning Staff to prepare secretly a scheme for the evacuation of 'W' Force at short notice, partly direct to Alexandria and part, for the time being at any rate, by the shorter sea route to Crete. A combined

---

[6] In charge of the base area.

staff to carry out this operation was also briefed, a wise precaution as it turned out.

Page 378:...Wavell was forced to return to Greece, where affairs had reached such a critical stage that a vital decision as to future policy was required. This was nothing less than whether the British force was to fight to a finish or once again ask the Royal Navy to get away what they could.

Wavell had, of course, realized for some days that he might be faced with this terrible problem and had done all he could to prepare for it. He had already made up his mind that if evacuation could be carried out honourably and without leaving his Greek Allies in the lurch, it was the wiser course. Whether it was possible was another matter. He took with him a small staff which had been studying the problem and which had skeleton plans already in hand. In Greece waiting for him, too, was one of his staff[7] who, landing with the first flight of transports, had been secretly working out plans for evacuation ever since.

Page 402: As soon as the Joint Planning Staff were, on Wavell's instructions, set to studying the evacuation from Greece, it became evident that Crete would have to be used as a half-way house to Egypt. Otherwise neither shipping nor escort vessels would suffice to carry out the evacuation in any reasonable time.

It will be seen that the above extracts give a most misleading — in fact a completely false — picture of the real facts. Wavell would not contemplate evacuation; took strong exception to plans to that end being prepared, and finally found me in

---

[7] 'Major (later Major-General Sir F.) de Guingand, who, in *Operation Victory* (Hodder and Stoughton) describes the part he played in the Greek drama.'

Greece, during the visit referred to in General Collins's second quotation, virtually against his orders.

I spent another day or so in Greece and then returned once again to Cairo, reporting back to the J.P.S. It was then decided that Colonel Norton, my Army colleague, and Wing-Commander Claude Pelly[8] should go over to Greece to assist as best they could during the evacuation. They did a fine job and had an interesting and exciting time.

About 80 per cent of the forces originally sent to Greece were evacuated, and this was made possible only by the superhuman efforts and courage of the Royal Navy. The expedition had put a terrible strain on them, but, in the face of great odds, they saw the thing through to the end. Their losses were, however, very severe and, as at Dunkirk, the Army lost all its transport and its weapons other than small-arms.

There was, not unnaturally, an outcry after this great failure and an inquiry was instituted. I never knew what happened to these deliberations. There was, however, one most disturbing feature of the business. Certain high-ranking officers, who should have known better, lobbied me in connection with the evidence that I was going to give. I recollect discussing the matter with Colonel Salisbury-Jones at the time, and both of us were very indignant about it all.

Some years ago I wrote to Salisbury-Jones and put certain questions to him. Here are my questions and his replies:

Question 1: Were you at the time Military Attaché in Athens? Or a member of the British Military Mission? Or both?
Answer: I was not Military Attaché in Athens at the time. I was G.S.O.1 to General Heywood, who was Head of the

---

[8] Later to become Air-Marshal and Air C.-in-C. Middle East.

British Military Mission. As such, I frequently deputized for Heywood in his absence and well remember sending telegrams to Cairo in which I stressed the many unhappy factors of the situation. I also sent a lengthy appreciation of the situation, based largely on talks which I had with General Papagos. I was never able to trace this report afterwards in Cairo and I felt at the time that it had been conveniently mislaid.

Question 2: Do you still believe that Wavell took an unrealistic view of the whole situation, and especially did not take into account the state of the Greek Army's equipment, morale, maintenance and strength?

Answer. As regards Wavell taking an unrealistic view, I hesitate to express an opinion. But I can affirm without hesitation that the risks of the situation and the state of the Greek Army as regards equipment, morale and strength were fully made clear by the Military Mission. Indeed, I have my records in front of me.

Early in February the Mission pointed out that Metaxas had considered the Greek resistance could not be protracted without substantial aid from outside, and that it would only be short-lived, if the situation in Albania were not liquidated first.

On the 20th February I myself informed Cairo that Papagos had warned me that if the Germans attacked before the Albanian situation had been cleared up, the position would be catastrophic. In the same report I stressed that unless the Albanian situation were first cleared up, only three Greek divisions would be available for the Macedonian front, where a minimum of two Corps would be necessary. The Greeks were particularly anxious that nothing should be done to precipitate a German attack before they themselves had reached Valona in Albania. Twenty instead of three Greek Divisions might then be available for the Macedonian front. Unless the situation in Albania could be improved in the above sense, there was every danger that Greek forces in Albania might be cut off if the Germans broke through on the Verria or Edessa front. I also pointed out that although it would be more economical to hold a line farther south it was questionable whether Greek morale would stand up to the strain of losing so much territory. On the same day I also stressed that since Greece was not prepared for war with Germany, the outbreak of a German offensive against her would place a severe strain on her morale. I drew attention to the importance of clearing up the Yugoslav situation, about which it was impossible to discover anything in Athens. Indeed this was not the task of the Mission anyhow.

So much for the efforts of the Mission to point out the situation and particularly its disadvantages. I know that d'Albiac left Cairo in no doubt as to the Air situation. In the light of the above, you may imagine my consternation when it came to my knowledge that a report by Force Headquarters had criticized the Mission for failing to represent the military position in Greece. Therein lies a sorry tale. There was no love lost between Force Headquarters and Heywood and as a result, the Mission and its advice were often ignored. I need say no more. Unfortunately Heywood was killed shortly afterwards and therefore unable to speak for himself. I did my best to speak for him by writing a true account of events in the above sense. This I sent to the War Office and I imagine that it must still be pigeon-holed among the records. I asked that it should be sent to the historical section.

Question 3: Do you confirm that the Greeks, even after the death of Metaxas, were not keen on our intervention, as they felt that what we could offer would be too little, too late?

Answer: The Greeks were never over-keen on our intervention unless we could provide at least four divisions. Indeed I myself pointed out in one of many telegrams to Cairo that at least two Corps would be required to hold the Aliakmon position.

Question 4: Do you recall any details of the inquiry in Cairo after the whole thing was over? What happened to the report of the inquiry? Was it ever published? My views on the show were so well known that before the inquiry I was lobbied with a view to my watering down criticism. Were you subjected to any like pressure?

Answer. On my arrival in Cairo, after getting away from Crete, I was appointed to preside over a committee to learn the lessons of Crete. The committee was later also ordered to write a report on the lessons of the Greek campaign. In regard to the campaign in Crete, I still recall the essence of our report. A copy of it was sent to England at the time but I understand that machinery was later set in motion to ensure that the report was completely ignored. Indeed I understand that another officer was appointed to write a new report. Exactly what happened in regard to this report I have never really known nor have I gone out of my way to discover. Naturally, however, I was none too pleased. I believe that at least one eminent individual in London, who did see the report at the time thought that it was just what was wanted. In the light of subsequent information which has come to hand, there is little that I would alter in our report. We were particularly critical of the lack of work which had been done during the six months' occupation of Crete. We also drew attention to the fact that no less than six different commanders had been appointed during this period. We further pointed out that even if Crete was originally occupied as a base for offensive operations, it was an elementary principle of war that operations are only conducted from a secure base. No serious attempt had been made to make Crete secure. I remember, in particular, that we drew attention to the fact that no attempt had been made to construct pens or similar works to protect our aircraft on the ground. We were told that such a suggestion was impracticable. And so this point was ignored as indeed were most of the other points in our report, elementary though most of them were. A year later, when the first modern fighters reached Malta, no adequate ground protection had been arranged and they were mostly shot up on the ground within a few hours of their arrival. It was only then that they got down seriously to digging pens and making other suitable arrangements to protect these aircraft on the ground.

I suggest that Salisbury-Jones's comments reinforce the views I have expressed. He was right on the spot and 'knew the form'.

When I was at the Camberley Staff College I remember the big exercises that were held, in which we students were allocated certain appointments, such as C.-in-C., Chief of Staff, etc. In most of them a member of the Directing Staff used to take the part of a politician, who would do his level best to make the service chiefs do something which was militarily unsound. We were all taught the lesson that we must rightly expect the political heads of government to press us to undertake this or that in times of war, but that if the proposal was impracticable, from the military angle, we must say so and stand firm on the issue.

I suggest that the Greek episode is the classic example from the last war of how the military considerations were given insufficient weight, and it should figure in every staff college curriculum. The whole dismal story shows this to be the case, and I'm afraid the blame must be laid on Wavell. He found himself unable to say 'No' to the politician, and agreed to an operation which was fundamentally unsound. The politician, however, can hardly be blamed, for he was entitled to accept the views of a soldier who had at that time, because of the desert victories against the Italians, reached the pinnacle of prestige in the eyes of the British people.

The cost of our intervention in Greece was very heavy in resources; apart from that, it endangered our whole position in the Middle East. Our losses included (exclusive of Greek losses)[9]

(a) CASUALTIES:
  Killed: 903
  Wounded: 1,250
  Prisoners: 13,958
(b) TANKS:
  Light Tanks: 52
  Cruiser Tanks: 52
(c) GUNS (exclusive of guns in Tanks):
  A.A.: 40
  Field: 192
  Anti-Tank: 164
(d) MACHINE GUNS:
  Heavy and Light: 1,812
(e) TRANSPORT:
  About 8,000 lorries of various types.
(f) RADIO EQUIPMENT:
  Virtually the lot.
(g) SHIPS SUNK:
  Lost by air attack — 26 (including H.M.S. *Diamond* and H.M.S. *Wryneck*).
(h) R.A.F.:
  209 Aircraft.

I only met Lord Wavell once after the war, and that was at a dinner party at the Rand Club in Johannesburg, given by Sir Ernest Oppenheimer. He had been made a director of De Beers. As General Collins made clear in his book Wavell was a man of few words. After the dinner had ended he walked out of the room, passing down the line of guests; when he came opposite me, he stopped, poked a finger in my chest and said,

'There was more in the Greek business than you knew about.'

---

[9] *Authorities*: The Library, War Office, London. Winston Churchill's *The Second World War*, Vol. III.

But my subsequent inquiry produced nothing further from this taciturn man.

As far as I know, I have read everything connected with the campaign and I have talked to numbers of people who played leading roles, but I have never been able to find any evidence to suggest that it was a reasonable military risk.

CHAPTER TWO: CRISES IN THE MIDDLE EAST

In analysing Wavell's military decisions, it is important to describe the disastrous result of stripping the Western Desert of the resources necessary to ensure security in that region.

On 27th February, *over five weeks* before the Germans invaded Greece and Yugoslavia, the Chiefs of Staff in London sent Wavell a warning about enemy reinforcements that were to be expected in North Africa. And, what is more significant, it was then known that German armoured formations were on the way over. But Wavell did not seem unduly alarmed or worried in his considered reply.[10] He had made his decision regarding intervention in Greece and his mind was now inflexible. It should be noticed, however, that this ominous message from the Chiefs of Staff arrived several days before there occurred the chance of withdrawing with honour, and with Greece's approval, from our promise of help.

After a halt had been called at Benghazi, with advanced elements positioned around Agheila, Wavell made a surprising change in command. He withdrew General O'Connor, the experienced victor of the recent desert battles and posted him to command the British Troops in Egypt. This was, of course, a welcome reward, but it was hardly wise in the circumstances. General Neame, who was then stationed in Palestine, was given the desert command. It was not long, however, before Neame expressed his anxiety about the scarcity of his resources, particularly in view of the latest reports of enemy

---

[10] *The Second World War*, Vol. III, Winston Churchill: page 174.

reinforcements on the way from Europe. As to the strategical layout of our forces in the desert, Wavell never appeared to understand the weakness of holding in strength the Benghazi bulge. Wavell's orders to Neame were to withdraw to Benghazi if attacked, which was an indication of his lack of strategical sense, for it meant Neame could be easily by-passed and trapped by Rommel using the desert tracks south of the Benghazi bulge.

When Rommel eventually attacked, Wavell acted in an odd way. Realizing that a commander of desert experience was needed, he attempted to place O'Connor once again in command, but as the latter was unwell, posted him as deputy and 'adviser' to Neame. Such action did not show great confidence in Neame at a most critical stage and, in any case, a sort of dual control is at best not a very satisfactory arrangement.

The subsequent operations are well known. Rommel defeated our forces in the Agheila area and then thrust across the desert country south of the Jebel towards Tobruk. Some of our forces were cut off and defeated and in the process both Neame and O'Connor were captured.

No one will deny that Wavell, in his position as Commander-in-Chief Middle East, had an extremely difficult assignment, for one crisis and complication followed another. There is no doubt that the failure in Greece had shaken him considerably, and in the case of Rashid Ali's revolt in Iraq we now find him resisting political pressure to send a force to Habbaniyeh, but in this particular case the politicians and the Chiefs of Staff in London were right and Wavell was to be proved wrong.

The new pro-German Prime Minister in Baghdad adopted a hostile attitude towards the British at the end of March, and in

April refused to give permission for further landings of troops at Basra from India; on 2nd May fighting began around the R.A.F. Station at Habbaniyeh. It became vital to reassert our position in Iraq in order to safeguard the supply of oil which ran through the pipe-line to the Mediterranean, and the great refinery at Abadan was of vital importance to our war effort. There were something like 9,000 civilians in Habbaniyeh, many of whom had been evacuated from Baghdad. Auchinleck, then C.-in-C. India, was full of fight and eager to send reinforcements to deal with the situation, but Wavell who was, of course, not so well supplied with resources, was against taking any action, and suggested a negotiated settlement. The following extract from Churchill's book demonstrates his mood:

> Your message takes little account of realities. You must face facts... I feel it my duty to warn you in the gravest possible terms that I consider the prolongation of fighting in Iraq will seriously endanger the defence of Palestine and Egypt ... I therefore urge again most strongly that a settlement should be negotiated as early as possible.[11]

In one of his messages to Churchill he even offered to resign because of disagreement with the policy. He had no doubt learnt his lesson, but it was a pity that he had not applied this resistance when faced with the militarily unsound expedition to Greece. Thus, in the case of Greece, Wavell apparently carried out the politician's wishes although the project was militarily unsound: in the case of Iraq, however, he decided to fight political pressure in a matter where the military possibilities supported their view rather than his. Even allowing for the effects of cumulative strain in the last few months, these

---

[11] *The Second World War*, Vol. III, Winston Churchill: page 228.

paradoxical actions of Wavell must suggest that he has been overrated as a commander and as a strategist, and that his military judgement was wrong.

The British Prime Minister was very dissatisfied with Wavell's attitude, for in a minute to the Chiefs of Staff Committee he says,

> I am deeply disturbed at Wavell's attitude. He seems to have been taken as much by surprise on his eastern as he was on his western flank... He gives me the impression of being tired out.[12]

In the end the Chiefs of Staff had to take over the responsibility themselves and a message to Wavell on 6th May reads,

> Chiefs of Staff have therefore advised Defence Committee that they are prepared to accept responsibility for the dispatch of the force specified in your telegram at the earliest possible moment.

Even after this Wavell still stuck his toes in and suggested a political solution should be sought. But Churchill and the Chiefs of Staff were determined in their policy, and in this they were proved overwhelmingly right. The ubiquitous Jumbo Wilson was given the task and as Churchill states in his book, 'The result was crowned with swift and complete success.'[13]

Crete

In practically every paper that the Joint Planning Staff produced upon Middle East strategy, the importance of Crete

---

[12] *The Second World War*, Vol. III, Winston Churchill: pages 228-9.
[13] *The Second World War*, Vol. III, Winston Churchill: page 237.

was stressed — particularly by its Naval and Air Force members. It was very obvious that in enemy hands it would strengthen their position in the Eastern Mediterranean, and it was also clear that, if Greece was lost, its defence would not prove an easy matter, because of its distance from our air bases in Egypt, and of the fact that the only developed harbours were situated on the Aegean side of the island. It is not my purpose to examine the role that Crete might have played in the Middle East war, but rather to spotlight Wavell's failure to take the necessary steps to ensure that everything possible was done to prepare for its defence. It was certainly not through lack of prompting by the other Commanders-in-Chief or by the Staff.

Nearly six months elapsed from the time the Greeks allowed us to send troops to the island (December 1940) until the Germans started their attack, and the efforts made to organize and strengthen its defence were truly lamentable. Admittedly, resources were meagre, but virtually nothing was accomplished until it was really too late. For instance, there was no continuity of command; as has been pointed out by Salisbury-Jones, six commanders were appointed in turn, each with different ideas of how to proceed with his task. Little attempt had been made to build up reserves of ammunition; to prepare airstrips on the southern side of the island; or to improve communications and to develop the smaller ports. We can scarcely doubt that had such obvious measures been carried out while there was plenty of time, Crete might have been held, knowing, as we do now, how near the German invasion was to failure. Whether holding on to the island would have proved a running sore is another matter. But the overall policy was to hold Crete; Churchill appreciated its importance from the very start, and drew attention to this fact on a number of occasions. Admittedly, the Germans stressed the strength of the defences in the battle report of the 11th Air Corps, but it is not unusual for commanders to over-emphasize the strength of defences that they have ultimately overcome!

Churchill in his *The Second World War* admits that he was 'very discontented with Wavell's provision for the defence of Crete, and especially that a few more tanks had not been sent.'[14]

There is no doubt whatever that more could have been done, and the blame for lack of preparedness must be laid on Wavell.

Salisbury-Jones's comments on the Crete problem are also interesting.

In 1941 the situation in Syria was such that the War Cabinet and the Chiefs of Staff decided that, in spite of the other commitments already undertaken in the Middle East, it was essential to assist the Free French forces in gaining control of that important area.

This is another example of Wavell saying 'No' when the answer should have been 'Yes'.

At one stage he offered to resign, but the differences were smoothed over and, once again, because of Wavell's opposition to the project, the Cabinet agreed to 'take full responsibility' for the decision; in fact he was told that if he still felt unwilling to carry out this policy, then arrangements would be made to meet his wish to be relieved of his command. Once more he was showing the firmness towards politicians he ought to have shown over Greece; and once more his *military* appreciation of the situation was utterly wrong.

Wavell, however, now complied and the campaign was successful, the Vichy Commander surrendering on 12th July.

---

[14] *The Second World War*, Vol. III, Winston Churchill: page 308.

The Battleaxe offensive was carried out in the Western Desert on the 15th-17th June, 1941, at Wavell's insistence. It was a total failure, and the loss of tanks was nearly fatal.

General Collins in his book discussing 'Operation Battleaxe' writes:

> To what extent the Battleaxe offensive was a political battle is not a question which can be discussed as yet. But whatever extraneous pressure was exerted over Wavell to undertake an offensive in the heat of the summer, with the known relative strengths of the two forces, especially in armour, he, as Commander-in-Chief, Middle East, was master of his own plan. All commanders — in the last resource — if they are convinced that an operation politically desirable, is not militarily feasible, have the well-known, though difficult and unpleasant course open to them. They can ask that someone else shall be entrusted with the task. In Wavell's case it would appear that, tired out as he was, he may have yielded to extraneous pressure, which since it was urging him to attack again, suited his temperament and his inclinations.[15]

This is hardly an excuse: it is, in fact, an indictment. Surely a decision of paramount importance must be based upon the chances of success, and not upon a C.-in-C.'s personal temperament and inclination. Here was a case where Wavell should have stood up to political pressure, and used the threat of resignation to counter this pressure, as he wrongly did in the case of intervention in Iraq and Syria. For not only had a lesson been learnt in the abortive offensive undertaken in May, but he had expressed himself as having little confidence in the outcome. The conception of the operation was bad; no one had confidence in the result, and to take such risks, knowing

---

[15] *Lord Wavell*: pages 435-6.

what we were up against at that particular time, was altogether pointless. It was Greece all over again on a much smaller scale.

Let me describe briefly the sequence of events. After the failure in Greece and the disastrous reverse in the desert, which forced our army back to where it had been before the successful December offensive, the need to defeat Rommel before he became too strong was, from every point of view, a most desirable objective. Wavell was therefore asked by the War Cabinet to prepare for offensive action as soon as possible. Churchill laid on a brilliant operation called 'Tiger Cub' which aimed at sending a convoy, containing a large number of tanks, via the short Mediterranean route to Egypt. High hopes were entertained as to the effect of this substantial reinforcement. As Intelligence reports suggested that the enemy had weak resources in the forward area, Wavell decided to order a preliminary attack to be carried out, before the tank reinforcements arrived. It was launched but was a complete flop, costing us heavy casualties in both men and tanks and the objective of joining up with the Tobruk garrison and driving the enemy to the west of the fortress was never achieved. The fighting did, however, show how quickly Rommel could react and what a formidable weapon the Germans had in their 88-mm. anti-tank gun. But I am afraid this lesson did not appear to have percolated through to G.H.Q. Wavell decided to call off the battle and to try again after the arrival of the additional tanks. And so the days passed by.

Through the truly magnificent efforts of the Royal Navy and the R.A.F. the convoy got through, but many of the tanks were found to be in poor mechanical condition, and because of this and of the time required to make them desert-worthy, there was considerable delay before they were ready for battle, and this enabled the enemy to bring up additional reinforcements.

When one recapitulates the various factors having an adverse bearing upon 'Operation Battleaxe', it is very hard to understand why Wavell agreed to its taking place. These were:

(a) The lessons of the 15th May attack were there as a warning of what to expect, i.e. Rommel's tactics and the power of the 88-mm. gun.

(b) Our intelligence indicated the considerable reinforcements that were arriving to strengthen Rommel: the 15th Panzer Division was on its way. Advanced elements, I believe, had actually arrived.

(c) The 'I' tanks were too slow and in other ways unsatisfactory for desert warfare.

(d) The inadequacy of the armour fitted to our armoured cars rendered reconnaissance difficult.

(e) The enemy attacked on 26th May and turned us off our positions around Halfaya.

(f) Confidence in the coming battle was at low ebb. One heard criticism on all sides, and the J.P.S. produced a paper drawing attention to the poor prospects of success. (But I don't suppose that anyone who mattered read it!)

That very intelligent soldier Major-General Dorman-Smith, who was, I believe, Director of Plans at the time, was very apprehensive about the prospects of 'Operation Battleaxe', and he then had considerable influence with Wavell.

One has only to read Wavell's message sent to the C.I.G.S. on 28th May — over two weeks before 'Battleaxe' — to realize how little he thought of his chances of success. It was always a cardinal feature with Montgomery and Alexander that before a big battle, all those taking part must be enthusiastic and confident.

Here is the message:

28th May, 1941[16]

All available armoured strength, which will be a deciding factor, is being put into 'Battleaxe'. Various difficulties have delayed reconstitution 7th Armoured Division. Earliest date for beginning of forward move from Matruh will be 7th June, and may be later.

2. I think right to inform you that the measure of success which will attend this operation is, in my opinion, doubtful. I hope that it will succeed in driving the enemy west of Tobruk and re-establishing land communications with Tobruk. If possible we will exploit success further. But recent operations have disclosed some disquieting features. Our armoured cars are too lightly armoured to resist the fire of enemy fighter aircraft, and, having no gun, are powerless against the eight-wheeled German cars, which have guns and are faster. This makes reconnaissance difficult. Our infantry tanks are really too slow for a battle in the desert, and have been suffering considerable casualties from the fire of the powerful enemy anti-tank guns. Our cruisers have little advantage in power or speed over German medium tanks. Technical breakdowns are still too numerous. We shall not be able to accept battle with perfect confidence in spite of numerical inferiority, as we could against Italians. Above factors may limit our success. They also make it imperative that adequate flow of armoured reinforcements and reserves should be maintained.

It is my recollection that further messages to London preceding 'Battleaxe' were certainly no more optimistic.

Eventually the battle started on 15th June and nothing went right, and we returned to the defensive on 17th, having lost nearly a hundred tanks and suffered a thousand casualties.

Churchill, in his war history, says with reference to the failure of 'Battleaxe': '...which Wavell had undertaken in loyalty to the risks I had successfully run in sending out the "Tiger Cubs".'

---

[16] *The Second World War*, Vol. III, Winston Churchill: page 304.

This I suggest is not a very good military reason for undertaking an offensive: there should surely have been other favourable factors as well — but there were none.

This additional failure finally decided the War Cabinet to relieve Wavell of his command. He did not go into the limbo of obscurity, however, but was appointed Commander-in-Chief in India instead.

CHAPTER THREE: DISASTER IN THE FAR EAST

It is not my normal practice to write about events in the last war of which I did not have an intimate and personal knowledge. I consider however that in this study of Wavell his record after his replacement as C.-in-C. Middle East calls for mention. I will confine myself only to a brief account of his leadership during the closing stage of the Battle of Singapore, for I suggest it provides another example of faulty decision.

While fully appreciating the frightful problem that the defence of Singapore involved, I do not consider Wavell, as the soldier who had Churchill's confidence and who had been appointed Allied Supreme Commander in South-East Asia, gave sound advice or appreciated the situation as he should have done.

He realized the weakness of Singapore's defences from the landward side, but it was Churchill who eventually got something done about strengthening them. From the start Wavell seems to have been aware that it would be hopeless to attempt to defend the island once Johore was lost. However, he did not make his views at all clear, and almost at the last moment, when disaster appeared inevitable, his outlook suddenly became more optimistic. Even Churchill, thousands of miles away, at one point thought seriously of giving up the island, thus saving resources for Burma and elsewhere. I consider the final error of reasoning was to commit the major portion of the 18th Division to Singapore, virtually just in time for the capitulation. One would have thought that any experienced soldier would have foreseen the inevitable outcome at that stage. I remember Auchinleck in Cairo sending a message expressing the hope that this well-equipped division would not be used at Singapore. To all of us the end appeared close at hand. Here is the gist of what took place:[17]

> *16th January, 1942*: Wavell draws attention to the defence weaknesses both as regards attack from the Johore side and fortress cannon unsuitable for counter-battery work.
>
> *19th January, 1942*: Wavell informs Churchill that '…number of troops required to hold the island effectively is probably as great as or greater than number required to defend Johore'.
>
> He also stated, 'I must warn you, however, that I doubt whether island can be held for long once Johore is lost.'
>
> *20th January, 1942*: Chiefs of Staff instruct Wavell to institute various defence measures on Churchill's initiative.
>
> *20th January, 1942*: Churchill urges Wavell to ensure that there must be no surrender 'until after protracted fighting among the ruins of Singapore City'.
>
> *20th January, 1942*: Wavell informs the Chiefs of Staff that 'the situation in Malaya had greatly deteriorated'. It is in this message that he gives this somewhat vague opinion, 'If all goes well hope prolonged defence possible.' But the whole tenor of his message is that things are going anything but well.
>
> After reading Wavell's message of 19th January Churchill, full of fight as always, began to wonder whether it would not be better to divert the reinforcements to Burma, as it now appeared that if landed in Singapore they would be doomed, but as he says, 'The direct initial responsibility lay with Wavell as Allied Supreme Commander.'
>
> No clear or incisive recommendation, however, came from that quarter.
>
> *5th February, 1942*: Wavell reports three out of four aerodromes in Singapore subject to artillery fire, but ends his

---

[17] All quotations from Winston Churchill's *The Second World War*, Vol. IV.

message with, '…Singapore which there is every intention and hope of holding'. This was hardly an opinion warranted by the facts.

9th February, 1942: General Percival reports to Wavell that the enemy had landed on the west coast during the night and had penetrated about five miles. He goes on to say that 'the advance stopped temporarily by use of *Command* Reserves'. More landings occurred during the 9th and considerable losses were suffered. Percival was now thinking in terms of the close defence of Singapore itself. What else could he do — poor fellow!

10th February, 1942: Churchill sends a message to Wavell stressing the numerical advantage he considers General Percival has over the Japanese. He advocates stern measures for the troops and civilian population. He also stresses the role of the 18th Division.

Wavell reports to the P.M. his views after a visit to Singapore. He says that the battle for Singapore is 'not going well': that 'the morale of some troops is not too good, and none is as high as I should like to see'. He also says 'that everything possible is being done to produce a more offensive spirit and optimistic outlook, but I cannot pretend that these efforts have been entirely successful up to date'. He also reports that all aerodromes are out of use.

The whole trend of the message is one of pessimism and my experience in war suggests that it is quite impossible for a commander who is himself pessimistic to instil optimism in the troops under his command.

By 14th February the water supply to Singapore was only sufficient for twenty-four hours, a probability that was there for all to see; and about a million people were now concentrated within a radius of three miles of the city.

13th February, 1942: General Percival sends a very foreboding report to Wavell. He is, however, giving facts which to any receptive man would show the impossibility of the situation. But Wavell still orders fighting to the bitter end.

14th February, 1942: Churchill gives Wavell freedom of action as to what instructions he should send to Percival. And on 15th February Wavell finally gives Percival authority to surrender, when no further fighting is possible. The garrison capitulated on that very day.

In spite of all this Wavell ordered the remaining portion of the 18th Division to be landed only a few days before capitulation.

Thus, to sum up, the more I study Wavell's record of command, the less I am impressed with his military judgement, although I would be the first to admit that he was commanding both in the Middle and the Far East during most difficult periods. I submit, however, that our fortunes might have worked out better if he had not given such bad advice, and if he had approached problems more realistically and with greater skill.

His fundamental faults lay in his inconsistent approach to his relations with his political chiefs and in a military judgement that was often either wrong or vacillating. If it was right for him to threaten resignation over Iraq, it was more so over Greece — unless he really did believe the expedition had a chance of success, which would be the most serious indictment of all, and which, in view of his ostrich-like attitude to plans for evacuation, does seem possible. During his Middle East Command, which made his reputation, he had six major decisions to make — the scope of O'Connor's desert offensive; the taking of Tripoli; Greece; Iraq; 'Battleaxe', and Syria. It can be argued that, in the case of O'Connor, Wavell wished to keep that offensive in 'balance' with those of Cunningham and Platt. However, the remaining five out of the six decisions were wrong, and two — Greece and 'Battleaxe' — were disastrous.

PART TWO: MONTGOMERY— FROM THE LIFE

CHAPTER FOUR: SAVED BY ROMMEL

I have often been asked to relate exactly how I became Montgomery's Chief of Staff in the Eighth Army and later the 21st Army Group. I gave a brief account in my book *Operation Victory* and the Field-Marshal explains the reasons for his choice at some length in his *Memoirs*. But there is a little more to it than all that and my position was, in fact, anything but secure after Montgomery took over command of the Eighth Army, and I can truthfully say that I was consolidated in my post by Rommel!

After I had been appointed Director of Military Intelligence (Middle East) by Auchinleck in February 1942, I used to accompany the Commander-in-Chief on some of his visits to the Western Desert. One of these trips was somewhat prolonged, and that was after Ritchie had been relieved of his command of the Eighth Army and Auchinleck decided to take over command himself. Then followed exciting yet critical days when we were using everything we'd got to stop Rommel around El Alamein. The situation was very fluid at the time and one just didn't know what was going to happen next. When one heard the noise of tanks from the Army's Battle Headquarters, for instance, there was always the fear that they might prove to be those of the Afrika Korps! But gradually, thanks to the indomitable qualities of our fighting soldiers and to the tremendous help given us by the Desert Air Force, Rommel's steam started to run out and the position began to stabilize, and then suddenly we woke up one morning to realize that Cairo and the Middle East Base were safe — at least for the time being.

Auchinleck has never been given sufficient credit for his leadership during those anxious days. It was a situation that required great determination and courage. I admired him very much during this period and really enjoyed — if that's the right word — that exciting time in the desert. In a later chapter I give some impressions of Auchinleck as Commander-in-Chief.

When the front had finally been stabilized, and Eighth Army had its flanks securely protected by the sea and the Quattara Depression, I decided that it was about time for me to return to my Headquarters in Cairo, where a lot of work was awaiting my attention. I was D.M.I. Middle East and so the desert front was only a part of a pretty large parish. The War Office was pressing for various appreciations and views regarding this and that and so I asked the 'Auk' to allow me to return. He agreed.

I would not have been human had I not experienced some pleasurable thoughts as I climbed into the small aircraft that was to take me back to Cairo. A comfortable flat, hot baths and all the wartime gaiety of that cosmopolitan city were awaiting me.

That evening, as I sat eating a delicious dinner with friends at the Mohamed Ali Club, it hardly seemed possible that such a change could have taken place in a matter of hours. But little did I know what was in store for me and how the whole pattern of my existence for the rest of the war was shortly to be changed. I was in for a sizeable and severe shock.

The next day was spent in trying to bring myself up to date with all the paper-work that had accumulated during my absence, and with the various intelligence reports that had flowed in from many sources. The day passed quickly and pleasantly, for it was interesting work.

The following morning I arrived at the usual time in my office, to be briefed by my people for the daily Staff

Conference at which reports from the main branches of the Staff were made and at which the Commander-in-Chief was normally present. As he was now commanding the Eighth Army, on this occasion his Chief of General Staff, General Corbett, took his place.

On my table lay a signal for 'de Guingand's eyes only', and after sitting down in my comfortable chair, I ripped open the envelope and before I had read very far my eyes were literally popping out of my head.

It read something like this:

Brigadier de Guingand,
G.H.Q., Cairo.
    Request you hand over duties of D.M.I. to your Deputy and leave immediately for Headquarters Eighth Army to take up appointment of B.G.S.[18]

I rang the bell and showed it to my faithful Personal Assistant, Christopher Gowan. I think he was as shaken as I had been myself.

I remarked, 'The Auk must be round the bend.'

To take over such an important job at a time like this, when I had had no previous staff experience in the field, other than odd assignments, seemed at that moment quite beyond my own capacity and hardly fair to the Army itself.

I sat and thought about the problem and then decided to go and have a talk with the Military Secretary, who was responsible for recommending and making such appointments. I walked down the long dingy passages in a sort of numbed state and entered Andrewes's office, sat down and placed the signal on his desk. He read it and looked at me, saying nothing.

---

[18] Brigadier General Staff, an appointment which after Montgomery's arrival was changed to Chief of Staff.

So I gave him my views and I suppose rather unflatteringly he agreed and said:

'I think he's mad. Not a good move to appoint you B.G.S. at this time — too risky.'

'What shall I do?' I asked.

'Do nothing. I am flying up to see the C.-in-C. today and I'll deal with the matter when I get there.'

I thanked him, much relieved, and returned to my office and got on with the morning's work.

I enjoyed an excellent lunch at the Gezira Sporting Club and went back to my office, with the thought that if things went well in the afternoon, I might try and take an hour or so off and play a few holes of golf, as I was badly in need of exercise.

I had just been given a cup of tea when a signal was brought in by Gowan. I glanced at it and sat back with a jerk. It was from the Commander-in-Chief; it was short and precise and left no room for doubt as to what was required of me. It was also quite clear that Andrewes had failed in his mission.

Again I must rely upon my memory, but it read like this:

Seen Andrewes, you will report Eighth Army forthwith. C.-in-C.

So there it was, back to the sand and the real war and an end to the phoney life in Cairo. The only real problem was my very genuine fear that I would prove quite inadequate for the task ahead. Now there was no comeback; it was just a matter of getting there as quickly as possible.

I went up to see Tedder, who was Air C.-in-C., and told him of my impending move. He didn't express any particular objection or concern, which was reassuring, and I asked him for an aircraft to fly me up and this was soon arranged for the next morning.

The evening was spent in handing over to my Deputy, clearing things up at the flat, and packing up; for I had no idea when Cairo would see me again.

The next morning I took off in a Boston; not the most comfortable of aircraft. The passenger usually sat in the nose in the bomb-aimer's compartment made of perspex. I was most uncomfortable and very hot.

We flew to one of the landing-strips within the Eighth Army area and then drove up to where Auchinleck had his Headquarters and I reported to him for duty. I spent the next few hours in taking over from the existing B.G.S., Jock Whiteley; and then started some hectic days during which I tried to learn something about my new job. And so, to put the record straight — for there has been much controversy over this point — a great deal of the Staff's time was taken up in carrying out the studies necessary for producing plans for a future offensive against Rommel.

I have just related how I happened to be B.G.S. (Chief of Staff) of the Eighth Army when Montgomery arrived to take over command. In a previous book I have described how I met the new Army Commander at the cross-roads outside Alexandria on a hot and sultry August morning and how I drove up with him to our Battle Headquarters, and of the brilliant way in which he took a grip of things from the first moment of his arrival.

Montgomery, in his *Memoirs*, graphically describes his arrival in the Eighth Army and the drive up to our Headquarters. As we drove along a track on the open desert he writes: 'We were quiet now and I was thinking; chiefly about de Guingand, and I have no doubt he was thinking about me and his own future.'

He goes on to explain his mental process directed at choosing a Chief of Staff who would suit him. In fact, whether I was the right man to fill his requirements. He sees us as opposites.

In his own words:

> We were complete opposites; he lived on his nerves and was highly strung; in ordinary life he liked wine, gambling, and good food. Did the differences matter? I quickly decided that they did not; indeed, differences were assets.

The story goes that he originally included a liking for women as another 'opposite'; but the publishers advised against this — a bit dangerous!

He then says some very flattering things about me and having, as 'Monty' invariably did, 'analysed the problem' and made up his mind, he wrote: 'Before we arrived at Eighth Army H.Q. I had decided that de Guingand was the man; I would make him Chief of Staff with full powers and together we would do the job.'

And, sure enough, when he spoke to the Staff on that first evening on the Ruweisat Ridge as the sun was setting, he announced that he favoured the Chief of Staff system and that I would act as such with full powers from him, the Army Commander.

Later, however, he must have had some doubts, or at least found himself in a slight predicament. I must tell my version of what transpired.

Several days after Montgomery's arrival I was crossing the area between my caravan and the operations' vehicle, when he stuck out his head and in that rather shrill staccato voice, which later I got to know always prefaced something important, cried:

'Freddie, come along here. I want to have a word with you.'

So I climbed the steps into the caravan and sat down opposite him.

As was his custom, he got straight to the point.

'Now I don't want you to be hurt by what I have to say, but I feel I must tell you that I had a Chief of Staff in England, whom I trained myself and who knows my ways. Before leaving England I told him I would probably get him out here as it would save me a lot of trouble. So if this does happen, please don't get upset for it's no reflection on you personally and I will certainly see that you get any job you would like to have.'

Well, there it was. I might add this was not entirely unexpected and having said, 'That's quite all right, sir,' I left the caravan and continued my walk to the operations' vehicle. Strangely enough I didn't, at that moment, feel any great sense of disappointment; in fact I felt a certain wave of relief engulf me, for I was far from sure that I could hold the position satisfactorily, especially under a man of Monty's reputation, for he demanded a great deal from his subordinates.

Within three or four days, however, Rommel attacked — his last desperate thrust to capture Cairo and the Middle East Base. It was the usual 'right hook', but it failed and after some savage fighting Montgomery won his first victory — the Battle of Alam Halfa. He had anticipated exactly Rommel's intentions and had skilfully deployed his forces to meet the threat.

His immediate appreciation of the vital importance that the Alam Halfa ridge would play in any defensive battle was a classical example of what Napoleon called the '*coup d'œil militaire*'. Here is a quotation from his (Napoleon's) *Memoirs*:

> There is a gift of being able to see at a glance what prospects
> are offered by the terrain ... one can call it the '*coup d'œil
> militaire*', and it is a gift which is inborn in great generals.

And from that day in the caravan until long after the war, I
never heard the subject of my departure mentioned. Neither of
us referred to it, and how serious Montgomery was on that
occasion I shall never really know, but I have always felt a
certain gratitude to Field-Marshal Rommel, a great soldier by
any standards, for ensuring that I enjoyed an unforgettable
experience as Chief of Staff to one of the greatest British Field
Commanders of all time.

CHAPTER FIVE: LETTERS FROM MONTY IN NORTH AFRICA

Recently I have been sorting out a mass of old papers and among them found a number of letters written to me by Field-Marshal Montgomery. The majority were received after the war was over and are extremely interesting in that they give some vivid, caustic and often profoundly revealing comments on current events. As the Field-Marshal held the appointment of C.I.G.S., Chairman of the Western Union set-up, and then Deputy Supreme Commander of the NATO forces, he was in a position to be in close touch with the centre of things. These letters are, unfortunately, not for publication — at least not yet. And in any case they might invite legal proceedings which would prove altogether too costly! There are, however, a few letters which he wrote to me during the Desert War. They are few because we used to conduct our business by personal contact and the telephone and rarely by letter. We were usually in daily touch and we got to know each other so well that there was little need to commit anything to writing. They were mostly written when I was away from our H.Q. because of ill-health. These letters are, however, interesting in that they show a different side of Montgomery's character — a softer and more human angle to this great commander's make-up.

I have selected six for reproduction — all written in his own handwriting — and I propose to describe the events or circumstances that surround them.

The first is a short note written on the 9th December, 1942, from the British Embassy in Cairo. Here is the note:

British Embassy,
Cairo.
9-12-42.

My dear Freddie,

I enclose a copy of the treatise on how to fight battles. The printing people have done it very well.

Get well quickly and come back to me.

Yrs. ever,
B. L. Montgomery.

Perhaps I had better explain the background to this and the next two letters.

After the battle of El Alamein had been fought things moved very quickly. The major break-through occurred on the night of the 3rd/4th November, and then the fun started. Would we be able to cut off the mobile elements of Rommel's forces before they could clear Benghazi and so reach the comparative security of the Agheila position? Tedder, Air Vice-Marshal Coningham and others tried to persuade Monty to send a powerful force across the desert along the routes used by Dick O'Connor when he cut off and annihilated the Italians. In fact, early on in the battle, I had the transport and supplies already organized for such a move. But Monty was determined not to risk a reverse in view of the defeats we had had in the past in this area against Rommel, and in any case the units belonging to this task-force had to a large extent been absorbed into the main battle before the actual break-out occurred. It will be remembered that twice before the enemy had checked our advance at this bottle-neck among the salt-pans of Agheila. It was from this area that Rommel first gained desert fame, when he counter-attacked with great success with comparatively weak forces, on 31st March, 1941.

Our Battle Headquarters' having by-passed Tobruk, reached Martuba about the 14th November. In this rather pleasant locality we remained some days while the advance south of Benghazi took place. We had now temporarily left the desert and were situated in the 'Jebel' country where green scrub and grass were to be found. It rather resembled the moors in Scotland.

Towards the end of November Montgomery decided to move forward in order to discuss future plans with General Leese who commanded 30th Corps which was now in contact with the enemy. We took our two caravans, map lorry, wireless sets and a small Mess. Accompanied by the A.D.C.'s and Liaison Officers we set out on a lovely November morning for Benghazi, spending one night en route in a small and sheltered valley. It was wonderfully relaxing to get away, even for a few hours, from the hectic atmosphere of operations and plans; to leave an environment where one could not call one's soul one's own; being at everyone's beck and call during the whole twenty-four hours. That evening stands vividly in my memory, for I could luxuriously reflect upon the past few weeks, and I believe it was only then that I realized to the full what the Eighth Army had achieved. It was pleasant to gossip quietly with my Chief while our batmen got busy with our evening meal. Before we retired to bed we obtained a 'Situation Report' over the wireless, and, later, Montgomery's Liaison Officers arrived to tell their story. Things appeared to be going well south of Benghazi.

The next morning we drove leisurely into Benghazi via the agricultural centre of Barce. It was quite astonishing to find to what good use the Italians had put this comparatively fertile zone bordering upon the desert. For only a few miles to the south stretched countless leagues of sand.

It was, for both of us, our first visit to Benghazi and I certainly was thrilled to pace its streets, for here was a tangible result of our Army's efforts — a modern city and port now safely in our hands. After a drive down to the harbour to see the damage caused by bomb and gale, we paid a visit to the Cathedral — a fine building which had not been seriously marred by war. We chatted amiably with one of the Church dignitaries and then drove a short distance to a point from which we overlooked the port, and ate our picnic lunch. I remember pondering, as I topped off the meal with some Italian wine, how different would have been the entry into a captured city by some Commanders. Today saw no fuss, no pomp, no ceremony; and no security arrangements. Montgomery behaved more like a tourist than a victorious Army Commander.

After lunch we drove southwards along the road that traversed many miles to Tripoli, and towards dusk reached Leese's 30th Corps Headquarters — a mere collection of tents, caravans and cars dispersed around the desert.

Our caravans had already arrived and had been allotted their plot of sandy space.

Little time was lost in getting down to business and our future plans were discussed in great detail. How could we turn the Agheila position? How long would it take to concentrate sufficient force and adequate administrative resources? There was also the question of establishing the Desert Air Force far enough forward to ensure adequate air support to cover the next advance.

We ate a good dinner in Leese's Mess, after which George Walsh (B.G.S., 30th Corps) and I got down to detailed planning as a result of the decisions arrived at between our respective chiefs. About 11 p.m. I strolled over to my caravan to turn in, and hardly had I got undressed than I experienced an attack of acute pain — a repetition of several I had had over the last year or so. After some time it eased but I felt on the point of collapse. My trusted Chief Clerk, Harwood, who was with me all through the war and used to sleep under a lean-to attached to the side of my caravan, heard some peculiar noises and arrived to find me in a pretty poor condition. He rushed off to find the Corps H.Q.'s doctor who arrived in due course and gave me an injection which soon gave me some blessed sleep.

I was awakened the next morning at about 6 by the pom-pom fire from Bofors guns. Although half-doped, I struggled up to see what was the trouble, only to find that an enemy low-flying marauding aircraft was streaking in from the East. As I looked out of my caravan window three bombs dropped. The first went off and gave the side of my 'residence' a good pasting; the second and third bounced and then rolled across the gravel, but luckily they had been released so near to the ground that there had been insufficient time for them to become 'armed'. I saw one of the bombs rolling gaily along until it came to rest at the entrance to a small bivouac tent located near by. I was watching in a fascinated sort of way when suddenly from the small tent came loud and prolonged laughter, and out of the other end emerged Geoffrey Keating, the gallant and entertaining commander of the Eighth Army Film Unit and subsequently in charge of our public relations in the field. He patted the bomb affectionately on its side and came over for a chat. He told me that he had been lying peacefully in bed gazing out of the far end of the tent when he spotted the aircraft coming straight towards him. He witnessed the first bomb burst and then he saw the second bounce and start rolling towards his bivvy. Spellbound and glued to the ground he awaited his certain end, and, during those split seconds he engaged in a most remarkable self-examination — the result of which added up to something not altogether reassuring! With the failure of the bomb to explode, he realized that the Almighty in His mercy had decided to give him another spell on earth for most necessary atonement! The whole thing struck him as highly amusing, and I found his story and laughter so infectious that I managed to pull myself out of my lethargy.

After breakfast I was once again examined by the doctor who decided that I must be evacuated to hospital in Cairo. As it happened these attacks repeated themselves several more times during the war and after. It fell to a brilliant radiologist — Dr. Eric Samuel of Johannesburg and now of Edinburgh — to locate finally the source of the trouble. It was, as I had always thought, a gallstone.

By coincidence, this very same Dr. Samuel had occasion to X-ray Montgomery's back soon after the war ended. The engines of the Field-Marshal's small plane cut out just as it was about to land and as his back appeared injured he was flown to London for examination. When the X-ray photographs were developed, a large stone in his gall-bladder was visible. The medical experts discussed the matter and suggested that it should be taken out.

'How long has it been there?' he asked the surgeon.

'Oh probably for twenty-five years or more,' came the reply.

'Then it can stay there for another twenty-five years,' was the Army Group Commander's decision!

But back to my caravan at 30th Corps Headquarters. I was naturally very distressed and bitterly disappointed at being invalided back to Cairo, for I began to conjure up thoughts which spelt the end of my time with the Army I had grown to love so well; to say nothing of the end of my association with its remarkable Commander. I handed over to my friend Bobby Erskine (B.G.S., 13th Corps), which was reassuring for I knew he would prove a first-class Chief of Staff.

An aircraft was sent up to take me back to Cairo and I flew there with my batman Lawrence, who took a very favourable view of these developments. By the evening of the next day I was tucked up between cool sheets in the Scottish Hospital, somewhat bewildered and extremely miserable.

After about a couple of weeks' treatment a Medical Board dealt with my case, and I was told that they would recommend three months' sick leave and suggest a rest in South Africa. So this was the end, and I began to picture spending the rest of the war as a 'Base Wallah'. But I had not at that time appreciated fully the amazing determination or the character of my Chief. He flew to Cairo about the 8th December and came along to see me. I told him of the decision of the Medical Board and, in that typical way of his of refusing to accept anything which interfered with his plans, he asked me when I thought I would be fit to rejoin him? I replied that at the moment I did not feel too good but I guessed two or three weeks' rest might do the trick.

'All right, Freddie, I'll talk to your doctors,' he said. The talk produced miraculous results, for my three-months' sick leave was changed to three weeks on the condition that I was 'worked gently' to start with. So, in a matter of hours, the outlook entirely changed and I felt I had received a high-powered injection of some new stimulant.

This was the background to that short note sent from the British Embassy in Cairo on 9th December, 1942. The 'get well quickly and come back to me' was simply put and yet made me feel I was wanted once again in the Eighth Army. The reference to the 'treatise on how to fight battles' was a pamphlet Montgomery had prepared embodying all the lessons we had learned up to the end of the Battle of El Alamein. Some old 'Blimps' and the anti-Monty school tried, as usual, to suggest that this was merely an effort for self-advertisement. How wrong they were! 'Some brief notes for Senior Officers in the conduct of battle' was a most realistic and intensely valuable study, full of practical information and advice.

After the original Medical Board's decision, and as I had been 'walking-out' for some time, I decided to take this opportunity to get married. I left hospital on 16th December, and our wedding took place on the 17th, after which we flew to Jerusalem for my three-weeks' leave. The wedding was a quiet affair and was followed by a lunch party at the Mohamed Ali Club — Bill Norman, my old sailor colleague on the Joint Planning Staff, acting as my best man.

Shortly after arriving at the King David Hotel in Palestine I received the following letter from the Army Commander:

> Eighth Army
> 18-12-42.
>
> My Dear Freddie,
>
> I was glad to hear from you and to learn that you may be back in one month. I gather you are now out of hospital. I would certainly get married and have a quiet honeymoon in Jerusalem; but you must *be* quiet and not rush about to parties, etc. All goes very well here. We faced up to the Agheila position, and were just about to set about him when he decided it would be best to pull out. But he was not quite quick enough. The N.Z. Div. got across the road about 10 miles N.W. of Marble Arch on evening 15 Dec. and cut his mobile rearguards in two: Between there and Nofelia the road was thick with M.T. moving west; and in between the N.Z. Div. and 7 Armd. Div. was 90 Light, 15 and 21 Panzer Divs.,

and other odd units. It looked at one time as if we would have a really good bag. But the two Panzer Divs. and 90 Light broke away westwards through gaps in the N.Z. positions; very heavy toll was taken of them and the whole party was severely mauled. The air had a very good day with the stuff on the roads and the Bostons went over every ½ hour.

Now we are up to Nofelia and I shall have to halt the main bodies there, while I build up some maintenance.

I have had a good look at the famous Agheila position. It is immensely strong and we have been saved considerable casualties by not having to attack it seriously; it was a complete mass of mines, especially on the approaches, and we have had a good many chaps blown up; we had to concentrate most of the R.E. in the Army to clear the mines and get safe roads through.

The Bosche must have been very annoyed at having to give up this very strong position. Its strength lies in the ground, which forces an enemy to approach it in certain ways.

Harry Arkwright is back, and looking very well.

Jorrocks came up to see me and stayed two nights. He said that the 'G' staff in 10 Corps was quite frightful; no proper system; no organization; most of the G.2's complete duds. He is cleaning it all up. He is very pleased with Peake as B.G.S.; I have sent —— to 13th Corps.

Don't overdo it on leave.

Yrs. ever,

B. L. Montgomery.

This was really quite a long letter for Montgomery and starts with giving his blessing to my marriage. In view of his one-time maxim 'You can't make a good soldier and a good husband' this advice was somewhat unexpected and I have always wondered what would have happened if he had taken the opposite viewpoint! For it will be seen that the letter was written on the day after my wedding took place!

I'm afraid I did not feel hearty enough to go rushing about to parties, but the warning had a nice fatherly touch!

The very clear account of the operations around Agheila is interesting because the enemy were manoeuvred out of this position with very little loss to ourselves, and, looking back upon the operations from the end of El Alamein until we reached the Mareth Line, I am more than ever certain that Montgomery felt confident that he could deal with the remnants of Rommel's army without having to take any unnecessary risks. The left hook flanking movement carried out by the New Zealand Division was a pretty ambitious affair, and I still vividly remember getting a first-hand account of this operation from their gallant Divisional Commander — Freyberg. It was rich entertainment to hear him describe the actions of his beloved division — nothing was left to the imagination.

Montgomery was always most careful with regard to equating the operational side of his plans to his administrative resources. Unless forced to, he was not prepared to take risks in this respect. The reference to having to halt his main bodies at Nofelia bears out this point.

My Chief was a little disappointed that he had failed to cut off the enemy at Agheila and, no doubt, a psychologist would say that his references to the operation in the second paragraph of the letter savoured of self-justification to cover such disappointment. And, of course, they might be right!

Harry Arkwright was our Brigadier Royal Armoured Corps (Tank Adviser) and had suffered from a breakdown some weeks back.

'Jorrocks' is, of course, General Brian Horrocks, that lovable Commander of the 13th Corps at Alamein. After that battle — much to his disappointment — he had been left behind to 'tidy up' the battlefield. A week or two later, however, to his joy, he was back in the chase again in command of an Army Corps.

The references to the 'G' Staff of the 10th Corps are, perhaps, not wholly deserved. It is one of those things, that new Commanders, when they take over formations in war, are apt to be critical of the existing Staff, and somewhat naturally want to have some at least of their 'own chaps' around them.

Feeling a bit more robust after ten days spent in the Holy City, I felt I had better try to get some exercise and so harden myself up for the work ahead. By the kindness of that enlightened Monarch, the Emir Abdullah of Trans-Jordan, and also with the help of my old Staff College colleague, Shakir Al Wadi Bey, who was then Iraqi Consul General in Jerusalem, I arranged to pay two visits to the Jordan Valley to shoot.

The Emir, as was his custom each winter, had established a very commodious camp in the Jordan Valley, where at this time of the year the climate was extremely pleasant. We had a good talk followed by a spacious midday meal in true Arab style. My Cockney batman, Lawrence, did not live up to his name and found the company and the food anything but to his liking. He was catered for in splendid isolation away from the main dining tent, and, when I collected him after the meal, found him pea-green and unhappy. He considered 'these 'ere sheeps' eyes and what-nots are definitely not my cup of tea'. I told him, however, that the little programme that had been arranged for the afternoon was just what he required — a nice little walk after partridge in the Trans-Jordan hills!

I had warned Lawrence before he left the King David Hotel that I hoped to go shooting, and advised him to wear some robust old boots. I was somewhat surprised, therefore, to find that he was wearing a pair of rather thin-soled patent leather shoes. He explained, however, that they were 'just the job — nice and easy on the feet'.

Abdullah had arranged for my wife to go riding and she was rather shaken to find a mounted escort of some half-dozen keen-featured warriors, armed to the teeth, waiting to accompany her, in order to see that no harm came to the General's wife. She had a couple of hours' exercise, but found it difficult to admire and take in the rugged beauty of the countryside; for every time she broke out of a walk there was an immediate redisposition of the escort to ensure that she did not get away on her own. Actually, I felt she obtained a certain satisfaction from the episode, with the idea that perhaps she was looked upon as a juicy morsel for some tough and hard-riding Arab Sheik!

The shooting party drove off to a suitable area and my hosts then indicated the ground where game was likely to be found. As usual, in this part of the world, there were many hills to climb and the ground was particularly rough. After an hour's hard work I found myself puffing and blowing on the top of one hill, nearly out of cartridges, with Lawrence in a similar state of exhaustion sitting on another hill to my left. I shouted across and asked him to bring some ammunition which he was carrying in an old army haversack. He didn't appear to realize the significance of my request, and it was only after I had shouted myself hoarse that it dawned upon him what all this involved. I heard an indignant 'What — me! — Who does he think I am — a fluffing goat' come floating across the valley and I then witnessed the patent leather shoes making very heavy weather of the journey. I am certain that Leigh-Mallory's last climb up the north-west col of Everest can hardly have been more painful. When he had regained his breath, Lawrence told me exactly what he thought of shooting — 'I can't make out 'ead or tail of this 'ere shooting, sir — it seems bloody stupid to me!'

However, after that Lawrence took good care to keep reasonably close up in order to avoid another 'Calvary' that afternoon. But I am afraid he was never made for the outdoor life and his presence gave one the jitters. Every time he saw any sort of feathered creature take off — be it a sparrow or hawk, a cry of 'Look out, sir, there goes more of them bleedin' partridges!'

It was really a wonder that I connected at all.

And so back to Abdullah's camp for a cup of green tea and to witness that impressive moment when the Emir and his retinue met for evening prayers just as the sun flicked the craggy Palestinian hills.

I received a kind note from Abdullah after my visit. He was a warrior at heart and took a tremendous interest in Eighth Army's fortunes.

Translation of Abdullah's letter to the author.

Amman 6.4.1943.

Dear Brigadier de Guingand,

I thank you for your letters and remember with delight your visit to me with your wife. I am grateful for the photographs; wishing you victory and success in the coming actions.

Please present my compliments to General Montgomery.

Your friend,

sgd. (ABDULLAH)

I am anxiously awaiting the 8th Army's attack on the Afrika Korps across Gabes, and wish the triumphant 8th Army and their Officer Commanding decisive victory, by the will of God.

sgd. (ABDULLAH)

With improving health I began to worry more and more about the Eighth Army and the campaign ahead. I again got an attack of that unwanted feeling and wondered whether my old job was still open to me. But, early in the New Year an officer arrived with a letter from Montgomery and all my doubts and anxieties fell away. Here is the letter:

Eighth Army.

1-1-43.

My Dear Freddy,

I am delighted to hear all is going well. Here we are all getting tee-ed up for the big stuff. My leading troops are only about 200 miles from Tripoli, and 200 miles is nothing to us!!

I shall be delighted to see you back again. If you join up here by 14th January it might be worth your while. But get well first as life will be somewhat hectic about that time. I expect you will read between the lines.

We are now in contact with the Bosche on the line of the main Buerat position about 40 miles west of the Waid Gebir.

Yrs. ever,

B. L. Montgomery.

The letter starts with a nice note of optimism and confidence and then suggests the date by which I should return, i.e. 14th January. This second paragraph amused me for it finishes with: 'I expect you will read between the lines.' As the advance to Tripoli was booked to start on 15th January, very little was left to the imagination. But, no doubt, my Chief felt he was being very security-minded.

It was convenient, however, to have a target date to give my doctor, and he did wonders during the remaining period. So much so, that we were back in Cairo on the 12th, and on the 14th I found myself sitting in the bombardier's seat, isolated in the nose of a Boston aircraft, en route for the 'Marble Arch' airfield. Air-Marshal (as he then was) Sholto-Douglas very kindly gave me a lift. From here I was transhipped to a puddle-jumper which took me to an airstrip located alongside our Headquarters. It was good to meet old friends again and to hear all the gossip. Montgomery took me to his caravan and explained with his usual extraordinary clarity the plans for the advance to Tripoli. I had to admit, somewhat grudgingly perhaps, that everything had gone along very well without me — a sobering and useful experience!

However, by the time Tripoli had been captured — I felt once more at home in the saddle and we then started to concentrate all we knew upon how we should tackle the formidable Mareth Line.

In the midst of the preparations for the attack on the Mareth Line, Montgomery sent me back to Cairo with the ostensible object of arranging for the printing of yet another of the pamphlets which he issued to his Army from time to time. I appreciated that there was really no necessity for a Chief of Staff to handle such a simple matter, but I knew that it was his way of camouflaging a very kindly gesture. He no doubt thought it was about time that a newly married officer should see his wife again!

Once again I enjoyed the wonderful contrast of the comfort of this city with the rigours of the desert, and after landing at the air base, I drove as quickly as possible to the flat where my wife was living. It was situated in a large modern block on Gezira Island which was affectionately known as 'the Elephant'. There were two such buildings next door to each other, which were christened by someone 'The Elephant and Castle'.

After the appropriate greetings were over, I lay enjoying the luxury of a hot bath. Life felt very good indeed at that moment. But a little later on, while I was relaxing in my dressing-gown and sipping a king-size dry martini, my wife broke the news.

'Madame Catroux insists that she sees you at the earliest possible moment. Something very important, she says.'

Looking to see the effects of her words she added, 'And I had to promise faithfully that I would bring you along.'

For those who have never met this remarkable woman I will make the introductions. Margaret Catroux was the wife of General Georges Catroux, who was a magnificent product of the French military school. Before the war he had held the position of Governor-General in Algeria. He was one of the most charming and cultured men I have had the good fortune to meet, and his wife was in every way cast to take her place at his side and share his great responsibilities. Able, intelligent and possessing an almost fanatical loyalty to his beloved France, Catroux was no collaborator and had joined the Free French Movement, and at this particular time headed their affairs in the Middle East.

Madame Catroux was known affectionately as 'La Reine Margot'. She was an extremely strong and forceful personality and woe betide anyone who served under her husband and ignored her advice or scorned her patronage. General Pierre Kœnig once described to me her influence during the time he served on Catroux's staff in Algiers as a young man. There were some delicious stories of how she dominated the lives of these young officers, even to the point of having a say in their love-affairs and marriages.

As much as I admired 'La Reine Margot', and I most sincerely did, I didn't at that moment feel like paying social calls on my first evening back in Cairo. Eventually, however, my wife persuaded me to get dressed so that she could fulfil the promise that she had made.

'In any case, darling,' she said, 'her flat's only two floors down and the General is away from Egypt at the moment, so the old girl is probably feeling a bit lonely.'

We knocked at the door and were shown into an attractive sitting-room which contained some of the treasures that the Catrouxs had collected during their service in France's dominions overseas. We were not kept waiting long before 'La Reine' appeared in all her grandeur. She was certainly an impressive woman. On this occasion she was dressed in some sort of Eastern outfit — from Indo-China I presumed. She reminded me of a Chinese Empress or of someone out of "The Mikado." She expressed pleasure at seeing me again, adding that she had been looking after my 'little wife' — and I bet she had! She then told me that there was a matter of extreme importance which she wished to discuss with me. I smiled and politely asked what it was all about and then waited for her reply.

'Le Ligne Mareth — how are you going to attack? What is your plan?'

I must admit that I was just a bit surprised, for this information was naturally highly secret and even with so staunch an ally as Madame Catroux, one had to be careful to draw the line somewhere.

Before I had time to collect my thoughts and decide what answer I should give to this rather embarrassing question, she literally swept me towards a table situated at the end of the room, upon which were spread two large maps. I glanced down and noticed that they were French maps of the Mareth Line and the surrounding country. They looked old and well used. My interest was immediately alerted, particularly as I spotted various pencilled notes and other markings.

Without further ado, 'La Reine Margot' started to give me an extremely lucid description of the problem with which we were faced — of attacking the defences from the East. She went on to explain how during Catroux's period of Command in North Africa, he had conducted manoeuvres and exercises to test the strength of the position. I became very interested and listened attentively for we were, at that very moment, gathering all available information as to the feasibility of outflanking the defences from the landward side. A lot would depend upon the type of ground and the degree to which motor vehicles could traverse the hills and sandy wastes.

It was then my turn to speak, and I bombarded my hostess with questions. Apparently the exercises had shown that the Mareth Line was by no means invulnerable to a flanking attack, even in the days when vehicles and tyres were nothing like as desert-worthy as they were in 1943. Movement had been found to be quite possible.

Eventually *la séance* came to an end and we left the maps and sat down in comfortable chairs to drink a well-mixed cocktail. We chatted for about half an hour, during which Madame Catroux brought me up to date with the latest happenings in Cairo and how the struggle by the Free French to maintain their country's honour was progressing.

We got up to go and the strength of her personality was so great that one was almost tempted to walk out backwards as one left the presence of 'La Reine Margot'! All this information about the Mareth Line from the French, who had built it, made my Cairo trip really worth while from the military point of view after all.

And so the campaign rolled on, and further successes added to the glory of our Desert Army. Medenine, Mareth, Gabes, Sfax, and Sousse fell to our troops; these to be followed by the final assault upon the Axis Bridgehead around Cap Bon to which Hitler, in his wisdom decided to commit a quarter of a million of his troops without any hope for their evacuation. On 12th May the end came and the din of battle died down over the North African coast. Yet another blow had been struck on the road to complete victory. But the weary troops of Eighth and First Armies had by no means finished their task. There was much yet to be done — Sicily and the 'underbelly of the Axis' were glittering objectives, and there was no time to be lost if Sicily was to be invaded before the autumn weather in the Mediterranean made the operation too hazardous.

By agreement with General Alexander, and in order to accelerate the preparations for the Sicilian assault, it was decided that I should return to Cairo as Montgomery's deputy and get busy with our plans. I arrived there on 15th April for that purpose, not altogether disappointed at my fate; for once again Cairo and the fleshpots sounded an excellent alternative to the desert. I'd begun to get just a bit scruffy!

On arrival in Cairo I got straight down to planning at our specially guarded Headquarters called 'George', where I first met that fine sailor, Admiral Ramsay. Bimbo Dempsey, now commanding the 13th Corps, was also in the set-up, as his Corps was to be used for the initial assault. This was a happy time, for one could not have wished for more able or co-operative colleagues, besides which I was able to snatch a bit of family life.

It did not take me long to realize that the basis of the plan, prepared by a special planning staff attached to Eisenhower's Headquarters at Algiers, had some serious weaknesses. The main fault I found was that dispersal rather than concentration formed the foundation. The proposed Command set-up and other matters also appeared unsatisfactory. I therefore wrote an appreciation for my Chief and followed this up with a suggestion that he should fly to Cairo and acquaint himself first-hand with all the problems involved. This he agreed to do, and arrived in his Flying Fortress on 23rd April.

We held several meetings with the other Services and Dempsey, and, as a result, Montgomery sent a pretty stiff signal[19] to Algiers giving in no uncertain terms his views regarding the proposed plan, together with his suggested modifications. This, naturally, caused a bit of a hullaballoo and Alexander, now Eisenhower's deputy, wisely summoned a conference to take place at Algiers on 28th April. On the day before, however, I received a signal from my Chief to say that as he was ill in bed I must take his place at the coming Conference. After a few hectic hours of preparation I took off at 10 p.m. on the 27th in a special Hudson aircraft, and we were due to arrive in Algiers in time for the Conference the next morning. We had a perfect flight under a clear and starlit sky to our first refuelling stop, El Adem. The Station Commander met me and took me into the Mess for some sandwiches and a hot drink. While we were chatting an officer came in and reported that a desert mist had blown across the airfield and that, for the time being, no take-off was possible. This wasn't too good, as it was of the utmost importance that I attended this Conference. In about a couple of hours there was a slight improvement in the conditions, and I pressed very hard that an attempt should be made. I could see the Station Commander didn't like it but, in view of the urgency, and after a discussion with the pilot, he agreed to let us go. There were

---

[19] See account in *Operation Victory*.

no aircraft on the actual landing-ground and so it was arranged that a lorry should lead the aircraft over to the correct starting point for its take-off. As the pilot knew the length of the airfield, and as the aircraft would be above the mist within a second or two, it was felt that no particular risk was being taken.

I clambered back into the cabin and settled myself down on the temporary bed which had been fixed up for me. By good fortune I had arranged a goodly assortment of pillows around my head, which was pointing towards the aircraft's nose. Having taxied across the gravel, and after revving up our engines, we started our take-off run straight into the mist, which was, of course, made to look worse in the glare of the aircraft's landing lights. And that's all I remembered for many hours.

The only recollection that vividly invaded my mind was the strong smell of petrol. What had happened was that, either through an engine cutting, or owing to an error of judgement, the aircraft had dived into the ground just off the side of the airfield, after it had gained a few hundred feet of height. The aircraft itself was badly smashed up — I saw it a few weeks later looking a complete wreck. By some fortunate chance it had not caught fire in spite of the leakage of petrol. I believe this was due to the presence of mind of the pilot who switched off the fuel when he realized that control had been lost.

A Bombay Ambulance plane was flown up from Cairo and the crew, who had severe skull fractures, and myself were brought back to that city during the morning, where my wife met us at the airfield, naturally somewhat bewildered and distressed to see a procession of stretchers proceeding from the Bombay. She followed my stretcher into the waiting ambulance. As I was lowered into position I made some sort of noise and my wife understood me to say something about 'the black bag'. Having seen this object — which had all the Sicily plans in it — placed alongside my stretcher, she assured me that it was there. Satisfied with this information I then passed out once more. When the ambulance arrived outside our Cairo flat, she was met by a covey of red-tabbed officers who were formed up at the entrance. As she alighted from her car she was literally pounced upon with the eager demand: 'Where is the General's black bag?'

Luckily she could reassure them as to its safety. They departed with relieved expressions and the little black bag — the 'body' appeared to be of little importance — was taken upstairs to our flat!

Talking of black bags — it was the usual War Office issue — reminds me of another incident concerning this same bag. When living in London during the planning phase of 'Overlord' I had been lunching with my wife in a London hotel before an important conference with Eisenhower, Montgomery and the other Commanders-in-Chief. She had just packed up and, unbeknown to me, had at the last moment found a bundle of yellow knitting destined for our forthcoming baby. I rushed off, rather behind time, and arrived short of breath in the conference room to find that the proceedings had already started. Somewhat shaken I sat down, opened the black bag and yanked out all my files and papers. Imagine my surprise and embarrassment when out popped on to the table with these highly secret documents (the plans for 'Overlord') this peculiar-looking garment together with the knitting needles! This galaxy of Service Chiefs thoroughly enjoyed the joke, but I had some difficulty in explaining how the article could have got muddled up with these very secret papers. It was obviously useless for me to pretend that I had taken up knitting as a relaxation!

And now back to Cairo.

After two or three days of lying in bed, I received the following letter from Montgomery:

28-4-43.

My Dear Freddie,

I am terribly sorry about your accident. I am sending Belchem to Cairo. You are to stay in your house and be completely quiet.

Belchem will do the whole thing and can come and see you if he wants advice on any point.

It is absolutely essential that you take it easy and get well.

I am in bed myself with a temperature and sore throat, so the whole show is breaking up!!

Cheer up.

My kind regards to your lady wife.

Yrs. ever,
B. L. Montgomery.

I think it will be agreed that this is a very human letter, devoid of flap, yet comforting and fatherly. Receiving it did me a lot of good.

After various X-rays and treatment, two large-size bumps began to subside and my head felt less like the 'morning after the night before'. The doctors, however, decided that I must go away and rest for a couple of weeks before returning to the mêlée of our Headquarters. We decided, therefore, to visit Palestine and Syria — which we knew would be at its loveliest in the late spring.

The Middle East Headquarters were human enough to allow me to take my army car — a very nice Lincoln — for my sick leave. The faithful Lawrence spent a hectic few days learning to drive as I was forbidden to do so for a while, and so off we started early one morning in mid-May bound for Ismailia — the Sinai Desert and Jerusalem.

From Jerusalem we drove to Baalbek where I spent three days trout-fishing in the Orontes River, which gushes out of the Anti-Lebanon mountain range about midway between Baalbek and Homs. I had fished there before the war when stationed in Egypt and remembered how amazed I was to find this fisherman's paradise concealed in such an arid locality. You leave the main Homs road and drive across the virtual desert for several miles until you suddenly come up against a narrow gorge-like valley, at the bottom of which is to be found the icy cold, crystal clear, and fast-flowing Orontes. For fifty to a hundred yards on either side can be seen green cultivation and fruit trees, the land being irrigated by the ample waters drawn from the river. It was well-stocked with fine rainbow trout running up to several pounds in weight. The reason for this remarkable occurrence, in an otherwise hot and unsuitable country, is the fact that the great springs which start the river on its long journey to the Mediterranean are fed from the melting snows which often lie throughout the year on the higher slopes of the Anti-Lebanon. Within a matter of a few miles, however, the sun warms up the water beyond the temperature in which trout can live and breed; but during those first half-dozen miles excellent fish are to be found.

It was quite evident, after only a few miles' journey, that Lawrence's driving novitiate had been altogether too short — and the resting of my already rather shattered nerves was not assisted by this experience! However, the great point was that he appeared to enjoy himself to the full. On the return journey to Cairo we decided to fly back and leave the Lincoln in my batman's inexperienced hands. Three days after our arrival back, however, a somewhat crestfallen and bandaged Lawrence reported at 'George' with a tragic tale. The Lincoln was now lying at the bottom of some deep ravine in the Judean Hills and the military authorities, who had examined its condition, had reported it 'beyond salvage and repair'. So I suppose we had to feel grateful that the Almighty had watched over us on our outward journey!

This ill-fated Lincoln had a central window that could be let up and down in order to seal off the driver from his passengers. As my wife and I had many things to say to each other, which perhaps might have embarrassed my faithful batman, I had occasion to wind up the window. It was not long, however, before we sensed by the erratic driving that this development had not been favourably received by Lawrence. Eventually he turned round and knocked on the window. I wound it down as he slowed up to hear what was the trouble, and Lawrence replied: 'Y'know, you two needn't worry if you think I listen to what you say, because I don't. I never 'ear a word so you can keep the window open.' Not wanting to hurt his delicate feelings I therefore complied with his suggestion, and we were all once again on a more intimate basis.

Shortly after this incident I was quietly discussing with my wife a particular member of my staff. She did not entirely share my favourable views. The matter was, however, settled with little delay, for round turned Lawrence saying 'The General's quite right, Ma'am — Major is a very nice chap — all we blokes 'ave got a lot of use for him.' So that was that. It was nice to know that my views found support, but it said little for Lawrence's claims regarding the poor acoustic properties of our car! In the end we gave it up and the window was left permanently down.

Those three days relaxation by the Orontes River were unforgettable, and Lawrence found fishing a much saner occupation than shooting partridge in the hills. In fact, it was 'just the job'. The beer, rods, food and cushions were taken from the car to a shady spot on the river by a swarm of little Arab 'totos' and, this done, Lawrence's role was that of a watch-dog, which he filled to the complete satisfaction of the three of us.

After Baalbek we drove back to Beyrouth, knowing that within a day or two we should have to retrace our steps for 'George', and I can't say I was too happy, for I was still getting bad headaches. The day after our arrival, however, an officer came with a letter from Montgomery, and here it is:

British Embassy,
Cairo.
12-5-43.

My Dear Freddie,

I am in Cairo checking up on HUSKY.[20] Before coming here I visited Algiers and got various things agreed to as a result of the acceptance of my plan.

I then visited Alexander and got everything I wanted agreed to. There is now no need to worry on any matter. I have had conferences here and have explained the whole business to everyone; the foundations and framework of the whole project are now firm.

I am quite happy about the Air matters.

In fact everything is going along so well that I am myself going off to England on Sunday next, 16th May; Army H.Q. pulls out of the battle that day and goes back to the Tripoli area. Oliver will be in charge here while I am away; Belchem is running everything quite excellently. Richardson will be at Algiers as my representative at Force 141.

---

[20] Code word for the Sicily Operation.

Now about yourself.

It is absolutely vital that you should get quite fit *before* you come back.

You are not to worry about the business, or even to think about it. It is quite unnecessary for anyone to go up and see you, and keep you in touch.

There is nothing to worry about; everything is now splendid. You must stay where you are; amuse yourself; have a thorough good rest; and be back here on 1st June *and not before*. I will be back myself by 5th June at Tripoli (Main Army).

I shall come to Cairo about 8th June, and go off with Ramsay to the rehearsals about 11th or 12th June.

Show these orders to your wife and tell her that I rely on her to see them carried out. You are far too valuable to be wasted, and I would be 'in the soup' if you came back too soon and cracked up again later.

So stay where you are and be back here by 1st June.

Good luck to you,

Yrs. ever,

B. L. Montgomery.

It was, from my point of view, most satisfactory — our modifications to the Sicily plan had been accepted and all the planning and preparation had apparently gone ahead without hitch or trouble. Once again, Eighth Army appeared to be getting along very well without me!

The reference to the 'Air matters' concerned the original proposal for Command arrangements to which we took exception. We wanted to retain the same intimate relationship that previously existed between the Desert Air Force and the Eighth Army. And this weakness had now been put right.

This was the first news I had received that my Chief was off to England, and, from the date of the letter, it will be seen that the Eighth Army Commander left before the North African campaign finally closed. The reason was, of course, that elements of Eighth Army were allotted a holding role about Enfidaville, whilst a Corps was detached to take part with First Army in the final assault on the Cap Bon Bridgehead. In order that we should be ready in time for the Sicily operation (HUSKY) it was essential that Eighth Army Headquarters be concentrated near Tripoli, as there was a great deal to be done. Lieut.-General Oliver Leese, the successful Commander of 30th Corps, was left to hold the fort in that locality during our Commander's absence. Belchem was my G.1 operations and, as usual, could be trusted to carry out an excellent job.

Richardson, whom I had appointed as my deputy when I left for Cairo, had been sent to join Force 141 which was the planning set-up under General Alexander in Algiers. This body had been responsible for producing the original outline plan which we had at first found unacceptable.

The part about myself made pleasant reading. It was a relief to know that I was now to have time to get fit before my return to Cairo; and I was human enough to derive a certain amount of pleasure from the thought that Montgomery would be 'in the soup' if I cracked up — although, perhaps, in my heart of hearts I did not believe it! Anyway my wife, naturally enough, did not want much prompting to see that I carried out these orders.

These instructions meant that I had close upon a fortnight's more leave, and so we decided to spend a week at a small hotel tucked far away in the Lebanon Hills. Here we would be cool and would find peace and rest.

It was very near heaven to be among the trees and hills in this lovely country. We could really be idle, and at last I found myself 'running down' and my headaches became less. I made a mental note to return here one day, for in the early mornings and late evenings you could hear the partridges calling in the hills around us, and there was a stream near at hand reported to contain some excellent rainbow trout.

Before leaving I decided that I must throw just one fly on this stream to test its quality, and so my wife, Lawrence and I drove down a primitive road over hill and dale until we reached a river running swiftly through woodland slopes. One could not have wished for more charming surroundings. Cypress and cedar trees covered the gentle undulating country and wild flowers grew in profusion amongst the carpet of green grass. The river had plenty of water and there appeared to be a number of tempting pools. I regretted that I had not visited this little paradise before. After a preliminary reconnaissance, I decided to try my fortune in a turbulent-looking run. I clambered down a very steep bank, positioned myself somewhat precariously on some rocks, proceeded to wet my fly upstream, and then taking out the necessary length of line slowly let my fly down into the fast-running water. The fly having reached the end of its journey, which was just alongside a half-submerged rock, I started to work gently towards me. In a flash my rod bent temptingly and, before I realized what had happened, my line was singing from the reel. I was well stuck into a very sizeable fish.

I had left my wife and Lawrence preparing to occupy a comfortable position on the green turf near by; the latter being in charge of my landing-net which was attached to a four-foot pole. Having got over my surprise, for I had inwardly approached this river with very little hope of success, I started to shout at the top of my voice for my wife who eventually heard me and asked what I wanted. I should explain that she was inexperienced in the art of fishing and, in fact, was already, like so many other wives in this world, beginning to wonder whether it wasn't about time she put her foot down on all this nonsense.

I cried out that I wanted the landing-net and was told that Lawrence had it.

'Then tell the flipping idiot to bring the blasted net down here,' was my heated reply.

I was shattered, however, to hear that Lawrence had drifted away on a tour of exploration. I took little time in issuing instructions for his immediate recapture, stressing the extreme urgency of the situation, for I was experiencing considerable difficulty from my delicate perch in keeping control of my yet unseen quarry. As my wife rushed off to do my bidding I bellowed myself hoarse in the hopes that my cries might reach Cpl. Lawrence in time. I now got down to the problem on hand with all seriousness. I was beginning to get in some line and my fish was coming nearer when it suddenly decided to try its luck upstream, and before I knew where I was, I saw a few yards of slack line and a splash in a dark pool at my feet. I looked down to see a fine trout of well over two pounds. The effort of gathering in my line and the shock of seeing so large a fish, were too much for my equilibrium, and before I knew where I was, I had slipped off the rocks, bounced gracefully off my bottom, and was soon floundering up to my waist in the pool. Lifting the point of my rod upwards, however, I was thrilled to find the line was taut once more and the fish careering down towards the rock where he had been lying. After an agony of waiting I heard a voice behind me, and turning my head saw my wife, a slim figure in blue slacks and gum-boots, sliding down the steep bank with the blessed net in her hand. I shouted to her to position herself alongside the stream and began to bring my precious trout in towards her. The water was running very fast and so netting by an experienced gillie would not have been easy. Slowly but surely I succeeded in reeling in until my fish was within striking distance of the net — the word 'striking' turned out to be, alas, only too apt an adjective. I called to my wife to net the fish, but the current made it difficult for her to manoeuvre the net into a position that would fulfil its task. By this time I was getting desperate and my nervous tension was of a high order. My instructions became very different from those that should emanate from an officer and a gentleman, and ended with 'For —— sake finish off the —— fish!'

Glancing sideways I saw my wife's expression change and a look of grim determination took the place of one of apprehension. To my horror I saw her lift up the net and bring it down with a mighty crack on the fish's head! She had carried out my instructions to the letter! A dreadful silence reigned as I contemplated my sagging line with its length of broken gut. I regret to say that I then completely lost my temper and I now shudder to think what invective I hurled at my poor, unfortunate wife. Perhaps keen fishermen who read this story will understand and have compassion. I have had to use the air-crash and my bruised and damaged head as a salve to my guilty conscience.

I arrived back in Cairo on the last day of May to find the city both hot and stuffy and 'George', our office, a veritable inferno. Great progress had been made and it looked as if we should be able to complete all our preparations in time. Montgomery had returned from his triumphal visit to London and was busy visiting his troops who were scattered in an area bounded by Tunisia in the west to Egypt, Palestine and Syria in the east. And, in addition, the First Canadian Division, which was to take part in the initial assault, was located in England. But, of course, Montgomery had been able to visit this formation during his recent trip home. About three weeks before the assault was due to take place I received the following letter from Montgomery, written in Tripoli:

20-6-43.

My Dear Freddie,

I am staying here to see The King's visit through. General Alexander has given me permission. I shall be quite glad when he has gone as it is worse than a battle and is somewhat of a responsibility.

I have all civilians in Tripoli and area confined to their houses.

We have had parachutists doing damage at Benghazi and Sholto tells me they failed to catch them all and some are still at large.

You must present our plans at Algiers and will do it very well.

I leave here for Cairo on early morning of 23rd June and will be at the Embassy that night.

My kind regards to Ramsay.

Yrs. ever,
B. L. Montgomery.

With the campaign over it was decided that the King should fly out to visit his forces which had won such fame and were now being prepared to conquer new fields. It was a great honour for which we were all duly grateful, but it put a tremendous responsibility upon the various Commanders and meant certain adjustments in our carefully phased programmes. There is no more loyal soldier than Montgomery but even he describes all the business involved as 'worse than a battle'.

The mention of my having to present our plans at Algiers refers to a 'most Secret' conference summoned by Eisenhower at which all the Commanders concerned — Army, Navy and

Air — described their plans in detail and brought up any matter which, in their view, required modification. In this way it was possible to effect the maximum degree of co-ordination before it was too late.

Montgomery spent a very busy time in Cairo on this occasion, as also during the visit mentioned in his previous letter. The rehearsals mostly took place in the Gulf of Suez and made us realize how complex combined operations were when conducted on a major scale, and how much more we had to learn.

It was extremely interesting to meet my Chief again after his visit to London. I noticed a subtle change. He had left for North Africa as a General comparatively unknown to the British public, and had found on return to Britain that he had virtually overnight become a national hero. He received a tremendous ovation wherever he went; in the theatre, stepping in or out of the War Office, crowds would shout 'Good old Monty!' 'God bless you, Monty!' Walking across the Horse Guards Parade to his Club he would be followed by hundreds of his fellow countrymen, all pressing forward to shake his hand or at least to get a glimpse of him. What all this must have meant to a somewhat lonely man is easy to understand. Not to have enjoyed it would not have been human. He did, and sometimes asked for more. It was also a good thing for the Army, which had sunk so low in the public's esteem. It needed this favourable reaction — and it needed a successful General. The main changes which I noticed were: firstly, Montgomery had, perhaps, lost a little of his simplicity, and, secondly, he now realized that he was a real power in the land and that there were few who would not heed his advice. In fact, he realized that in most cases he could afford to be really tough to get his own way!

During his visit to Cairo in early June, my wife rang up Montgomery to ask him to a small lunch party in our flat, to which Ramsay and Dempsey had also been invited.

He was on the top of his form after his London visit and asked her: 'Have you heard all about my visit?'

'No,' replied my wife.

'Well, I will send round John Poston (A.D.C.) right away to give you a full account — all the details. It was a remarkable success!'

There is no doubt that Montgomery was intensely pleased that he had made the grade with his King and countrymen. And who can blame him for that?

The lunch party which followed had its amusing side. Montgomery is not a very easy man to feed. In the first place, he is a very meagre eater, besides being somewhat choosey — the latter not being through inclination but through necessity. If he eats pig, shell-fish or eggs, they are apt to disagree with him. I would guess that this trouble stems from the gall-stones that I described earlier.

A *spécialité de la Maison* was a type of prawn cocktail to be eaten as a first course, and this had been ordered before I had told my wife about my Chief's allergies. She, therefore, ordered our Egyptian cook to prepare, in addition, a small kidney sauté with some rice.

When we had taken our seats the prawn cocktail, straight from the refrigerator, was placed before the guests, and then along came the kidney sauté for Montgomery. Imagine my wife's horror when she realized that this had received treatment similar to the prawns and had been served up in a fruit cocktail glass having spent its allotted span in the Frigidaire. The result was altogether unpleasant — a cold, soggy, greasy-looking mess. The gallant General would not hear of my wife's protests that he should ignore this loathsome dish, and proceeded to consume it without delay. I am glad to say that I never had the misfortune to eat iced kidney sauté and rice; but I can assure my readers that I have it on the very best authority — Montgomery's! — that it's not too hot.

It was on a warm and sticky morning in early July that I sailed from Alexandria for Malta with Admiral Ramsay in his flagship. Our great amphibious adventure was under way. I joined up once again with my Chief and we saw the conquest of Sicily and the invasion of Italy, and then flew away together from an airstrip situated near the Sangro River on the last day of 1943. We were bound for the 'Second Front'.

CHAPTER SIX: EUROPE 1944 — A SIGNAL THAT SAVED THE TEAM

The relationship between the Allies in the Second World War was truly remarkable for the small amount of friction that occurred. The Commanders and their Staffs worked as a team in a way that must serve as an example to future generations, if they are ever again unlucky enough to be involved in a major war. Compared with the bickerings and crisis-upon-crisis which occurred between the British and French during the First World War, it was wellnigh miraculous. And this harmony can largely be attributed to two men — Winston Churchill and Dwight Eisenhower. The former managed to maintain a practical understanding between the politicians and the service chiefs; whilst the latter demonstrated his extraordinary ability to exact intense loyalty and devotion from those serving under him.

I don't mean to suggest that we all saw eye-to-eye the whole time. Far from it, for there was constant divergence of views. But these were rarely allowed to reach the dangerous stage. With a number of able and forceful commanders it was inevitable that, from time to time, opinions would differ, but in spite of this the leading figures of the team that Eisenhower built up around him in the Mediterranean theatre remained together until victory was won.

Having said all this, however, I must qualify it with one exception and that occurred during the hectic days when von Rundstedt led that last gamble through the Ardennes in December 1944. It produced a crisis in allied relations that could have proved disastrous, and it was one in which I personally played a part. It was ended by a signal sent by Montgomery to Eisenhower; but for a time I was fearful that an irrevocable rift had occurred in the Allied High Command, and that Monty would lose his command of 21st Army Group. The events leading up to this all-important and vital signal are well worthy of being placed on record, as a page of history that has as yet not been fully written.

It is necessary to go back a bit in order to trace Montgomery's views on the High Command set-up in the North-West Europe Campaign, for this had a considerable bearing on the Montgomery-Eisenhower-Bradley relationship throughout these operations.

Shortly after some of us had arrived in England to take up our various appointments for the Second Front Campaign, Eisenhower decided, primarily for simplicity's sake, that the assault on 'D-Day' and the initial period of fighting in the inevitable bridgehead areas should come under 21st Army Group's Command, of which Montgomery was Army Group Commander. He was also, no doubt, influenced by our Chief's proven experience and ability at preparing for and fighting a dogged battle. It was, however, made perfectly clear that this arrangement in no way meant that the American 12th Army Group, under Bradley, would not subsequently take over command of the American formations. And with this end in view our plans were laid. For instance, I decided against a completely integrated British/American staff, which would obviously have been the most economical as far as the number of officers employed was concerned. Instead I built up parallel staffs — British and American — in order to cater for the day when the 12th Army Group would start to function on its own. This meant that all those Americans holding key appointments would be completely in the picture when the time came, and would be able to commence their work with 12th Army Group with a minimum of disruption. In planning the flow of equipment across the Channel to Normandy, we took into account the need to have all the 12th Army Group Headquarter's vehicles concentrated in France by a certain date, which, as far as I can remember, was to be 'D' plus 21.

Now Montgomery, although he knew and approved of all these preparations for the day when Bradley was to open up his own Army Group Headquarters, never, I believe, thought that that day would come so soon. Possibly, as always, he thirsted after the simple solution, and, therefore, hoped that the initial command set-up was there to stay for a long time. He was, I think, apt to give insufficient weight to the dictates of prestige and national feelings, or to the increasing contribution of America, in both men and arms to the European theatre of war. It was obvious, however, to most of us that it would have been an impossible situation for a British General and a British Headquarters to retain command of these more numerous American formations indefinitely.

When it was made clear that the introduction of the new Army Group was to become an accomplished fact, Montgomery, of course, accepted the position, but I sensed that from that moment onwards he began to think in terms of an overall land force commander under Eisenhower, the Allied Supreme Commander.

At first glance this might have appeared to have been the right solution — a tidy pyramid with Eisenhower sitting at the top, with his Naval, Land and Air Force Commanders working directly under him.

Montgomery made his own views known in no uncertain manner — to the Supreme Commander himself and also to the British War Office. And it is only natural that he should have thought that he himself would be the right man for such a post. At one stage, however, he told Eisenhower that he was prepared to serve under Bradley if that would help a solution. Eisenhower was, however, completely opposed to such a development, and unfortunately this became a cause of friction, which luckily never reached dangerous proportions until the Battle of the Bulge. But Bradley was human enough to feel a little bit put out by these known views of my Chief. Controversy upon this issue of the command arrangement went on when the war was over and even to this day there is no official or agreed solution.

I will here digress for a moment and quote what I said about this difficult question of the High Command set-up in a review I wrote for a London daily on Eisenhower's book *Crusade in Europe*.

> General Eisenhower vigorously defends his decision not to appoint a Land Force Commander. Field-Marshal Montgomery disagreed with this view. Theoretically and considering the immense burden Eisenhower shouldered, Montgomery's view appears logical. In practice, however, it is not as easy as all that. Everyone appeared satisfied — Montgomery included — with the initial set up, whereby my Chief commanded and co-ordinated the first phase in Normandy.
>
> It is only fair to say that the Supreme Commander made it clear from the start that he would bring in General Omar Bradley's Army Group when General Patton's Army entered the field.
>
> Montgomery, I think, was disappointed when, after the successful turn of events in Normandy, his powers of co-ordination were taken from him.

The best answer would have been to appoint a land commander from the start, but by the end of August this would have been difficult.

I sent a copy of my article to Eisenhower, who was then (1949) Chief of Staff in Washington, and received a long letter in reply. In this Eisenhower firmly maintained that the appointment of a Land Force Commander would have served no practical purpose. Such a person would have found himself between the Supreme Commander and the Army Group Commanders without any useful role either in the formation of general strategy or in the particular applications of this strategy in such a large field of operations.

In such matters one is inclined to be fully influenced by personalities, and there is no doubt that my judgement was to some degree influenced by the great ability of my Chief. After some years of reflection on this knotty problem, however, I have veered to Eisenhower's view. An Army Group Commander should be able to handle all that is required on his sector of the theatre of operations, in accordance with the general strategic direction of the Supreme Commander. The overall strategy must remain the chief responsibility of the Supreme Commander, and the insertion of a land force commander between him and the army groups would not produce a tidy answer. Russia organized her theatre into 'fronts' or army groups and Generalissimo Stalin handled the overall strategic plan and dealt directly with his various 'front' commanders.

General Bradley, who commanded the 12th U.S. Army Group, was obviously still feeling some bitterness when he wrote *A Soldier's Story*, for this is what he said about the High Command controversy:

That unfortunate August split never completely healed. It persisted throughout the winter war in a subtle whispering campaign that favoured Monty's restoration to overall ground command. And eventually it came to a head during the Battle of the Bulge, when the Montgomery protagonists declared von Rundstedt's break-through might have been avoided had Eisenhower echeloned his Army Groups into a single ground command. Those might-have-beens, however, are refuted by the record, for on the eve of von Rundstedt's offensive, Montgomery unwittingly admitted that he was no more occult than the others of us.

Although once again Montgomery could have curbed these backers, he carefully ignored them. Indeed he even intimated during that phase of the campaign from the Seine to the Reich that if ground command were vested in him, he would shorten the span of war. Monty thought SHAEF too distantly removed from the shooting to direct the day-to-day campaigns of the three independent Army Groups. He would remedy the situation and relieve SHAEF of its labours by creating a super ground command to be headed by him as an additional echelon between Eisenhower and the Army Groups.

Because of this attitude, Monty lent substance to the canard that Eisenhower functioned in Europe primarily as a politician commander, unfamiliar with the everyday problems of our tactical war. The inference was grossly unfair, for Eisenhower showed himself to be a superb tactician with a sensitive and intimate feel of the front. With Bedell Smith to shoulder a generous share of his administrative duties, Eisenhower directed his major effort to operations in the field. His tactical talents had been demonstrated years before at Leavenworth where he finished at the head of his class in 1926. It is at Leavenworth that the army's most promising officers are schooled in the tactics and logistics of senior commands.

Because Ike's tactical labours were largely confined to private conversations with the Army Group Commanders, only Montgomery, Devers and I could attest to his rare astuteness in this role as field commander. Quite often the working level at SHAEF G.3 was unaware of the issues involved in these private discussions. And similarly the officers of my G.3 staff were cut off from these conversations. After October Eisenhower and I were in almost daily touch by phone, and he was fully informed of my every move at Group. Quite frequently our long-range plans evolved during late night conversations at Ike's C.P. or mine. Sometimes we would sit until two or three in the morning, swapping opinions and discussing plans for successive phases of the campaign. For this reason, historians may find it difficult to ascribe to any individual commander his views of credits for key tactical decisions: Eisenhower contributed more than he benefited from these exchanges; I need not belittle Montgomery nor deny him any of his lustre to rate Eisenhower his superior as a field commander.

During the winter campaign Eisenhower was astonished to learn that Montgomery aspired to overall command of the Allied ground forces. At the same time, Montgomery did not wish to surrender his Army Group Command to become Eisenhower's deputy for the ground at SHAEF. He would retain 21st Army Group, and take on the role of super ground force commander as an added function.

'Monty,' Ike said in exasperation, 'wants to have his cake and eat it, too.'

Reverting once more to Montgomery's rooted views on the command set-up, those who know him well realize that when he has convinced himself that a particular course is right, he feels justified in bringing all influences to bear in order to win his point: in fact, the end justifies almost any means. Those who do not agree with his conclusions, however, are apt to be critical of his methods.

In addition to the friction which was undoubtedly created because of Montgomery's views on the need for a Land Force Commander, there were other contributory factors which from time to time caused difficulties between Montgomery, Eisenhower and Bradley.

There was the well known difference of opinion between Eisenhower and Montgomery regarding the grand strategy to be followed once the Allied Forces had broken out of the Normandy bridgehead. The Supreme Commander wished to advance on a broad front, employing both Army Groups, while my Chief favoured all available resources being concentrated to allow a narrower thrust being made deep into Germany via the Low Countries. Then there was a certain amount of rivalry between the two Army Groups when the great advance across the Seine to the Dutch frontier was set in motion. Montgomery and Bradley were both asking for the lion's share of the somewhat limited administrative resources. I think, on balance, the 21st Army Group won this contest, and I guess Bradley, and particularly Patton, one of his Army Commanders, felt they had been harshly treated. But Chester Wilmot, in his excellent and careful study of this particular aspect of the operations, suggests that Patton did better in this connection than he permitted Eisenhower to know. In his *Memoirs* Montgomery suggests that if his policy had been adopted, the war might have been won in 1944.

The 'glorious failure' of Arnhem — I think we dwell too much on failure in the story of British arms — sucked in a considerable slice of Eisenhower's general reserve and the American commanders argued that this fact was forgotten by Montgomery when he was criticizing the slowness of Bradley's offensive in the late autumn of 1944 in the area of Aachen, the Roer River and its dams. There was thus from D-Day onwards a background of rising tension.

Before I proceed to relate the events that led up to the real crisis and how the crisis was resolved, I feel bound to mention, with some reluctance, a factor which did much to pour salt upon the wound of Anglo-American relations, to say nothing of making my task as Montgomery's Chief of Staff a great deal more difficult. I do so because it provides a lesson for the future. There was a certain high-ranking officer in the War Office, who had been one of 'Montgomery's men' in the old days. In many ways he was most efficient and in certain directions his contribution was first-class. On the other hand, I am sorry to say that he went out of his way to encourage Montgomery in pursuing a proposal which I considered impracticable, unrealistic and altogether unfortunate — the appointment of a Land Force Commander. He was apt to lean towards agreement with my Chief whenever possible, and was not averse to belittling the American effort as well as their commanders. As a great deal of my time was spent in removing points of friction and smoothing over problems of human relationships, I was more than worried by these activities. I certainly viewed with apprehension this officer's visits to our Headquarters, for I inevitably found my Chief less easy after his departure. He became known to my intimate circle as 'Busy Breeches'.

I recollect one occasion shortly after 'Busy Breeches' had left us, and after he had spent a night at SHAEF on his return to Whitehall; the Field-Marshal handed me a letter from 'Busy Breeches', saying 'Read this'. I did so — and nearly burst a blood vessel. It contained petty criticism of Eisenhower's Headquarters: the fact that they were housed in buildings; the comfortable way the staff lived and other bits of gossip and tittle-tattle. It struck me as an attempt to put over what, in his opinion, he thought Montgomery would like to hear. I told my Chief exactly what I thought of the letter. There was a bit of an atmosphere between us for a time.

This simmering situation between Monty and the Americans came to a head during Field-Marshal von Rundstedt's initially successful surprise offensive in the Ardennes. Luckily, air attacks, and their own shortage of supplies and fuel and heroic fighting by the Americans — particularly their defence of Bastogne — held them up.

Eisenhower temporarily transferred General Hodges's 1st Army and other troops north of the German bulge to Montgomery's command. The procedure was quite logical, for Bradley, owing to the severance of his communications, would have had difficulty in exercising his proper functions. The decision, however, was never meant to be anything but a temporary expedient.

Montgomery handled a difficult military situation with remarkable skill. It is probable, however, that he felt this crisis had produced the opportunity to introduce a Land Force Commander into the Allied High Command system. No doubt he also felt that recent events had clearly demonstrated the need. It was significant that this line was now taken up by the British Press, and Montgomery was depicted as the man of the hour who had saved the situation after an American Commander's failure. The American Press naturally took the opposite view, and the long and the short of it was that Bradley's position became increasingly difficult. His troops, for instance, received ample supplies of the British daily newspapers and there was, therefore, a great danger that they might lose confidence in their Commander.

I soon realized that an extremely dangerous situation had developed, and that unless something was done, and done quickly, a crisis would occur in the sphere of inter-allied relationships. Having obtained an alarming report from one of our liaison officers as to the strength of feeling which existed in the 12th Army Group, I rang up my old friend Bedell Smith (Eisenhower's Chief of Staff) and sounded him regarding the situation. The reply I received was anything but reassuring; in fact so much the opposite that I decided to fly off immediately to SHAEF to learn at first-hand how matters stood.

However, when I put down the telephone receiver on my desk at our main Headquarters in Brussels, and looked out of the window, I realized that this trip to SHAEF was easier said than done, for there was thick fog outside, and intermittent blizzards were sweeping across the city. I called in my American aide, Bill Culver, and told him that I wanted to get away as soon as possible and would he go straight off and see my pilot. He returned a little later to say that flying was impossible at the moment, and that similar conditions existed all over France, and, incidentally, over the Ardennes battlefield — which prevented us using our formidable air power to check the enemy's offensive. This was extremely serious. My normal rule was to accept my pilot's advice as to whether or not conditions were suitable for flying. But this was a very unusual situation, and so I called Jack Race to my office to discuss the position. When he arrived I explained that this was a vitally urgent matter, and he must do his best to get me to SHAEF that day.

After an early lunch Race rang up from the airfield to say that he felt he could take a chance, so we immediately drove out there. The weather conditions looked most uninviting:

snow on the ground and very low visibility, interspersed by bitter snowfalls.

In we got, and the aircraft took off into the fog. Until we reached the area of Paris, we could see no farther than our wing-tips, and when over Paris, Race got such bad reports on the weather that he decided to fly towards the sea, hoping for conditions which would enable him to get down to within sight of the ground. It was beginning to look hopeless, and my pilot was even thinking of flying to some airfield in England, where better weather prevailed, when, by good fortune, we got a momentary glimpse of the Seine. Down we spiralled and started flying up the river in search of Paris. From then onwards things were comparatively simple, and, choosing our moment when the runway was clear of snow flurries, we landed at the Orly airstrip to find Bedell Smith's A.D.C. waiting with a car.

I drove straight to Bedell's office and discussed the situation with him. He explained the repercussions of the British Press campaign and Montgomery's alleged 'naughtiness'; there was now a state of affairs which looked as if Eisenhower, Montgomery and Bradley could no longer work in essential harmony. Bedell gave me to understand that the matter had practically reached a stage where nothing more could be done about it, and that some higher authority would have to find a solution. He concluded by saying, 'I think we had better go right over and see Ike, otherwise it will certainly be too late.' We walked across to the small house in the SHAEF grounds that the Supreme Commander used for his living and office quarters. It was the period during which, much against his will, he had been forbidden to leave his quarters because of the threat from Skorzeny's paratroopers.

It was now quite dark. Passing a sentry on duty outside the door, we entered Ike's office to find him at his desk looking very serious indeed. Tedder, the Deputy Supreme Commander, sat near him to the right of the desk, sucking away as ever at his pipe, apparently reading a document. I think Eisenhower's military assistant, Jimmy Gault, was also present.

They all looked up as we entered, the fire flickering on their faces in the sombre light of the room. Eisenhower said, 'Hello, Freddie — please sit down.'

I did so and Bedell Smith explained that I had come to see if I could help over the dangerous situation which had arisen, and that I could perhaps throw some new light on the problem.

The Supreme Commander looked really tired and worried. He very quietly started to explain how serious matters were. He told me that Bradley's position had become intolerable, and that there was every chance that he would lose the confidence of his troops. This would be most unfortunate and might mean his losing one of his ablest commanders. He asked me whether my Chief fully realized the effects of the line taken up by the British Press, and how Monty himself had helped to create this crisis by his campaign for a Land Force Commander and by the indiscreet remarks he had passed. Eisenhower went on to say that he was tired of the whole business, and had come to the conclusion that it was now a matter for the Combined Chiefs of Staff to make a decision. It was quite obvious that with Montgomery still pressing for a Land Force Commander it was impossible for the two of them to carry on working in harness together. He had already prepared a signal to General Marshall, Chairman of the Combined Chiefs of Staff in Washington, which was, in fact, being vetted at that very moment. He handed over the draft for me to read.

I was stunned by what I read. In very direct language, it made it crystal-clear that a crisis of the first magnitude was indeed here. I was determined to prevent this signal being sent, for I felt sure, given the time, that I could put things right, and the alternative was too frightful even to contemplate. For the Allies could ill afford to lose Eisenhower or Montgomery or indeed Bradley, with the reputation they had built up. It was clear, however, that the Supreme Commander had decided to make an issue of the matter and was quite prepared to go himself, if the Combined Chiefs of Staff considered this to be the right solution. Since the Americans were the stronger ally, it really meant that Monty would be the one to go.

I then made my little speech, and I was in deadly earnest. I said that in the first place I was absolutely convinced that Montgomery himself had no idea that things had become so serious, and that I was certain that once it was explained to him, he would cooperate to the hilt. I was aware that the Supreme Commander knew very well how difficult it often was for my Chief to understand the atmosphere of events outside his own zone, and how his refusal to leave his own Headquarters except to visit his formations was largely responsible for this. I said several other things which I felt might ease the tension; and finished by imploring Eisenhower to delay sending the signal for twenty-four hours so as to give me an opportunity to solve the impasse. At first neither Eisenhower nor Tedder appeared inclined to agree to this, and they stressed the damage which had already been done. Bedell, however, advised delay, and to my intense relief it was finally agreed that the signal should be held up to give me an opportunity to act. But it was quite a time before they came round to this point of view.

I thanked Eisenhower from a very grateful heart, and then left the room. As I closed the door behind me I remember thinking what a magnificent smoke-screen Tedder could produce from his pipe, for the visibility appeared no better in there than it was outside on this miserably cold evening.

When I thought of what had just taken place, I really sweated. What an incredibly lucky piece of timing — if I had not decided to fly to SHAEF, or had arrived a few minutes later, the consequences might have been disastrous.

I walked over to the Chief of Staff's office and sat there waiting for my friend to tidy things up for the night. I felt exhausted. While waiting I sent off a signal to Montgomery saying I was now at SHAEF and would be flying to see him at his Tactical Headquarters the next day with a most important matter to discuss.

Bedell and I then drove out to his little house situated in the forest a mile or two from SHAEF, and on arrival there gratefully accepted one of his servants' inimitable 'Old-Fashioneds'. And by that time I must say I needed it! Before leaving SHAEF I had told Bill Bovill, my personal assistant, to arrange our start back early in the morning, weather permitting. Bill Bovill, Bill Culver and my two pilots then disappeared for the night — with Paris a few miles away they did not ask for official entertainment!

As usual, I stayed with Bedell Smith. I used to enjoy those evenings immensely, for not only was he a charming host, but it also gave us an opportunity to discuss many common problems. I never left without feeling that we had made good use of our time.

The next morning I was rung up by Bill Bovill to say that there wasn't an earthly hope of our getting off yet awhile, for the fog and snow-storms were still with us. Realizing that we might be delayed several hours, I passed a message to Jack Race to locate the landing-strip nearest to Montgomery's Tactical Headquarters so that we could fly straight there and so save time. I also had a signal sent to ensure that my car would be at his Headquarters, in case circumstances necessitated that I travel back to Main Headquarters in Brussels by road, and not by air.

We spent a most irritating morning waiting for the weather to clear and by noon I had developed a very bad attack of nerves. I think it was shortly after one o'clock when we were eventually allowed to take off, and then, after two or three hours of unpleasant flying, Jack Race put my Dakota down on the advanced airstrip. A car was waiting and I immediately drove off to see my Chief.

I arrived at the little house which he was using as his Mess at about 4.30 p.m. to find tea being served. He greeted me in his usual cheerful way and I remember thinking, 'Oh dear — you just don't know what's coming to you!'

Before I had been there very long, he realized that I had something important on my mind and that something must be wrong. As he left the table, he said, 'I'm going upstairs to my office, Freddie. Please come up when you have finished your tea.'

I followed him up after a minute or two and found him reading some papers. I sat down and waited until he had finished. During the flight up I had made a note or two and was perfectly clear how I should present the picture. I had decided that I must be absolutely frank with my Chief and make him realize the seriousness of the recent developments. His part in the successful stemming of the von Rundstedt tide had, I think, made him more or less oblivious of the forces that were gathering outside against him.

So I started off like this:

'I've just come from SHAEF and seen Ike, and it's on the cards that you might have to go.' I added that I had for some time been telling him that this agitation for a Land Force Commander was dangerous and impracticable. It was one of the few times that I saw Montgomery really worried and disturbed, for I believe he was genuinely and completely taken by surprise and found it difficult to grasp what I was saying. He naturally asked me to explain what it was all about; this I proceeded to do, describing my mounting fears and ending up with my interview with the Supreme Commander and the signal that was waiting to be sent off to Washington. I told him that I believed the situation could be put right, but that it required immediate action.

Montgomery found it extremely hard to believe it possible that he might be relieved of his command after his successes and the tremendous prestige he had gained, particularly in the eyes of the troops and the British public. In answer to his remarks I replied that if it came to a choice between Eisenhower and him, then the Combined Chiefs of Staff would in my view retain Eisenhower. America was now producing by far the greatest contribution in both men and munitions, and I did not believe even Churchill would be able to win a battle on his behalf. As to a successor in 21st Army Group there was always Alexander, and during my interview with the Supreme Commander, he had actually hinted at this very solution. In fact, I seem to recall that Alexander's name was mentioned in the signal.

I felt terribly sorry for my Chief, for he now looked completely nonplussed — I don't think I had ever seen him so deflated. It was as if a cloak of loneliness had descended upon him. His reply was, 'What shall I do, Freddie?'

I told him that I believed things could be smoothed over and suggested that he send a 'most immediate' signal off to Eisenhower. This he was eager to do, and as I had already prepared a draft in the aircraft of the type of signal I thought was required. He was able to use this as the basis.

Here is the signal:

Dear Ike,

Have seen Freddie and understand you are greatly worried by many considerations in these very difficult days. I have given you my frank views because I have felt you like this. I am sure there are many factors which have a bearing quite beyond anything I realize. Whatever your decision may be you can rely on me one hundred per cent to make it work, and I know Brad will do the same. Very distressed that my letter[21] may have upset you and I would ask you to tear it up.

Your very devoted subordinate,
Monty.

He checked through the signal once more, marked it 'For Eisenhower's eyes only' and 'Most immediate' — the highest priority possible; rang the bell and gave it to one of his A.D.C.'s to send off. I hoped it would be in the Supreme Commander's hands within a couple of hours. It had, of course, to be enciphered and there was the deciphering to be carried out at the other end; Montgomery's Tactical Headquarters had a direct wireless link with SHAEF, so there would be little delay on that account.

With this out of the way I suggested that an early visit to Bradley was of extreme importance, and Montgomery said he

---

[21] Letter sent to Eisenhower by Montgomery concerning the command set-up.

would try and fly to 12th Army Group Headquarters as soon as possible.

Another signal was then prepared and sent to Bradley. The visit was not a roaring success. The atmosphere throughout was distinctly cool. We stayed to lunch but few words were spoken other than were necessary for the transaction of business. When, however, the American troops were later withdrawn from Montgomery's command, he wrote a very pleasant letter to Bradley but I don't recollect whether he ever received a reply. Here it is:

> TAC. H.Q.,
> 21 ARMY GROUP.
> 12th January, 1945.

My dear Brad:

It does seem as if the battle of the 'salient' will shortly be drawing to a close, and when it is all clean and tidy I imagine that your armies will be returning to your operational command.

I would like to say two things:

> *First*: What a great honour it has been for me to command such fine troops.
>
> *Second*: How well they have all done.

2. It has been a great pleasure to work with Hodges and Simpson; both have done very well.

And the Corps Commanders in the First Army (Gerow, Collins, Ridgway) have been quite magnificent; it must be most exceptional to find such a good lot of Corps Commanders gathered together in one Army.

3. All of us in the northern side of the salient would like to say how much we have admired the operations that have been conducted on the southern side; if you had not held on firmly to BASTOGNE the whole situation might have become very awkward.

4. My kind regards to you and to George Patton.

Yrs. very sincerely,
s/ B. L. Montgomery.

So far so good — things had been set in motion to solve this problem of personalities but there was still the acute danger that the Allied Press would continue to aggravate the situation. I therefore got on the phone to our Main Headquarters in Brussels and instructed my B.G.S. Operations (Belchem) to lay on a conference with the War Correspondents Committee, of which Alan Moorehead was the Chairman. It was now dark, so I had to drive back by car and the roads were very icy; the journey was likely to take three or four hours, so I gave 8.30 p.m. to 9 p.m. as my estimated time of arrival.

Having completed my business I said good night to Montgomery, closed the door quietly, walked down the stairs and found Bill Bovill chatting to the A.D.C.s. I stayed a few minutes with them and drank what I felt was a well-earned whisky and soda. While warming myself up for the cold drive ahead, I heard the evening reports coming in, the situation in the Ardennes front seemed to be swinging our way.

The drive back to Brussels was tedious owing to the cold and the icy surface of the roads, but we made fair time although my estimated time of arrival turned out to have been over-optimistic. We drove straight to our Main Headquarters through the blacked-out streets, and then to my enormous office on the top floor, which until the liberation of Belgium had been occupied by the German Commander-in-Chief, Field-Marshal von Falkenhausen. David Belchem as well as Bill Williams, the Head of the Intelligence Branch, were waiting there, and they told me that the War Correspondents Committee had arrived and were ready for the conference. So I got straight down to business.

In walked Alan Moorehead, Paul Holt of the *Express*, Christopher Buckley of the *Telegraph*, who was so tragically killed in Korea, and Alexander Clifford of the *Daily Mail*. We knew each other well and had met together many a time to find a solution to some knotty problem. Once a month they would invite me to dinner, and wherever we happened to be, whether in the shell- and bomb-destroyed area of the Normandy Bridgehead or in Brussels itself, the food and wine produced were all one could desire. These people certainly knew their way about.

As always, I was perfectly frank with them. It is no use being anything else with intelligent War Correspondents — a fact often forgotten by some Commanders. I told them that a major crisis had occurred in the High Command and explained how this had come about and how the Press in England and America were making matters ten times worse. I then proceeded to analyse the Ardennes Battle and showed how, in spite of the story now being put over in Britain, the Americans had borne the major share of the fighting and their Commanders and troops had behaved magnificently. I went on to explain why Eisenhower had rearranged Command on a temporary basis, and that as for the appointment of a Land Force Commander, this would not take place. It would certainly not be acceptable to America, and if the controversy went on, public opinion in the States might demand that in future no American troops should be placed under British Command. Such a step would, of course, be tragic and would completely fetter the Supreme Commander's hands.

They appreciated the points I made and agreed to help in improving the situation. I therefore asked each of them to get in touch with their respective editors at once and explain the trend of events and ask them to take a less dangerous line in future. They agreed to do this and I felt that a good day's work had now been completed.

After clearing up urgent business, I left the office and drove to our mess in my car where Corporal Lawrence was awaiting my arrival. He was on excellent terms with our cook and it was not long before we were all sitting down to a good dinner. The popping of a champagne cork told me that Bill Bovill felt that there was some cause for celebration — well, perhaps there was!

Before turning in I rang up SHAEF and found that the signal had been duly delivered. Bedell Smith told me that Ike had been most touched and that the signal to Washington now reposed in the waste-paper basket. I said a small thanksgiving prayer that night before getting into bed. Although Bradley never really forgave Montgomery, the crisis in the Allied Command was over, and the same team went on together to final victory over Germany.

Shortly after these events took place I went to pay Bradley another visit at his Headquarters, for there were a lot of things to be tied up between our two Army Groups in connection with future operations. This visit provided a comic sequel to the previous near-tragic one.

The 12th Army Group, or more accurately, Bradley and his immediate entourage, were housed in a château. I arrived in the evening. It was a dreary old place and at this wintry time of year altogether unattractive. Our conference, to be attended by a number of Bradley's staff, was fixed to take place at 8.30 the next morning.

An A.D.C. showed me up to my room, which was typical of its kind — dark and dismal, and crammed with old furniture, including an enormous bed with a forbidding-looking canopy over it. It looked as if it had not been dusted since the war started.

I tumbled into bed hoping that I would have a good night's rest as I was extremely tired. However, the odds were against me, because at this period I was sleeping very badly. I suppose the strain of five years of war was beginning to tell.

It wasn't many minutes, however, before I lost consciousness. But soon I was awake again, aware of an odd noise — nothing much, but an irritating one all the same. It was a sort of scratching, clicking sound, and at first I thought of rats and mice. By now I was fully awake and concentrated on the problem. It was so regular that I decided that rats and mice were out. Eventually I got out of bed to investigate and then I realized what it was. Most surprisingly this ancient château had been installed with one product of the modern age — an electric clock.

Satisfied that I had tracked down the culprit, I got back into bed once more and again tried to sleep. But I found this quite impossible, for, as so often happens, when you try to forget or ignore something, you concentrate on it all the more. And so the night wore on and I became quite desperate, for I knew I should have to be alert for tomorrow's important discussions.

Finally I could stand it no longer. I switched on the light, leapt out of bed and examined the clock once again. How could one stop it? It was then I noticed a very thin wire that obviously led the current to the clock. It was cunningly concealed along the edge of a fine carved wooden panel which was covered with wall-paper. There was only one thing to do and that was to interrupt the current, and so I went to my dressing-table and collected my nail scissors and returned to the scene of operations. At the time I wondered whether I might receive a bad shock, but that risk had to be taken and I selected an inconspicuous place and gently snipped the wire. It was beautifully done; I could see no sign whatever of the cut. Immediately the clock stopped — peace reigned at last, and I returned to bed and slept fitfully until it was time to get up, shave and have my bath.

I arrived downstairs about 8 a.m. and ordered breakfast. I appeared to be the first arrival. Later another member of the staff walked in, said 'Good morning' and asked for his breakfast to be brought as quickly as possible. As he sat down, he told me he had overslept because the clock in his room had stopped.

Then it suddenly dawned upon me that the little operation which I had carried out had not only affected the local circuit but had produced repercussions farther afield! This was to be confirmed only too clearly within the next few minutes, for various officers dashed in at intervals, each complaining loudly about the stoppage of his clock. It was now quite plain that I had put the whole system out of action.

I said nothing and went on with my scrambled eggs and bacon. The result of this little trouble was that the conference was put back half an hour.

I'm afraid I acted like a coward and left after we had completed our deliberations without owning up to the cause of the great clock failure.

To find the fault must have been an extremely difficult business and I always wondered how it was traced and whether I had been suspected of deliberate sabotage.

Perhaps someone who reads this story may have been present in the château on that occasion. I should be grateful if he would get in touch with me and set my mind at rest!

PART THREE: LIFE AT MONTGOMERY'S H.Q.

CHAPTER SEVEN: A PIG AND A CONSCIENCE

You cannot spend all your time working and thinking about the war even when you are living through great events or planning tremendous operations. Life at a big headquarters has its amusing, human side; it has to have, or everyone would go round the bend. Some of the amusing incidents I want to describe show Monty off parade. Others show the comradeship of chaps of different kinds in the same team that makes the army the interesting life it is.

The opening scene is our Tactical Headquarters during the campaign in Italy. We had just occupied Bari and as the weather was very hot, you had a bathe in the sea whenever there was a chance, or, if this was geographically impossible, a bath either in a canvas contraption in your caravan or in a proper bath if you were lucky enough to find one.

This particular evening our victorious Army Commander was taking his bath in the dimly-lit bathroom of a small tumble-down house which happened to lie on the axis of our advance. He had reached the squatting stage and was ready for a good sluice-down before getting out to dry himself. The plumbing was not functioning and so he shouted for his servant to bring him a can of cold water. The batman, who was standing poised to fulfil Montgomery's every wish, jumped to it and moved over to where several jerrycans were stacked close to the go-down were the A.D.C.s slept. Unscrewing the top he entered the bathroom and handed the container over to the bather, who promptly started to pour the contents over his body with relish and gusto.

The operation had not gone very far when our Chief knew something was wrong. It didn't feel like water, it didn't look like water and it certainly didn't smell like water. Let's face it — it smelt like wine!

Realizing the truth, Monty let out a bellow for the batman to remove the offending can. A veritable sacrilege had been committed and you could take your choice whichever way you looked at it. Was it a crime to pour wine on a teetotaller or was it an unforgiveable waste of good wine?

An inquiry was, of course, initiated as a matter of the highest priority and then the truth came out. Johnny Henderson, Monty's A.D.C., had come across a wrecked building in a battle-scarred village and discovered in the debris a vat of Marsala wine. He sampled it and found it very much to his liking. What a pity to waste it and how welcome it would be to some of his friends at TAC.! So a little substitution took place — wine replaced the water in several jerrycans carried in his Jeep. And on his return to Headquarters he placed them outside his tent, pending the arrival of a suitable occasion.

Well, it was no good trying to make excuses, and it was no use claiming that there had been a second miracle of the water and the wine — he just had to own up. And the Army Commander, having decontaminated himself, and being a very human person, forgave him.

The episode naturally caused much amusement and some wag remarked:

'Anyone but Monty might have been tempted to drink his bath water!'

Before I tell the story of a pig and a Staff Officer's conscience, I think that I had better explain how Montgomery organized his Headquarters to suit his particular methods of exercising command. He himself lived at Tactical

Headquarters, which was located as far forward as possible in order that he could keep in close touch with his various commanders. In the rear of this was the Main Headquarters, which in an Army was of modest dimensions, but in an Army Group grew to a colossal size, staffed by hundreds of officers and men. Behind this, and sometimes positioned in close proximity, was the Rear Headquarters, which again was a massive set-up. It was sometimes necessary to divide both Main and Rear Headquarters into two echelons to suit a particular situation, but Tac. H.Q., although undergoing a process of evolution from the time of El Alamein, remained a separate entity throughout the war. It was designed to be extremely mobile and to contain the bare minimum of personnel and transport for the needs of the Army Commander or the Commander-in-Chief as the ease might be. At Alamein it was a small affair sited in the sand-dunes on the shores of the Mediterranean, and close to the Army Corps Headquarters. We had a small Mess tent and lived in our caravans. There was an Armoured Command Vehicle (A.C.V.) and a map lorry where all information was kept up-to-date on large-scale maps surrounding its walls; there were also the signal vehicles. At the opening of that battle, Montgomery, myself, two A.D.C.s and a couple of 'G' Staff Officers were to be found at Tac. H.Q.

In North Africa Tactical and Main Headquarters would often join up during quiet periods, but as the months and years rolled by, Tac. H.Q. became something quite apart and Montgomery operated in splendid isolation although, of course, he frequently saw members of his staff, who came up from both Main and Rear Headquarters. I used to keep a caravan at Tac. H.Q. for use when I worked and stayed up there.

There was much criticism from time to time about Montgomery's way of living apart from his staff, but although it put a considerable strain upon a number of us, his great success as a Commander proves that this system had a lot to commend it. Rommel, during a battle, exercised command from a very mobile Battle H.Q. and there is no doubt that my Chief stole a leaf out of this brilliant German Commander's book.

With the coming landings in Normandy and the campaign in North-west Europe before us, the composition of a Tac. H.Q. suited to Montgomery's needs as an Army Group Commander required a great deal of consideration. It had to be larger than hitherto in order to cater for his new responsibilities. There had to be, for instance, a sizeable 'B' Mess for all the officers who were not part of his immediate entourage; a separate Intelligence set-up with a hand-picked officer to run it; additional signal links; accommodation for the few important guests whom Montgomery would allow to visit him and a transport unit capable of looking after the motley collection of vehicles. His personal staff and L.O.s were also increased and consisted of two British A.D.C.s, Johnny Henderson and Noel Chevasse, who had succeeded John Poston, now an L.O.; a Canadian and an American personal L.O., in addition to a military assistant in the person of Kit Dawnay, who was as efficient as he was charming. It was a very happy party and Montgomery obtained much needed relaxation by chatting with these young men. He has been criticized for surrounding himself by this younger element, but I believe that on the whole it was not a bad thing. James Gunn has painted a delightful conversation piece of Montgomery sitting at his dining table in the Mess tent of his Tac. H.Q. surrounded by his personal staff. It was exhibited at the Royal Academy and it certainly portrays a relaxed C.-in-C.

Because of the enhanced status of this Tac. H.Q. it was decided that a specially selected officer should be appointed to be in charge. It was naturally thought that selection for this job would be a great honour. I therefore went to a great deal of trouble with the military secretary to sift through those names which he had proposed for consideration. It was a key appointment and I couldn't afford to make a mistake. Eventually I decided upon a brilliant young officer whom I thought would fit the role. The only possible objection was the fact that he had, as yet, not been fortunate enough to take an active part in one of the great campaigns, nor had he served with the Eighth Army, which, as things were at that time, carried the hall-mark for advancement in Montgomery's eyes. I felt, however, that this particular officer possessed the necessary qualifications that would enable him to surmount these drawbacks. He was interviewed by the C.-in-C. and confirmed in his appointment.

Tac. H.Q. was one of the first invasion echelons that concentrated in the Portsmouth area close to Southwell Park, and every vehicle was put through the process of waterproofing. As it was probable that Montgomery would move over to Normandy soon after the initial landings, these vehicles were ordered to be loaded into the landing-craft before the invasion fleet sailed from the shores of Great Britain. I had underestimated my Chief's urge to follow up the assaulting troops during the invasion of Sicily and got a severe rocket for my lack of foresight. He had suddenly decided to leave Malta for Sicily a few hours after the landings commenced, and I regret to say that his Tac. H.Q. vehicles had not been loaded at the time and the Army Commander had been forced to spend about twenty-four hours on the island without a home of his own. A tortoise without its shell!

With news of the initial success on the Normandy beaches, Montgomery was straining at the leash and on 8th June, two days after the invasion started, he decided to go over to France. This time, I am glad to say, Tac. H.Q. was there to greet him. Main Headquarters remained in England until the situation permitted this great and unwieldy organization to cross over gradually by echelons. There was soon a good cross-Channel telephone system in operation and Eisenhower kindly gave me a Dakota aircraft with an American crew for my personal use for the duration of the campaign, so I was able to keep in close touch with my Chief and with events in the bridgehead.

A week or two after 'D-Day' Montgomery came through on the phone to say that there had been some trouble at Tac. H.Q. — would I please come over straight away and deal with the matter. There was no point in going into details over the wires and so I ordered my aircraft and prepared to fly over for a couple of days.

It was only a matter of minutes after take-off that one got a view of the amazing scene that the assault beaches presented with the artificial harbours ('Mulberries'), the balloon barrages, the numbers of ships of all sizes, the airstrips surrounded by dust and the tremendous activity taking place on every side. In the middle distance, only a few miles from the shore, one could see signs of battle in one sector or another — shelling, and burning vehicles belching black smoke into the skies.

There was a car to meet me at the airstrip and we drove straight off to Tac. H.Q. where I found my chief in his map lorry, studying the latest situation which had just been chalked up by one of his liaison officers on his return from Dempsey's sector of the front. He saw me approaching and shouted out,

'Hello, Freddie, you haven't wasted any time. Come along inside.'

I climbed up the steps and sat down beside him.

'Now, what's the trouble?' I asked.

'Well, Jones (the brilliant Staff Officer appointed to Tac. H.Q. — I'll call him Jones) has accused me of looting, or rather of condoning looting. I won't have him here a moment longer. I think he's gone mad! It's all to do with a pig, but you'd better get Johnny to tell you about it and then come and see me again.'

I left the map lorry and sought out Johnny Henderson, finding him in the Mess tent with some of the other boys. I asked him what all the trouble was about and he told me the story.

It has been the custom throughout the ages, when soldiers are hungry and see some tempting addition to their fare running round the countryside, to procure it with few formalities. The usual procedure, when commandeering considerable amounts of food, is to hand over a signed requisition form enumerating the articles in question. Later these forms are exchanged for cash by the appropriate authority. In this rich countryside the farms had suffered greatly during the first week or two of 'Operation Overlord'. Bombs and shells had played havoc with the livestock, and wherever one looked one could sec the bloated carcasses of cattle and pigs which smelt to high heaven. Poultry were wandering about scratching up food where they could find it, and I am afraid that quite a fair proportion found their way into the bellies of deserving soldiers without the formalities of the requisition form. Because of the interdiction programme carried out by the Allied Air Forces, which aimed at cutting the railways and isolating the whole of the assault area from the rest of France, abundant farm produce had piled up in barns and warehouses because of lack of transport. For instance, there were tens of thousands of Camembert cheeses literally rotting.

It was one of the duties of the A.D.C.s to see that their Chief was well-fed, and I heard that some excellent ducklings had figured on the 'A' Mess menu a couple of nights before my arrival. The next day another and more interesting opportunity came the A.D.C.s' way. It was reported that a nice, plump little pig had been seen carrying out a personal reconnaissance very close to the forbidden ground of Tac. H.Q. It was therefore not long before a hunt was organized, and a Commando, armed to the hilt, moved off to deal with this threatening situation. The result was completely successful and a delicious little pig was handed over to the mess sergeant. Unfortunately Jones heard of these activities and was simply horrified. Having received no satisfaction from the A.D.C.s, he felt it was a crime of such magnitude that he formed up before the C.-in-C. and asked that disciplinary action be taken against these offenders who had transgressed the Army Act. Under the Act, an officer who leaves his commanding officer to go in search of plunder is liable for penal servitude, but if *not* on active service, can be cashiered!

I should love to have been present at the interview which, I gather, went something like this:

'Yes, what do you want? Anything important come through from 1st Corps front?'

'Well, I am afraid I have a very serious matter to report and it concerns your A.D.C.s.'

The C.-in-C. looked up sharply, for he was ever-watchful of the discipline and behaviour of his personal staff.

'There has been a very grave case of looting.'

Jones then went on to explain about the pig and the utter lack of contrition on the part of the A.D.C.s. Montgomery told me that he sat fascinated as the tale was unfolded, and when stern disciplinary action against the offenders was demanded, he burst out laughing.

'I thought he was tight!' Monty told me.

When Jones took exception to the attitude of the C.-in-C. and showed his displeasure, Montgomery told his Staff Officer to leave his caravan and not to be such a fool.

Having heard the full story, which I found highly amusing, and after inquiring whether we were due for a succulent dish of roast pork that evening, I left the tent to look for Jones, feeling reasonably hopeful that I should be able to put matters right and in their true perspective, and so avoid any change in this key appointment at this important juncture. I soon came across Jones and asked him to come for a stroll and tell me his story. When he came to the end I was rather worried, for there was no doubt whatever that Jones had taken the whole business very much to heart and was determined to see that punishment for this flagrant violation of the rules of war should be imposed. And, what is more, he made it crystal-clear that the Army Group Commander was included as an offender!

At first I tried to reason with this highly-principled officer. However, I soon became quite angry as I tried to make him see how small this technical offence was in comparison with the momentous events that were taking place. I asked him whether he had thought about our gallant Russian Allies, who lived off the country as a means of staging their fantastic offensives. I suggested that if he had seen the devastation I had seen in North Africa, Sicily and Italy; the misery and hardships suffered by the inhabitants of these countries, where countless thousands had lost everything they possessed, and had in addition suffered great cruelty at the hands of a ruthless enemy, he would perhaps consider the shooting of a small pig something so insignificant as to be forgotten in the immensity of modern warfare. I finished by explaining that no rules or regulations could stop such a modest scale of looting.

But my words fell upon deaf ears, for Jones was determined to see that justice was done. So in the end I had to tell him that he was to be relieved of his post, but that I would do my best to ensure that he obtained a good appointment after he left Tac. H.Q. However, the whole business of looting had got under his skin, and in deadly seriousness he told me that he would not rest until he had exposed Montgomery's 'disgraceful behaviour' and seen that retribution came his way; he would have the matter raised in the House of Commons, and so on. I think my only comment was to observe that I could hardly believe that the British people would be prepared to pillory such a successful commander, who had already become a national hero, for so small a technical offence. Finally, I told him that I thought he was being terribly foolish. However, nothing would cool his wrath or his resentment, and so we parted; he with anger in his heart, and I irritated that so much of my time had been wasted.

The ex-Tac. H.Q. Staff Officer was as good as his word, and did all in his power to see that Montgomery was hauled over the coals for the pig incident. When the Field-Marshal went to the War Office as C.I.G.S. in 1946 a file was presented to him — quite a bulky one — full of minutes about this unfortunate porker, which had added so much to the gastronomic enjoyment of a number of us.

There is a postscript. A short time ago I was dining with Montgomery at a little restaurant in Soho in which Johnny

Wright, the old Tac. H.Q.'s cook has a stake. He is also the chef. Needless to say, we had first-class attention and excellent food. We reminded Wright about the pig incident, and his account of the day he cooked the animal was extremely funny. Apparently the farmer had heard of the fate of his pig. 'But,' added Wright, 'he was a bit late, sir. You see, I was just engaged in browning the bristles.' This was, in fact, the first time I had heard that the farmer had come into the picture!

Now in case the reader feels, by any chance, that my Chief's behaviour was not in the best traditions of the British Army, I would like to say that in practice he was bitterly opposed to real looting, and if ever this subject raised its ugly head, he dealt with it most sternly. I remember one occasion in which I was involved.

I had always been most meticulous in setting a good example, as Chief of Staff of the Army Group, and never once accepted the excellent cameras and binoculars which were often to be had for the asking. I am rather sorry now that I didn't! One day, however, when we were operating in Germany, one of my personal staff heard of an abandoned Mercedes car going begging. I believe it had belonged to a high Nazi official. It was brought along and the suggestion made that we might keep it as a V.I.P. car and that I could use it when necessary. I was given a run in it and I must say that it was a superb motor car. Thinking there was no harm in commandeering it, I gave Bill Bovill the O.K. It was only the next day when I was talking to Montgomery at Tac. H.Q. that he suddenly raised the question of this car. How he got to know about it so soon I have no idea — the grapevine must have been operating particularly efficiently at that moment! Very nicely, he suggested that my action might possibly be misinterpreted by those under me, and that in the circumstances he felt I had better give up the car. I saw his point and on my return to Main Headquarters gave instructions for the car to be handed over to the appropriate authorities.

But in spite of Montgomery's attitude, and the uncompromising instructions issued on this subject, there was a certain amount of looting of a larger kind that fell outside the category of the small pig incident. It was quite extraordinary how many Mercedes, soon after the war, found their way into private hands, and eventually arrived in the United Kingdom. No doubt documents were available in most cases to show that they had been correctly purchased. After I left 21st Army Group I heard many tales of cars hidden in barns and haystacks on the route of our advance, which were eventually salvaged after the cessation of hostilities. There was a case in which a beautiful grand piano was placed in a sealed lorry and sent back to a certain station in England via the cross-Channel ferry! I also believe that when we overran the stud farm area of Normandy, one or two mares were flown home in Dakotas. Some horsy types must have thought it was a pity to leave them to face the rigours of peace! Then there were several cases of large consignments of wine being flown back to England and disposed of on the black market. But cases of bad looting were, I think, on the whole few and far between.

I should be dishonest if I did not tell you the story of how I acquired a picture which I suppose falls more or less under the category of loot. It was not an old master, nor a painting by any well-known artist — just a picture which I came to love and which cheered me up on many a bleak occasion, and it just 'fell into me hands' as they say!

This is how it happened.

The anxiety and difficulties of the Normandy bridgehead were at last a nightmare of the past, and our victorious forces had crossed the Seine and were driving northwards at a shattering pace, with Brussels as a major objective. Although we had lived in tents or caravans since Alamein, it had become clear that because of the tremendous size our Headquarters had now reached, it would in future have to be housed in buildings, and that large office facilities must be found for both Rear and Main Headquarters. So I issued instructions that we should ear-mark suitable accommodation in Brussels itself, and suggested that the ex-German Headquarters would probably prove the right answer.

Harry Llewellyn, of international show-jumping fame, was now one of my liaison officers, and to him I gave the task of moving forward with a small party in the van of the advance, so that he would be able to stake our claim in Brussels. Harry, who had been an L.O. in the Eighth Army, came back to join 21st Army Group Headquarters and became my personal assistant. But I soon realized that this type of work was quite unsuited to his temperament, and so I set in motion the machinery which made Harry G.S.O.1 in charge of our liaison staff; Bill Bovill came to me as my new Personal Assistant, remaining with me until the war ended.

So, during the great advance to Brussels and the Dutch border, Llewellyn and his party moved with the Guards Armoured Division, which was leading Dempsey's spearhead. He arrived in time to take part in the hectic festivities that took place in the Belgian capital. It must have been a memorable experience, for the people went quite mad with joy, and the celebrations started as the enemy were still leaving the city. One factor which helped to produce the party spirit was the finding of a German Army liquor dump, in the woods on the outskirts of Brussels. As far as I remember this Dionysian treasure consisted of close on four and a half million bottles, and it had quite an effect upon the progress of operations.

Harry Llewellyn carried out his task with great efficiency. He claimed, in the name of Army Group Headquarters, the buildings that had just been vacated by the German High Command. There was, of course, no official hand-over in the terms of King's Regulations! The Army Group and the 2nd Tactical Air Force commanded by 'Maori' Coningham divided up the buildings between them, and it was satisfactory to find that the offices were equipped with an excellent telephone system.

When I arrived in Brussels I was shown up to my office which happened to be the one recently vacated by the German C.-in-C., Field-Marshal von Falkenhausen, who, I understand, had carried out his difficult role in Belgium with reasonable fairness. It was an enormous room on the seventh floor. Windows stretched along the whole length of a wall, and at one end there was a large desk on which were a number of differently coloured telephones. But what riveted my attention was a picture — the only one in the room — which was hanging directly behind the desk. The sun's rays, slanting through the windows, lit up a charming scene, which I took to be a Parisian boulevard in the spring. It had the composition of a Renoir, and I found it altogether enchanting. It was the gayest of pictures, painted in oils in the free style of the Impressionist school. The trees were at their best, and looking at it one could almost hear the noise of the traffic and the laughter and chatter of the people. In the foreground, walking towards one, were two attractive young women, accompanied by their dogs and children, the breeze ruffling their skirts. It affected me profoundly, and all of a sudden, tired as I was, I felt a wave of confidence that we would be able to re-establish the order of things depicted in this picture.

I never forgot this occasion and whenever I felt depressed or down-hearted, I turned in my chair and looked up at the picture, to experience a return of my faith in ultimate victory.

I asked how this painting had got there and was told that it had been left behind by the Germans, so I then asked the *concierge* to come up and tell me about it. The answer that he gave suggested that it belonged to the German Commander-in-Chief, and that it had been given to him by a Belgian admirer, but had been forgotten in the rush of his hasty departure. I made many inquiries while in Belgium, but could never obtain any information as to the whereabouts of the artist and no one seemed to know the name which was so clearly painted in a corner of the canvas.

My personal staff soon realized what this picture meant to me, and wherever we set up our headquarters, there it was. Sometimes it was hanging in a tent, sometimes in a schoolroom — but it became an integral part of the office equipment.

The war in Europe was now over and the sad day arrived when I was to leave the 21st Army Group. All my goods and chattels were packed up and with a heavy heart I said good-bye to my many friends who had served with me since Alamein. My Dakota was ticking over on the airstrip; Bill Bovill reported that all were aboard, and we flew off to England and home.

We landed at an airport near London, and I drove off in a car that had been sent to meet me, whilst my 'chaps' were engaged in clearing my belongings through the customs. We headed for London — and Yeoman's Row where my wife had rented a charming little house.

Some time during the afternoon a lorry arrived with all my things which were carried up the stairs. During this operation I spotted a large crate which I had not remembered seeing with my other things in Germany before my departure. I asked Bill Bovill and my A.D.C. what it contained and they confessed that was my picture. They said that as they knew it meant so much to me, and as it had presumably belonged to the German C.-in-C., they felt it was one of the perks of war. Apparently they had told the story to the customs officers who had dealt very kindly with them. I must admit that I was delighted, and to this day it has remained a treasured possession, not because of any intrinsic value, but because it had meant so much to me during an unforgettable period of my life. And as I write these pages I am looking up at it hanging on the wall.

CHAPTER EIGHT: VODKA — AN AID TO PROMOTION

In contrast with the sad story of the over-conscientious Staff Officer and the pig, here is a story in which several factors helped a spirited young officer to promotion. The magnificence of Russian hospitality; the young officer's difficulty in surmounting its effects; and the Field-Marshal's stern yet human qualities — all go to produce rather a charming tale.

It is now well known how Montgomery stole a leaf out of Wellington's book by making a great deal of use of personal liaison officers in order to help him exercise intimate command of operations in the field. Of course, circumstances were very different from the days of Waterloo. Then it was possible for the Commander-in-Chief to sit astride his horse and view more or less the whole field of battle. The dispatch of an L.O. on his charger to report on any particular sector of the fight and his return, provided he escaped the shot and cannon balls en route, were merely a matter of minutes. But the principle was the same, for Wellington and Montgomery would often make vital decisions, while viewing events through the eyes of the elite band of young officers who served on their liaison staff.

During the last war, with the wide fronts and fast-moving operations, the liaison officer's task was no easy one. He had to have courage, determination and almost unlimited resource. He also had to possess a personality that was acceptable to commanders who might dislike being contacted during critical periods. This latter point was, however, of little consequence, for not only did the Commander-in-Chief select his L.O.s with the greatest possible care, but he backed them up to the hilt with his authority, and it therefore took a really brave commander to brush aside lightly any inquiries made by them.

It was the rule that all L.O.s reported back to Montgomery each evening. As I sat in his map lorry at Tactical Headquarters and listened to their reports and watched the coloured pencils bringing dispositions up to date, it was easy to forget, or even accept as commonplace, the toil and tribulations that these young men experienced in providing the answers to the questions set them by our Chief.

Churchill, in his history of *The Second World War — Triumph and Tragedy* describes these evening conferences when he visited 21st Army Group to see the battle of the crossing of the Rhine.

Churchill's descriptive powers cannot be bettered:

> At 8 p.m. we repaired to the map wagon, and now I had an excellent opportunity of seeing Montgomery's methods of conducting a battle on this gigantic scale. For nearly two hours a succession of young officers, of about the rank of major, presented themselves. Each had come back from a different sector of the front. They were the direct personal representatives of the Commander-in-Chief, and could go anywhere and see anything and ask any questions they liked of any commander, whether at the divisional headquarters or with the forward troops. As in turn they made their reports and were searchingly questioned by their chief the whole story of the day's battle was unfolded. This gave Monty a complete account of what had happened by highly competent men whom he knew well and whose eyes he trusted. It afforded an invaluable cross-check to the reports from all the various headquarters and from the commanders, all of which had already been weighed and sifted by General de Guingand, his Chief of Staff, and were known to Montgomery. By this

process he was able to form a more vivid, direct, and sometimes more accurate picture. The officers ran great risks, and of the seven or eight to whom I listened on this and succeeding nights two were killed in the next few weeks. I thought the system admirable, and indeed the only way in which a modern Commander-in-Chief could see as well as read what was going on in every part of the front. This process having finished, Montgomery gave a series of directions to de Guingand, which were turned into immediate action by the Staff machine, and so to bed.

I shall always remember John Poston as Montgomery's most colourful L.O. He started life with Monty as an A.D.C. shortly after he took over command of the Eighth Army. He came from that distinguished cavalry regiment — the 11th Hussars, 'The Cherry Pickers'; he and Johnny Henderson made a delightful pair, full of the fire of youth and its accompanying weaknesses. We were great friends, and they would often come to me with their troubles in the hope that I could either smooth things out with Montgomery or organize things so that leave was granted for some important purpose.

Johnny, many years after the end of the war, does not look a day older. He is married to a charming wife and they have three delightful children. His morale is still unimpaired and he is invariably very kind to me when I allow too many pheasants to fly over my head unharmed. On reading Montgomery's *Memoirs* I was very surprised to find that Johnny never received a mention but knowing how fond Monty was of his A.D.C., I'm sure it was just an oversight.

John Poston met a tragic end, virtually within striking distance of Montgomery's Tactical Headquarters, when we were waiting expectantly for the enemy flag to be struck. A handful of German soldiers, who were hiding in a wood, ambushed him while driving his Jeep on some mission for his Chief. I know how all of us who belonged to the original team felt his loss. Even Montgomery, with his iron control, found it difficult to disguise his grief. Every year he holds a reunion dinner with all those who were attached to his Tac. H.Q.s and when they meet thoughts go back to this gay and gallant young officer. John Poston is never forgotten.

The main character in this story joined the distinguished band of Liaison Officers after poor John Poston had been killed. He was a very likeable young man. Not long afterwards the war drew to a close, which, as far as 21st Army Group was concerned, dated from the German surrender at Lüneburg Heath.

It was then that we began to fraternize and make contact with our Russian Allies, and a series of banquets took place. Our Red Army hosts always surpassed us in the splendour and standard of their hospitality. They taxed one's head and stomach to a dreadful extent, and unless one had the firm resolve and frugal habits of a Montgomery, the after-effects were often painful and severe.

'Bimbo' Dempsey had invited Marshal Konstantin Rokossovsky, who was commanding the Russian front opposite his 2nd British Army, to a lunch party, the remains of German resistance having been squashed out from between us like jam from a sandwich. The return match was now to be played on the Russian home ground, and to this parade and luncheon Montgomery had been formally invited.

The Commander-in-Chief took with him Kit Dawnay, his Military Assistant, Johnny Henderson and the Young Liaison Officer, and they set off in his Dakota for the landing-strip adjacent to Rokossovsky's Headquarters.

Montgomery was received with due respect by a well-drilled guard of honour, after which he inspected a collection of Russian and enemy equipment. I had not been at Dempsey's luncheon, but he told me that he had lined up all the latest weapons and vehicles (British and American) in order to demonstrate Western ingenuity and strength. There were heavy guns, the latest anti-tank and self-propelled artillery, tanks of varying types, including amphibians, and an array of other vehicles. An interesting side-light on the Russian mentality was the fact that their soldiers and N.C.O.s accompanying the officers pointed to certain of the exhibits and said, 'Ah, so you have had to use some of our equipment', when the item in question showed quite plainly their country of origin. It was obvious that the Russian soldiers had not been told the extent of the help given them by their British and American allies.

It is best to pass quickly over the banquet. There was an abundance of food and drink, the caviar was of a superlative quality, and one could have had a bath in the amount of vodka consumed.

It was late in the afternoon before the guests were allowed to depart, and Dawnay began to organize Montgomery's party. Unfortunately, reports reached him that the latest-joined Liaison Officer had suffered considerably at the hands of his Russian hosts and their vodka. It was obvious that it would be unwise to let him join in the farewell formalities near the runway. Arrangements were therefore made to have this unhappy officer taken ahead independently of his Chief to the Dakota, and it needs little imagination to guess in which part of the aircraft he was deposited — it was, of course, the 'Lou'!

All went well, and after inspecting the Guard of Honour, our C.-in-C. stepped into his aircraft, accompanied by the best wishes of his Russian opposite number. As the aircraft was being prepared for take-off Montgomery turned round and questioned Dawnay regarding the young officer. Was he aboard? Kit could truthfully reply that he was, for he had had to talk continuously in order to drown the hilarious noises that were issuing from the 'Lou'!

It was then that the Russians started to fire their 19-gun salute in honour of the Field-Marshal. And it was this very procedure that produced such unfortunate results for our temporarily disabled friend. With that ingrained sense of military discipline, together with a desire to see that his Chief had his full share of respect, he pulled himself together, and, not to be outdone, drew his revolver in order to join in the salutation. Without warning, the shattering sound of several shots was heard above the roar of the engines. The L.O. had made his contribution very effectively by firing through the window of the lavatory. The aircraft then took off and he returned to his previous happy state.

As can be imagined, Montgomery sat up and took notice and Dawnay was subject to a bombardment of questions.

'What's he been doing — drinking?' shouted our Chief. 'Get him out of there at once.'

When seat-belts were unfastened, Kit went through the motions of looking into the 'Lou', but shut the door smartly and returned to the Field-Marshal. He made it clear that it was better to leave things as they were for a while.

'Well, bring him to see me directly we get back to Headquarters.' There was an electric atmosphere for the remainder of the flight, and not a little apprehension.

On arrival at the landing-ground, the Commander-in-Chief was driven off in his car accompanied by Johnny Henderson, while Kit Dawnay organized matters so that the L.O. could be escorted to his quarters with the least fuss and publicity.

Montgomery was not a man to let the grass grow under his feet, and was eager to deal with his young L.O. with as little delay as possible. Dawnay was therefore summoned to his office and questioned about this unfortunate incident. He had some difficulty in explaining to the austere Field-Marshal, with his well-known personal dislike of alcohol, how difficult it was to stand up against a well co-ordinated Russian attack armed with vodka. He also had to explain how long it took to get over the effects of this particular liquor, and how sudden contact with fresh air or the drinking of a glass of water was likely to produce delayed-action results.

Nevertheless, Montgomery was keen to get to grips with the matter and waved Dawnay aside, telling him to order the L.O. to report in half an hour's time for an interview.

Dawnay withdrew, but returned ten minutes later with a troubled mind. He had made a close personal reconnaissance and formed certain very obvious conclusions, the most important of which was that it was utterly impracticable for the C.-in-C. to interview the young officer in half an hour or even in an hour — it would be better to wait until the following day.

He explained the position to his Chief, expecting a minor atomic explosion to take place.

'Did you say tomorrow?' cried Montgomery.

'Yes, sir, I'm afraid I did.'

Then instead of the anticipated detonation, the Field-Marshal burst out laughing. I think he must have been intrigued and even fascinated at learning that alcohol could produce such an astonishing effect on so young and virile a man.

'All right, then I will see him tomorrow morning.'

But as things turned out forty-eight hours went by before the interview took place. A very crestfallen L.O. reported to receive his caning. He fully realized that with a man like

Montgomery, there was only one outcome. There were very heavy odds against his remaining an L.O. any longer, and the chances of a court-martial looked very probable.

Montgomery had given the problem his usual careful attention. His personal staff must be above reproach, and this officer's one lapse, admittedly under very difficult circumstances, meant that he could no longer remain with him. But Monty is really a very human and kindly man, and is particularly fond of youth.

The interview was short and to the point. The officer had erred and must therefore take his punishment. From that day he ceased to be a Liaison Officer and was to be posted elsewhere.

'I have instructed the Military Secretary to return you to your Regiment. Report to him at once. And let this be a lesson to you.' Then he added: 'I'm sorry this has happened.'

Then with a ghost of a smile, the young officer was dismissed.

And what was the sequel? The posting meant that in a very short time he was promoted to command a battery, with the rank of Major.

So although he was obviously sad at leaving the Field-Marshal, nevertheless, the war was at an end, and the chance of promotion was something well worth having.

I have always felt that this is a very good example of that very human side of Montgomery's character.

CHAPTER NINE: A PRESENT FROM ZHUKOV

International entertaining always possessed its hazards — even for the Russians. I remember such an occasion in November 1945, when I was Director of Military Intelligence at the War Office. Montgomery had asked me to visit him in Germany.

The C.-in-C.'s country residence, a *Schloss* near Ein Badhausen, was a most comfortable mansion and I was overjoyed to find myself back once more in the congenial atmosphere of the 21st Army Group, now the British Army of Occupation of the Rhine, meeting members of my old staff once again and also the Commander-in-Chief's personal retinue. It was all very refreshing.

Montgomery was engaged, with the help of the staff, in writing the factual accounts of the campaigns which he had so successfully conducted, and I had to spend a number of hours reading through the manuscripts. The diaries which he had kept so meticulously throughout the war were made available to me and I sat up for two nights until the early hours reading — they brought back many vivid memories.

Then we flew on to Berlin.

The flight to Berlin was uneventful, and we lunched with Sir Brian Robertson, one of the old team, who was then the C.-in-C.'s deputy there. Later he became the High Commissioner for the British Zone in Germany. After lunch, we all went off to attend a meeting of the four Commanders-in-Chief who between them controlled Occupied Germany. The meeting started at 2.30 p.m. and broke up about 4.30 p.m., when refreshments were served in an adjoining room. Eisenhower was away visiting America, and General Clay, Robertson's American opposite number, took his place.

It was most interesting to see the four Allies functioning together. Various matters were put up for discussion and it was quite evident, even from this meeting alone, to see that Marshal Zhukov had little power of final decision. Several times Montgomery, Clay and Kœnig agreed upon a certain course of action, but the Russian Marshal had to say that he would give his approval or otherwise only after reference to Moscow. I understand this procedure became quite a joke in the end, and it is said that finally Zhukov at one meeting said to the amusement of his colleagues: 'I agree, and will let Moscow know later!'

He was recalled and appointed to a minor post in Russia shortly afterwards.

One of the reasons for my visit to Berlin was to attend a dinner party that Montgomery was giving to the other three allied C's-in-C and their Chiefs of Staff. There had been numerous banquets and other high-level entertainment since the end of the war, and the Russians had been responsible for some particularly lavish displays. The British Commander-in-Chief had therefore decided to initiate them into the 'British way of life' in the form of a typical English dinner-party. It was a pity that Eisenhower was away, but Zhukov and his Chief of Staff, Sogolovsky, Clay, Kœnig and his Chief of Staff, and Robertson were invited.

Montgomery, with his usual care, had taken a great deal of trouble to ensure that the menu would be truly representative. There were to be two cocktails served before dinner — White Ladies and Dry Martinis. Smoked salmon was to be eaten with these drinks. An excellent *consommé* was to be followed by sole which had been flown specially from the Baltic. The next course was to consist of pheasant — beautifully presented with the cocks' tail feathers sticking out of the blunt end of the roasted birds. Then there was to be some sort of ice as a sweet, and finally a savoury and dessert. Suitable wines had been chosen for each course. An excellent dinner, one must admit, but it fell far short of the type of Russian banquet that many of us had attended.

The dinner-party had been fixed for this particular evening, and when the four-power meeting was through, Montgomery went over to where Zhukov was standing and, clapping him on the back, said through an interpreter: 'Now, Marshal, don't forget that you are dining with me tonight, and I want to make it quite clear that this is not going to be one of your Russian binges — it's just an ordinary little English dinner-party.' And without a moment's hesitation Zhukov smilingly replied: 'Well, I suppose that means that I shall have to have my dinner before I go!' We all liked this rugged Russian soldier, not only for his triumphs in the field, but because of his friendly and cheerful personality.

When these big-four meetings commenced it was decided that each nation in turn would be responsible for laying on the refreshments afterwards. I believe it fell to the British to start the ball rolling and, as might be expected, the whole business was handed over to the N.A.A.F.I. Although not wishing to belittle our excellent canteen services, the results, I'm told, were not very exciting: rather large and unappetizing sandwiches, cakes, tea and, of course, a bar where most drinks were to be had. I think it was the Americans who came next on the roster, and there was a distinct rise in the standard of living! Various tinned delicacies were offered in quantity; Virginia peach-fed hams and numerous other appetizing dishes. Next came the French and, of course, this sort of occasion was just up their street. The tables were covered with a delicious array of foods and the very best champagnes were there for the asking. But perhaps the most exciting touch was the presence of a carefully selected band of the French equivalent of our A.T.S. who had been imported, I believe, from Paris! They were beautiful girls with lovely figures, immaculately turned out and chosen for their proficiency in languages. It was not surprising that this party was a 'wow'!

On this particular day that I was in the party, it was the Russians' turn, and I shall never forget the scene that met our eyes when the great curtains were drawn aside. I am sure that the display could not have been bettered even when the Czars held sway. The tables were arranged in a long gentle curve with three projections jutting back to the rear. The food was out of this world. There were great silver bowls of caviar and even the red type from the salmon was not forgotten. Then we saw lying majestically upon their dishes smoked and fresh salmon as well as sturgeon. Every sort of herring was to be found: hams, boars' heads, turkeys, chickens, and the lot. And as for the drink, there was everything from vodka to champagne. It was terrific. Finally, a most impressive touch was given by a number of soldiers, both men and women, standing strictly to attention with folded arms in front of the tables. The men wore well-cut breeches with highly-polished black top-boots, shirts and Sam-Brown belts. The women wore skirts and boots, shirts and belts, just as the men. It was a really tantalizing display, particularly as I knew what was in store for us at the Villa Montgomery in two or three hours' time!

The Commanders-in-Chief were escorted to a room leading off from the main hall and were soon seated at a small table placed in the centre. The table was covered with a selection of foods, and almost immediately waiters appeared with caviar and vodka. Montgomery took a modest helping of caviar, but put up his hand when the sergeant made a move to fill his glass with vodka. Zhukov, seeing this gesture, said: 'Would you not drink to the health of Generalissimo Stalin, Field-Marshal?'

Without batting an eyelid our C.-in-C. replied, 'Certainly, if you would like me to do so.' And the glass was filled.

When everyone had been attended to the toast was proposed and Montgomery, in unison with the others, drained his glass at one go — no heel-taps in fact. In spite of the obvious surprise that his throat and stomach must have experienced from this quite unusual treatment, the Field-Marshal showed the greatest fortitude and stood up to this test extremely well, but he didn't ask for another glass.

Using all forces of self-denial, I was eventually led away by Montgomery without having seriously affected my appetite for the coming dinner.

In view of the growing standard of this post-conference refreshment, Montgomery decided that the time had come to stop further competition, and after this Russian triumph, agreement was reached with his colleagues to bring things down to a more modest level, and so our N.A.A.F.I. was saved a certain amount of embarrassment.

At 8.15 p.m. precisely, our guests started to arrive and they all appeared to be in excellent spirits. Johnny Henderson and the other A.D.C.s soon got busy seeing that everyone had the drinks they required. Zhukov brought his own interpreter and there were, I think, one or two others. As was usual on occasions of this sort, they sat on chairs behind those engaged in conversation. They would take great care to check each other's translations, so that no mistakes were made, and sometimes the flow of talk was held up while the interpreters wrangled over the precise meaning of some particular phrase or other.

Early on in this pre-dinner period it was noticeable that Zhukov and Sogolovsky, while accepting cocktails, were not actually drinking them. They would frequently put their lips to their glasses, but the level of the drink remained the same. This abstinence was quite unusual because, as a rule, the Russian Marshal was not very backward when good drink was on tap. The same procedure was followed during dinner; wine was poured into their glasses but the contents were virtually left untouched. It was all very odd especially as the other guests appeared to find the wines very much to their liking, except, of course, Montgomery who never drank them. It was fairly obvious that the Russian Commissar had given the Russian C.-in-C. and his Chief of Staff some rigid instructions on deportment before they set out. No doubt some sort of trap was expected: Montgomery wished to obtain information from them and therefore it would be better to keep off the drink so that the risk of any indiscretion might be eliminated. Such a suspicious approach was, of course, typical of the Russian mentality at that time.

Nevertheless, it was a very happy little party and conversation was bright and interesting and the food was obviously appreciated by everyone. After coffee, port and liqueurs, we got up and adjourned to another room. At one stage I found myself grouped with the two Russians and Montgomery, and we began talking about various Allied commanders and their methods. I happened to quote Montgomery's oft-stated comment that he organized things so that his Chief of Staff might go mad, but never himself! I added that it was a wonder that I had more or less stood up to the strain — but perhaps I hadn't, for people who go off their heads are alleged never to realize what has happened to them. I was trying to be funny.

Sogolovsky, however, turned to me and said with the utmost seriousness: '*I* would have enjoyed serving under your great Commander!' It was a charming little compliment and I am sure it was sincere, for the Russians held my Chief in great esteem. They recognized him as a fighter and one who understood the art of command.

Our host had arranged some after-dinner entertainment in the form of a team of pipers and dancers from one of the Scottish regiments, and we were asked to sit around the lounge so that things could start. It was rather a small room and it was with some apprehension that I observed several lusty Highlanders, resplendent in their kilts, march into the room playing some stirring tune. I delight in listening to pipes in the open, but in a confined space I believe one must have some Scottish blood in one's veins to be able to enjoy them. I watched Zhukov from time to time. To start with, he was beaming all over his face, but as one tune followed another, he began to look a little restless, and I must admit that at times the noise was terrific. The final part of the programme consisted of the sword-dance, beautifully executed by four enormous men. Naturally, we all applauded with great enthusiasm, partly for their skill and partly, no doubt, because peace and calm would now return to the villa.

The mess waiters then came in and, much to our surprise, it was Zhukov who first asked for refreshment.

'May I have a large whisky and soda?' he asked.

It had taken the bagpipes to break down the resistance of our Russian friends!

Zhukov was the chief actor in another post-war episode in my life. A kindly War Office had granted me several months' sick leave after V-E Day in order to repair some of the scars and strains that were inevitable after nearly six years' campaigning in several theatres, for in May 1945 I really believed I was almost qualifying for a breakdown. However, the crisp air, together with the peace and beauty of the Highlands, was producing remarkable results, and early August found me moving over the hills to Skye. Taking the little ferry steamer from the Kyle of Lochalsh I stayed for a few days at a charming hotel which was situated in the shadow of The Cuillins. It was near enough to allow one to enjoy the full magnificence of these rocky mountains, but far enough away to avoid being dominated by them.

After a short stay I moved farther afield to a lovely home north of Portree, which snuggled in a cosy hollow and yet was only a matter of yards from the sea. One could stroll out from the house and within a minute or so be looking over that magnificent stretch of water — the Sound of Raasay — and away to the north could be seen the islands where so many sea-birds make their homes, and where seals play around the rocky shores.

One evening we were returning late from a fishing excursion across the Sound and, having secured the boat, were climbing towards the house from the shore; all of us laden with quantities of fish. The sun had set but it was still quite light and the occasional flight of widgeon could be seen silhouetted against an opal sky; as we walked the frightened squeak of a solitary snipe let us know that we were not the only ones awake at ten o'clock of an evening in this beautiful Western Isle.

I was looking forward to the lovely supper which I knew would be awaiting us, and quickened my pace as the house came into view through a gap in the storm-blown fir-trees that lined the bank above the sandy beach. As I entered the house one of the little Scottish maids, dressed in her prim dark grey and white uniform, greeted me with:

'Oh, General, someone from Berlin has been calling you on the telephone.'

This took me by surprise, for I couldn't understand in the first place how anyone had been able to trace me to this remote point of enchanted isolation. I was even more surprised when, in answer to my question as to whether she knew who had been wishing to speak to me, she replied in a rather awed voice:

'I think they said it was a Field-Marshal, sir — Zhukov or some funny name.'

I must admit I was extremely puzzled, for if it really had been our old comrade Zhukov, the great Russian Marshal, and Number One Hero of the Soviet Union, I was quite certain that the last person he should wish to speak to was me! Therefore I presumed that the girl had got muddled up. On the other hand, I felt that I had better ring up the War Office to find out whether someone from Berlin was in fact trying to get in touch with me. And so I booked a call to that well-known Whitehall number.

As nothing had happened by eleven o'clock, and as I was feeling rather sleepy from a day in the open air followed by a wonderful meal of freshly-fried fish and a pink-coloured Scottish ham, I decided to give it up and go to bed. But hardly had I crawled luxuriously between the sheets and opened the book I was reading when the telephone bell rang, so I slipped on my dressing-gown and scrambled down the stairs, eager to know what might be behind this mysterious call.

Taking up the receiver I heard a rather tired and bored voice stating that this was the War Office — whom did I want? I asked for the 'G' Duty Officer, and after a few moments I heard his voice answering the ring of the telephone. It is quite a thing to hold this assignment for the night, and a young Staff Officer new to the task would feel a certain sense of importance and responsibility, for all signals passed through his hands. He would often be required to decide whether to wake up some rather senior General, or even a Cabinet Minister — knowing full well that if the awakened one did not rank the message on the same level of priority as himself, then there were likely to be some unkind things said the next day!

I gave my name, was fortunate to find that a young officer whom I knew quite well was there on duty, and quickly explained the reason for my call. The Duty Officer was fully aware of the matter and told me that a Liaison Officer at Marshal Zhukov's Headquarters had been trying to trace me all day, as he had a message from the Russian Marshal himself. Apparently the War Office had conducted a most efficient telephone hunt across Scotland and at long last had run me to earth on the Isle of Skye. I asked what the nature of the message was, and was told:

'Marshal Zhukov wishes you to attend a ceremony in Berlin on 10th August so that he can decorate you with the Order of Kutuzov, First Class.' An aircraft would be provided and the programme and instructions were being held by the War Office pending my decision as to where they were to be sent.

As the date in question was only three days off, and as I had been sent on sick leave with the strict instructions to lose myself in the country pursuits that Scotland had to offer and to refrain from all military activities, I considered that I was justified in declining to make the journey. I hoped, however, that my attitude would not be considered discourteous. All this I explained to the Duty Officer and asked him to get in touch with Montgomery so that he could explain the situation to this very likeable Russian soldier. I suggested that it might be possible to put off the ceremony for a month or two, or make some other arrangement. Then saying good night, I rang off and retired once again to my bed, relieved that this call was unlikely to result in my being uprooted from this happy existence.

The next day I received a long wire from my old Chief Montgomery saying that on no account was I to go to Berlin, but remain where I was and get fit. He had arranged everything satisfactorily with Zhukov and concluded by sending me his best wishes. So once again the horizon was clear and bright and I concentrated afresh upon such important matters as bait for the lobster pots, and how to lure those lazy salmon from a near-by river.

In due course I arrived back at our house in London and, as expected, found a veritable mountain of mail awaiting me. One particularly large and official looking envelope attracted my attention and, opening it, I found a written invitation to Berlin signed by the Marshal's Chief of Staff, together with a programme of the ceremony and subsequent proceedings. I must admit that I felt somewhat flattered at the honours which were to be showered upon a mere Chief of Staff.

I was to have been met at the airport with a guard of honour, and later driven to the Russian Commander-in-Chief's Headquarters, where the ceremony of the presentation of this Russian Order would have taken place. All this was to be followed by a luncheon and I knew something of these Russian banquets. They usually finished very late, and the most delicious and unproletarian foods and drinks were there to be consumed.

Together with these official letters was a note from our Liaison Officer explaining that Marshal Zhukov had sent the decoration with a letter to Montgomery, asking him to present it to me on his behalf on a suitable occasion. As I sat that evening sipping a whisky and soda, I started to wonder what sort of occasion Monty would choose. I began to day-dream and pictured myself resplendent in review order standing out in front of a well turned-out parade, facing the Commander-in-Chief of the British Army of the Rhine, the band playing a stirring tune as Montgomery pinned the medal on my chest. A proud moment this would be for the de Guingand family, details of which would be worthy of being passed down to my children. I eventually broke away from this reverie of self-glorification and started to get down to the many other letters that required my attention.

A few days later I had just returned to my house from a stroll in the Park and had asked my batman to brew me up a pot of tea, when the telephone bell rang. I answered it and found that one of the C.I.G.S.'s 'boys' was at the other end. After the usual preliminaries he explained that he wanted to know whether I was going to be home during the next hour or so, as there was an important letter for me from Field-Marshal Montgomery. It was 'Urgent' and so important that it had to be delivered into my own hands. I assured the young officer that I had no intention of moving from my house for the rest of the evening, so he had better send the document round right away.

This was not an unusual procedure, for I received many such letters and Montgomery was never dull on paper. Sometimes it might be a bit of gossip, or an inquiry about my health; or some query concerning a particular officer. There were also occasional questions regarding the campaign; for, as I have explained, my old Chief was at about that time writing up the factual account of the operations which he conducted from 'El

Alamein to the Sangro River' and from 'Normandy to the Baltic'.

I was sitting in a chair by the window reading the evening paper when the noise of a motor-cycle stopping at our door drew my attention. Glancing out of the window I saw a Signals Corporal jack up his machine, look up at the number, and then disappear from view as he moved forward to press the bell.

As I was waiting for my batman to show the Corporal to the sitting-room, it just crossed my mind that here might be the invitation to attend the ceremony at which I was going to receive the Order of Kutuzov. At that moment there was a knock at the door and, in answer to my call, in came the Corporal carrying a very important-looking sealed envelope. He brought out his little dispatch book, handed me the package and asked me to sign my name in the appropriate column.

Sitting back again in my chair, I opened the envelope. Inside was a letter together with a small sealed box. The latter I immediately started to open, and there before me nestled the high Russian Order — it was a star to be worn on the chest, and in the centre there was an enamelled miniature of Kutuzov himself. Slightly puzzled I proceeded to slit open the smaller envelope to find a letter from Marshal Zhukov to Montgomery, together with a translation, and here is a reproduction of it:

(The Peoples Commissariat for the
Defence of the U.S.S.R.)
The Commander of the Soviet
Occupation Troops in Germany

8 Aug 45
Dear Field-Marshal Montgomery,

I am extremely sorry that owing to illness Maj General Sir Francis de Guingand will be unable to come to my HQ on 10th Aug 45 in order to receive his Order of Kutuzov 1st Class, with which he has been decorated by the Soviet Government.

I should be very grateful to you if you could personally present the Order to him with my congratulations and my wishes for a speedy recovery.

Yours sincerely,
Marshal of the Soviet Union
G. Zhukov

To the Commander-in-Chief of
the British Occupation Troops in
GERMANY,
Field Marshal Sir Bernard Montgomery.

and there in my Chief's handwriting was a little note written in red ink across the right-hand top corner which read as follows:

Dear Freddie,
Herewith the doings!
Yrs. ever,
B.L.M.

Montgomery was always one for simplification!

CHAPTER TEN: VISITORS NOT WELCOME

One of Montgomery's strong points was the way in which he supported his Generals. His advice and experience were always at their disposal and he was particularly insistent that during a battle nothing must be allowed to happen which might take a Commander's eye off the ball. This included visitors and lookers-on who had no particular contribution to make.

The first real trouble Montgomery ran into in this connection was before the assault on the island of Sicily when the G.O.C.-in-C. of the First Canadian Army in England, General McNaughton, arrived in Malta with a party of Staff Officers, before the attack went in; with the object of crossing to Sicily at the first opportunity to see the First Canadian Division in action. The division was commanded by a first-class and able officer — General Guy Simonds. He was young and this was the first occasion that he had commanded his formation in battle, and so Montgomery decided to forbid McNaughton entry into Sicily, at least until things had reached a stage when no harm could be done. However, as he explained in his *Memoirs*, he first checked up with Simonds for his views on such a visit, and received an immediate reply — 'For God's sake keep him away!' And so the Canadian Army Commander did not see his division until the campaign in Sicily was over.

Montgomery undoubtedly made an enemy, but he protected Simonds from possible embarrassment during a delicate phase of the operations.

Another would-be visitor to Sicily received similar treatment about the same time. He was Major-General Drummond Inglis who became Chief Engineer of the 21st Army Group. I described this incident in my book *Operation Victory*:

> He arrived out with several others just before we landed in order to gain first-hand knowledge. Very strict orders were issued that no one was to land in Sicily until the Army Commander said: 'Go.' Inglis tried to beat the gun and sailed on a landing-craft from Malta. The news leaked out and he was faced with a message on the shores of Sicily saying that if he landed he would be placed under arrest! The reasons for these restrictions were again to ensure that no unavoidable worries were placed upon commanders until we knew things were properly launched. Inglis took it very well and served Montgomery with great ability in North-west Europe, receiving the K.B.E. shortly after the war ended.

After this the word got around that one could not gatecrash into any of Montgomery's battles. This did not mean that distinguished visitors did not arrive from time to time, but such visits were always preceded by a little probing, so as to ensure that the time was opportune and their presence welcomed.

I now come to the Battle of the Rhine. A few weeks before the assault the British Prime Minister, accompanied by Lord Alanbrooke and General Ismay, paid a fleeting visit to the front in Eisenhower's train and it pulled up for a few hours close to our Tactical Headquarters. Montgomery and I were invited to dinner, and although I was extremely tired I was delighted at the opportunity of once again meeting these great men. I also knew that the food and wine would be first-class and, of course, they were. Oh, I almost forgot the cigars! At the end of dinner a cigar cabinet was passed round which contained several sizes of cigars, from small Petite Coronas to that enormous variety of which Churchill is so fond. Unfortunately the small ones were closest to me, but with the risk of being considered rude or greedy, I stretched out my arm to its full extent and firmly grasped one of the very largest — I just couldn't miss such a wonderful opportunity!

When dinner was over Montgomery got up and said: 'Well, sir, I must return to my Headquarters.'

Churchill did not press him to stay and graciously excused him with some such remark as:

'I know the austere life you lead, Field-Marshal — good night, and more victories.'

I was very pleased at this development, for I was very weary and had a lot to do the following day. So I rose to my feet with the intention of following my Chief. But not a bit of it.

'Sit down, my boy.'

It was almost a roar! I sat down.

I briefly describe how the rest of the evening was spent in *Operation Victory*:

> After we had talked about various things, the coming battle which was to launch us over the Rhine was discussed. Then Churchill said he wished to see the operations and expected me to help him. He made it crystal-clear that this did not mean that he should be located in a safe place far from the crossing places, but that he must have a closeup view, and even pay a visit to the eastern bank. He would like to be allotted a tank and be hitched on to the early waves of the assault. I did not feel too sure of my ground, for I knew Montgomery's views about visitors during battles. I said I would do what I could, and would talk to the Field-Marshal about it, and that I thought something could be arranged. As the evening wore on I realized that the Prime Minister was absolutely determined on this project. He talked about the

battles he had been in during the last war, and that he insisted upon being in the thick of it once more. I even began to wonder whether this great man had decided that he would like to end his days in battle, at a time when he knew victory was upon us!

It was only recently that I read the second volume of Arthur Bryant's work which dealt with Field-Marshal Alanbrooke's diaries, and came across the following passages referring to the Prime Minister's request to see the Battle of the Rhine:

> Tonight we dined in the train and Monty and de Guingand came to dinner. Winston fretty because he was not allowed nearer the front, and trying to make plans to come back for the operation connected with the crossing of the Rhine!
>
> De Guingand, not knowing the P.M., unfortunately adopted quite the wrong attitude with him, and I at one time was afraid that we might have trouble. Winston was in deadly earnest in his desire to come back for the crossing of the Rhine and to be well forward in this operation. I knew we should have difficulty in providing for his security, but I was even more certain that de Guingand's rather grandmotherly arguments against Winston's wishes would ultimately lead to an explosion.

The next morning during my after-breakfast chat with the Army Group Commander I described what had happened after he left the previous night and the Prime Minister's request.

'Certainly not — never!' came the answer.

I stressed Churchill's earnestness and determination, but nothing I could say made any difference. So for the time being I left it at that.

A day or two later Montgomery casually told me that he thought Churchill should perhaps, after all, be allowed to come out to watch the battle but must be kept under control. I immediately guessed that he might have had a word from Alanbrooke on this subject for 'Brookie' was the one man whom Monty never tried to disobey or refuse. He went on to explain that we had better have a tank modified to take the P.M. around. It was decided to remove the turret and install a reasonably comfortable seat.

I now find that I was quite correct in my conjecture. Arthur Bryant records extracts from a letter that Alanbrooke sent to Montgomery soon after his return to London.

Here they are:

> As regards the P.M.'s proposals for his next visit, do not take this matter too light-heartedly…
>
> …de Guingand was working on the wrong lines after you left the night you dined, he was treating the whole visit as an impossibility…

I take a little unkindly to these comments on my handling of this difficult matter, because I knew my Chief's attitude to visitors, particularly valuable and unexpendable ones like Churchill. I was, in fact, merely carrying out his firm instruction, and his reception of the request the next morning merely confirmed this point. I am quite certain, however, that I told the P.M. that I would do my very best to obtain Montgomery's agreement. I realize that one seldom sees all one's weaknesses, but I was never aware that I possessed a grandmotherly touch in my make-up!

If I had taken an entirely negative stand, one would have thought that Alanbrooke would have intervened in the discussion and this he certainly never did. Also it seems strange that neither he nor the P.M. tackled the Army Group Commander himself whilst he was dining with us. Perhaps it was considered that the indirect approach through me might prove the best course!

About two days later I had to fly to London to take the Chair at a conference at the War Office in connection with the control of Germany after the war finished. I took over Belchem, B.G.S. Operations, and other members of the staff.

There was a large gathering of officers and after a full morning we had lunch and then started again. It was about 2.45 p.m. when someone entered the room and placed a message slip in front of me:

The Prime Minister would like to see you at his offices.

I looked up and told the officer who had brought in the message that I hoped the meeting wouldn't take much longer and then I'd come along. Within a very few minutes in came the same officer with another slip. The message was short and to the point:

From the Prime Minister,
You will come at once.

There was, of course, no come-back and I handed over the Chair to Belchem and drove over to the building where Churchill worked and often slept. I was led down by one of the Prime Minister's secretaries to a comfortably furnished room. There was a good fire burning and the great man was reclining in a large armchair situated at one side of the fireplace. It certainly looked as if he had had an excellent lunch. His eyes were closed and so I quietly occupied the other armchair.

I really didn't know quite what to do. I knew, of course, that he liked to have a nap during the day, but then, on the other hand, he had sent for me, and I was due to return to my

Headquarters that night. I decided, however, to give it a few minutes and so sat back and tried to relax. The room was pretty fuggy, what with the hot fire and stale cigar smoke; it wasn't very long before I began to feel drowsy myself.

Here was a fascinating situation; what if both of us were found asleep without having made verbal contact in, say, half an hour's time? It struck me as rather funny and I developed a terrible urge to laugh. I suppose we must have remained like this for five to ten minutes when with a grunt or two the Prime Minister began to surface — slowly at first, but there was a definite trend towards consciousness! The eyes began to open and he became aware that someone was parked in the other armchair. He then started to say something; I listened intently, and heard a mumbled:

'The news from Rumania is bad.'

I sat up and looked inquiringly at him, and then followed a few sentences of explanation. The latest Foreign Office telegrams were not encouraging as to Russian intentions in that country. We then had a few minutes rather halting conversation and I began to wonder whether Churchill thought the Foreign Secretary, Anthony Eden, and not I had come to see him. I didn't feel at all comfortable. Then, finally, he sat up with a comment that the danger to the Allies was in future going to be more from the Russians than from Germany.

Having got this off his chest the Prime Minister stuck his jaw out, glared at me and said:

'Now what preparations have been made for me to watch the battle of the Rhine?'

I felt anything but happy, for up to date nothing had really been done. But I could, however, truthfully tell him that my Chief was expecting him to be there and that we were preparing a tank for his use, so that he could watch without incurring unnecessary danger. He didn't appear to think too much of this but more or less gave his approval. I then told him that I would send over a liaison officer within the next day or two to report to him and explain the arrangements that had been made and the plan of battle. He appeared fairly satisfied with this, and once again stressed his determination to be there.

And so the interview came to an end and a suitable message was given me to convey to Montgomery and I left the hot and stuffy room very relieved.

All in all, I don't really see how I could have handled things much better, bearing in mind my Chief's views on visitors.

Well, the remainder of the story has been often told. Churchill flew over as planned and witnessed the start of this great battle from a close up vantage point on the evening of 23rd March. The opening was most spectacular with the massive airborne operation that supported the attack. The sky was almost black with aircraft — those that carried paratroops and those that towed the gliders.

Then on 26th March, in company with Alanbrooke and Montgomery, he crossed the Rhine and ate a picnic lunch on the east bank. He had achieved his object without mishap and had as always inspired all those with whom he came in contact.

CHAPTER ELEVEN: GAMBLING IS GOOD FOR YOU

In his *Memoirs* Montgomery stresses the fact that I like gambling. Well, that's quite true. I do. I have managed to keep the urge under control but whether they be horses or cards, I derive excitement and stimulation from a gamble, and I find it is an excellent way of making one forget one's worries and troubles, although unfortunately it is apt to produce others! My Chief never objected to our games of cards at Headquarters and in fact often used to watch with considerable interest and amused detachment. But that's not quite accurate, for there was one occasion when he did intervene in a spectacular way and I shall relate the incident later on.

Among my immediate colleagues in the Eighth Army and the 21st Army Group Headquarters, I found several kindred spirits. There was Miles Graham, who headed the Administrative Branch, Bill Bovill, my personal assistant, and Montgomery's two A.D.C.s, Johnny Henderson and John Poston. We were all old 'Le Touquetites' and *Chemin de fer* was our game.

We were prepared to play on almost any occasion: in the caravans, while driving about in our cars and in the Mess tent. Early on in the war someone had given me a miniature 'shoe' which used small patience cards, and I rarely travelled without it.

For chips we used matches and when they ran out, signed chits with our initials on them — I O U's, in fact. Settlement was infrequent and we used to keep collections of these and every now and then a swopping session took place, in order to reduce the amount in circulation. It sometimes happened that certain 'currencies' were at a discount, especially those belonging to temporary visitors who had left and, of course, during war, one's span of life was pretty dicey.

In 1954 I gave one of my annual dinners to Montgomery, to which I invited members of the old team which had served under him from Alamein to the end of the war, and after it was over we decided to reconstitute our old gambling school and retired to Geoffrey Keating's flat in Mayfair. It was quite like old times and we had a lot of fun. When the time came for us to break it up and go to bed, the settling took place and Geoffrey suddenly produced from his wallet several dirty scraps of paper, about the size of postage stamps. He laid them on the table with a smile. We recognized them at once as relics of the war. I spotted one of my unmistakable 'F. de G's' for £10, there was one with the initials 'M.G.' (Miles Graham) and another with 'P.B.' The latter represented the currency of Prince Bernard of the Netherlands, who served with the 21st Army Group, was most popular with us all, and was always ready for a game when he paid us a visit. Keating told us he was keeping this as a special souvenir, and I have no idea whether it has yet been redeemed. Somewhat grudgingly I had to honour my scrip and as my financial status had improved since the war, I felt bound to exchange it at par, in spite of the fact that so many years had passed since it was issued.

During active operations, I had to sit up in my caravan to keep in touch with the situation; several of us would get together and out would come the shoe. It helped to pass the time and also helped us to relax when conditions were none too pleasant. My faithful batman, Lawrence, would keep us going with brews of tea, sometimes laced with rum.

We had a marathon game when several of us flew with our Chief from an improvised airstrip at the mouth of the Sangro River on the last day of 1943. He used his personal Dakota and we landed at Algiers for refuelling before flying on to Marrakesh where Montgomery had a date with Churchill, who was convalescing there after an attack of pneumonia. The remainder of us transhipped to a Skymaster — a very new type of aircraft in those days — to fly to England. We played right through until we landed in Morocco, while the newly-appointed Army Group Commander relaxed in his seat, no doubt thinking out some of the great problems which he was now to face.

Another game that I remember very well was a twosome with Miles Graham. It was during the campaign in Sicily and our Tactical Headquarters were situated in some wooded country on the edge of the Catanian Plain. Bitter fighting was taking place and it was unbearably hot. Enemy aircraft were also very active at night and I found it difficult to get sufficient sleep. So I decided to play truant for a night and sleep in the cool of the hills that rose behind us. I asked Miles to join me in this expedition.

We set out in my car with a Jeep trailing along behind carrying our camp-beds, food and drink and a camp table and chairs. Our two batmen came along as well. I cherished nostalgic memories of my days in Central Africa with the King's African Rifles, where we spent many months of the year trekking about and living under the stars. It was then so wonderfully peaceful and at this moment I had an irresistible urge to recapture something from the past.

After climbing to a considerable height we selected a lovely spot to camp off the road in grassy country, with a few pleasant trees to give us protection from the wind. Alongside trickled a tiny mountain stream from which cool and crystal-clear water could be drawn.

The table and chairs were erected, electric lamps turned on and our beds were made up. When the sun went down, it became quite chilly and we collected wood and lit a fire. Then out came a bottle of whisky and some tumblers and we had our first drink of the evening. This was near to heaven: away from the noise, mountain air crisp and cool enough to permit sleep. Reeves, Miles's pre-war valet and now his batman, prepared the dinner which was quite excellent, and while we waited I produced the shoe and we played *Chemin de fer*.

It was a wonderfully relaxing occasion and by about ten o'clock our eyelids became heavy and we decided to turn in. I felt really at ease and slept better than I had done for several weeks. Early next morning we packed up the camp and descended to Tactical Headquarters, miraculously refreshed and ready for the work ahead.

From time to time distinguished visitors to our Headquarters soon found themselves taking part in our game. There were novices and experienced players. Some lost and some took our money.

I now come to the one time when our Chief took exception to our gambling. It was at his Tactical Headquarters which was at that time situated in a small villa west of the Rhine. He had retired to bed early, as usual, and out came the cards. The players besides myself were, I think, Johnny Henderson, John Poston and Bill Bovill. We may have been making a bit of a noise, but whatever disturbed him, Montgomery came down the stairs from his bedroom unexpectedly, finding us around the table in the throes of trying to break a formidable bank run by Bill.

For some reason, which only my illustrious Chief knew, his usual amused detachment had vanished. He went purple in the face and I have always described the ensuing scene as reminiscent of the Bible story of Christ flinging the money-lenders out of the Temple. Cards, matches and chits were swept off the table and scattered all over the room. I was given a stern order not to gamble in the Mess with his A.D.C.s. An uneasy silence prevailed as our Commander swung round and retired to his bed.

History does not relate what happened to the money-lenders after they had left the Temple. As far as we were concerned, however, the game was continued within a few minutes in one of the Mess waiter's 'go-downs'. I had, perhaps, taken my admonition too literally, for we were not playing in the *Mess*, and in any case it was really impossible to stop our gambling series so abruptly. We just had to give those of us who were down an opportunity to get their money back!

It is well known that Montgomery kept a betting book — you made any loose statements or claim in his Headquarters Mess at your peril. As likely as not you would be challenged and a wager struck, which would be duly recorded in the betting book. It became rather fashionable, therefore, to think up various excuses for laying a bet.

This particular one was made when Johnny Henderson was dining with some young friends of his in the 60th Mess. It had been a convivial evening and several bets had already been made. It was the winter of 1944-45 and the weather was bitterly cold. During the conversation one of Johnny's friends happened to mention that the low temperature was causing his Company Commander considerable problems concerning his 'water-works'. 'How many times a day,' asked Monty's A.D.C., and some spectacular figure was mentioned. 'That's nothing,' was Johnny's comment. 'You should just see how it affects my old man.'

As Montgomery was visiting the formation the next day a bet was made as to the number of times between 9 a.m. to 5 p.m., the runners in the race being the Army Group Commander and the Company Commander! The rules were quite simple — anything could be done by either party to encourage his particular 'horse', except telling him about the wager. It would be perfectly legitimate to persuade him to consume liquid refreshment and to draw his attention during the tour to any sanitary facilities that were available.

I doubt whether Montgomery had ever received from his A.D.C. such personal attention, such solicitude for his comfort.

From the moment the flag fell at 0900 hours, the game was on.

'Wouldn't you like a cup of coffee to warm you up, sir?'
'What about a cup of tea?'

were questions often heard throughout the morning. At lunch he was pressed to consume his favourite soft drinks.

Things got quite exciting towards the end because it was obviously going to be touch-and-go. Finally, however, Johnny's horse came home by a short head and he won his bet, but I'm afraid the winning number must remain a strict military secret.

At dinner that night at Tactical Headquarters, there was much joking; Monty began to smell a rat and, in the end, forced the truth out of Johnny.

His Army Group Commander, however, took it all as a great joke!

This reminds me of a good story Montgomery tells of Churchill. It was during the time that the Prime Minister paid us a visit during the operations on the west of the Rhine, and he was being taken round General Simpson's sector, the American Army Commander. His countrymen called him Sir William Simpson, K.B.E., as they considered him more British than the British.

During the tour, which was carried out on an icy day, Montgomery asked Churchill whether he would like 'a sanitary halt' — as he called it.

'How much farther is it to the Siegfried Line?' asked the P.M.

'About twenty miles,' replied the Army Group Commander.

'I'll wait,' came the gruff reply!

Perhaps it would be appropriate to end these stories of life at Montgomery's Headquarters with the letter he wrote to me when our long wartime association at last came to an end owing to my ill-health — those gall-stones again! Instead of taking up the post of Deputy to my Chief in Berlin, I was sent on a long period of sick leave.

This letter, I think, expresses that side of Monty's character that is not so widely recognized. It moved me greatly and I shall treasure it all my life.

Tac. Headquarters;
21 Army Group
21-5-45.

My Dear Freddie,

I feel I would like to send you a short note of personal thanks for all you have done for me during the time we served together. No commander can ever have had or ever will have, a better Chief of Staff than you were; you never spared yourself, and in fact you wore yourself out completely for the good of the show.

Together we achieved much; and together we saw the thing through to the end.

You must now have a good rest. And then, later on, together we will conquer fresh fields.

Thank you very much.

Yrs. ever,

B. L. Montgomery.

However, we never were to work together in peacetime, although Montgomery did, in fact, ask me to become V.C.I.G.S. when he was appointed C.I.G.S., but later changed his mind. But this is another story.

I was on sick leave in Scotland and was staying in a small hotel not far from Inverness. Only about half of my leave had passed, and I hoped to find an early run of grilse. Failing this, however, there were always trout and the numerous golf-courses to occupy my time.

On one particularly pleasant August evening my wife and I had played a round of golf, and after our bath had devoured a satisfying dinner of grilled salmon and good Scotch beef. Sitting over our coffee, we were discussing our plans for the following day, when a waiter came along to tell me that Field-Marshal Montgomery wanted me on the phone.

'The call is from Germany,' he added.

My old Chief never rang up without a very definite object, and, as I walked to the phone-box, I racked my brains to think what it might be about.

Lifting the receiver, I noticed that the waiter had positioned himself within earshot; this, however, was understandable for Montgomery's name at that time was almost magic in the ears of the men and women of Great Britain.

Speaking into the mouthpiece, I heard Johnny Henderson's cheerful voice over the wires, and was then connected to Montgomery himself.

'Is that you, Freddie — are you fit again?'

I replied that I was feeling much better and hoped that I should be in good shape by the time my sick leave was over. He made no comment upon this qualified reply, but went on to say:

'I'm coming over to London for a day or two next week, and I shall want to see you. Please come along to Claridges at 6 p.m. next Thursday. I'll give you all the news when we meet.'

And before I could think up a suitable reply, or how this request would fit in with my own plans, the conversation was brought to an abrupt close with: 'Well, I'm very busy — Good night!'

So that was that. London in August was not an attractive prospect, but I suppose my ingrained sense of discipline took command when I accepted the inevitable with reluctant obedience. My wife, who had never quite got used to this power that Montgomery exercised over his staff, subjected me to several minutes' verbal attack for not standing up to him. She didn't know the Field-Marshal as I did — so there was just nothing I could say.

I must admit that I felt slightly apprehensive before dozing off to sleep that night, for I could not help recalling a previous occasion on which Montgomery had interfered with the findings of a medical board — in Cairo in 1942. Was this going to be a repetition? I would know, of course, next week, but this time I felt confident that I would be able to resist any development of this kind; the war was over and therefore I could decide for myself. How wrong I was proved to be: having been separated from him for over three months had made me forget the influence he had over me. During the next few days, however, I found myself becoming more and more curious and ended up by being really eager for this appointment.

We travelled back to London by the night train, and a quarter to six the next evening saw me dressed in my best London clothes leaving our house in Yeoman's Row in a taxi-cab bound for Claridges — feeling just a little excited at the prospect of what might be in store for me.

One always gets a good feeling stepping into Claridges. The soft carpets, the cosy temperature, the exotic smells and, in fact, the whole atmosphere is very good for one's morale — or at least it has always had a very heartening effect upon mine.

Montgomery was still young enough at heart and honest enough with himself not to disguise his pleasure at staying in a suite at Claridges. He first went there in 1943, when he paid a short visit to London after his victorious advance from Alamein. Subsequently, when I asked him where he was staying in London — 'Oh, Claridges, of course — my usual suite — most comfortable — most comfortable' — was his invariable reply.

As I entered Montgomery jumped up, saying: 'Delighted to see you, Freddie — come and sit down.'

Johnny Henderson walked over to the drinks table and started to pour out a whisky and soda, which he knew I would want, but was brought up with a jerk by the brisk words: 'Now, please, leave us alone; he can have a drink when I am finished with him.'

I shall probably need it, I thought, as Johnny shot out into his adjoining bedroom.

As was his custom, Montgomery came straight to the point. He had been summoned to London by the Prime Minister and

Lord Alanbrooke, and had been offered the appointment of C.I.G.S. It had been arranged that he should take over from Alanbrooke on 1st January, 1946. Montgomery told me that he had accepted without hesitation. He had for some time expected such a development, and would in fact, have been very surprised if the offer had not been made. He had a burning desire to change a lot of things in the post-war British Army, and he appreciated that there was no other soldier — with the possible exception of Slim — who possessed the necessary experience to handle the difficult problems that would inevitably confront the armed forces after a long drawn-out war.

'I was then asked,' he continued, 'whom I should like to have as my V.C.I.G.S. I told them, you, provided of course that you were fit enough. How do you feel about it?' he added.

I replied that I was naturally very flattered at this suggestion and, as regards my health, well, I was feeling a lot better, and I thought that when my sick leave was over — I had another three months to go — I should be quite ready to start hard work again. Such a programme, however, did not fit in with Montgomery's ideas at all.

'Oh, we can't wait until then,' he said. 'It's all fixed up. As I have had no experience of the War Office during the whole of my service and as you were only there in the Secretary of State's Office for a few months in all, Alanbrooke has agreed that you take over the job of D.M.I. on a temporary basis until the end of the year, so that you can gain experience and know your way about by the time I arrive.'

'When do you expect me to start?' I inquired.

'Next Monday,' was the Field-Marshal's startling reply.

This was certainly a bombshell. Still the offer of V.C.I.G.S., with the rank of Lieutenant-General, was a tremendous jump for a junior Major-General, whose permanent rank was at that time only that of a Colonel. But the speed of the proposed events was somewhat overwhelming, and I recalled my determination to resist any interference with my full sick leave for a second time by my Chief. This was, however, something different from anything I had ever contemplated.

The upshot of it all was that I left Claridges having agreed to report at the War Office the following week to take up the job of D.M.I. I can't say that I was very thrilled with this immediate prospect, for I had had my fill of Intelligence during my time as D.M.I. in the Middle East under Auchinleck. However, there it was, and four months was not so long a period after all. Before I left I asked Montgomery what I had better do about the unexpired portion of my sick leave. How were the doctors to be squared?

'Leave that all to me,' was his reply, and I knew that the solution to this minor problem rested in very capable hands.

I thoroughly disliked once more putting on my uniform and entering the War Office as a member of that august establishment, and it wasn't long before I grew more and more unhappy. The War Office was rapidly readjusting itself from the days of war, and there was the inevitable strengthening of civilian and treasury control. It was, I found, a very different kettle of fish from working in an Army or Army Group in the field, where red tape was entirely lacking and where decisions were made and carried out rapidly and without question. At the War Office, no decision rests with one person alone. A number of officers and their civilian counterparts had to be consulted and brought into the picture, with endless memoranda and other types of bumph.

Each morning there was a conference in the C.I.G.S.'s office which the V.C.I.G.S., the D.M.O. and the D.M.I. attended.

Any matters of interest that had arisen during the past twenty-four hours were then reported. I found these dreary and uninspiring affairs. General Archie Nye was the V.C.I.G.S., and the D.M.O. had been at the War Office most of the war; I found that their approach to problems was somewhat academic and lethargic. They were, however, firm allies and determined to maintain the *status quo* of War Office procedure. I longed for the day when Montgomery would arrive, for one thing was certain — the effects of a new broom would soon be felt. I became more and more irritated and sometimes failed to control my temper, but I suppose that this sudden change of environment made such a reaction inevitable.

I found the cheerful team-spirit of my old Headquarters lacking, and several of those holding high appointments were bound up with their own particular futures. Army Lists were continually being brought out to see where they stood, and the findings of selection board meetings were studied with feverish anxiety and often with sour faces. There was, I am afraid, too much of that unpleasant vice, jealousy, to be found in the War Office at that time.

Amongst the older generation I was, I believe, looked upon with some suspicion and many no doubt guessed what Montgomery had in mind. I could sense an atmosphere in certain quarters. Among the younger element, however, I like to think that my arrival was welcomed, for I was certainly made to feel that this was the case. I became known as John the Baptist which, considering the circumstances, was not inappropriate!

One of my duties was to sit on the Joint Intelligence Committee. I had charming and delightful colleagues, and a representative of the Foreign Office took the Chair. Yet these meetings very nearly drove me insane. They used to go on for hours, and more than half our time was spent in drafting, in changing this phrase or that, and one word for another. In the field papers of this sort would be produced in a few hours and certain defects in presentation or composition were readily accepted by me or my Chief. I used to dread meetings of the J.I.C., although some of the subjects we discussed were most interesting. One of the many tasks which we undertook during that unhappy period was an appreciation on 'Russian Intentions'. And, if my memory serves me right, our conclusions fell not far short of the mark.

Then little things upset me, such as the tightening up in the distribution of official cars. I was suddenly informed one day that I should in future have to apply for pool transport for each specific occasion. This, to my mind, was a pointless economy, and one which would make one's task unnecessarily irksome. Over the last few years I had had several cars at my disposal and this sudden change of status was therefore particularly distasteful. I really believe we overdid this sort of economy, compared with other armies. The War Office did not seem to appreciate that a car was a necessity in that particular year of grace. I had many establishments to visit outside London; lectures to give, and meetings to attend away from the War Office. There were also innumerable official social events at which I had to appear, for one of my duties was to father all foreign military attachés, and hardly a day passed without some invitation arriving. I therefore decided to take a strong line, and informed the civil department in question that if I did not have a car for my sole use with a driver, I would in future refuse to attend any of these functions. After much argument it succeeded; I was allowed to keep my car, and some formula was worked out which satisfied those responsible for car allocations.

This reminds me of Montgomery's attitude when he eventually came to the War Office. Difficulties arose over living accommodation and servants. A most interesting file was started and the final shot fired by the C.I.G.S. was a minute to the effect that, unless he received satisfaction, he would bring up his caravans and station them in Hyde Park and live in them. Capitulation was the result and he was accorded the treatment merited by a distinguished and successful war leader, who now headed the British Army.

Various factors interfered with my taking up the appointment of V.C.I.G.S. In the first place, Mr. Attlee asked Lord Alanbrooke and General Nye to remain for an additional six months, and then my health deteriorated again and I spent a number of weeks in hospital. The yet undiscovered gall-stone was obviously being most active.

In view of all this Montgomery selected another to be his V.C.I.G.S. and with his assistance I retired from the Army towards the end of 1946 and sailed with my family for Southern Rhodesia to start life afresh. Looking back I am certain that although at the time I was rather disappointed at this turn of events I did the right thing. I entered the sphere of industry, and learnt the hard way, while my mind was flexible enough to readjust itself to an entirely new environment. I have found these post-war years most exciting, spent in a part of the world that offers mankind a very serious challenge.

If I had become V.C.I.G.S. in accordance with Montgomery's original plan I should probably have had to retire from the Army in 1952, by which time there would have been fewer opportunities for retired old generals.

On many occasions during the war I used to think how lucky I was to have so many able and delightful colleagues serving with me in 'Monty's Team'. They were a mixture of professional soldiers, territorials and men who had joined up from civilian life. I felt sure that because of their ability they would prove successful in any walk of life. It is, therefore, not without interest to see what happened to some members of this 'Team'. I realize it is invidious to select only a few of the many who served our Chief so well, but nevertheless the accompanying table gives the story of some of those with whom I was more closely associated.

1. *Name*: Air Chief Marshal Sir Harry Broadhurst, G.C.B., K.B.E., D.S.O., D.F.C., A.F.C., *Principal Appointments*: Commanded Desert and Tactical Air Forces, *Post-War Record*: Commanded NATO Air Forces at SHAPE and now Managing-Director, A.V. Roe & Co., etc., etc.

2. *Name*: Major-General David Belchem, C.B., C.B.E., D.S.O., *Principal Appointments*: G.S.O.1 Operations, Eighth Army; B.G.S. Operations, 21st Army Group, *Post-War Record*: Appointed Major-General and Chief of Staff to Montgomery 1948-1950.

3. *Name*: Lieut.-General Sir Geoffrey Baker, K.C.B., C.M.G., C.B.E., M.C., *Principal Appointments*: G.S.O.1 Eighth Army, 21st Army Group B.G.S., *Post-War Record*: Now V.C.I.G.S., War Office.

4. *Name*: Major Bill Bovill, *Principal Appointments*: My personal assistant in 21st Army Group, *Post-War Record*: Retired to his delightful country estate (lucky fellow!)

5. *Name*: Lieut.-Colonel Frank Byers, O.B.E., *Principal Appointments*: G.S.O.1 Eighth Army and 21st Army Group, *Post-War Record*: Became an M.P. and Chairman of Liberal Party and Industrialist.

6. *Name*: Major E.R. Culver, *Principal Appointments*: My American A.D.C. in 21st Army Group, *Post-War Record*: Head of his large family business in U.S.A.

7. *Name*: General Sir Miles Dempsey, G.B.E., K.C.B., D.S.O., M.C., *Principal Appointments*: Commanded Army

Corps in Eighth Army and 2nd British Army in N.W. Europe, *Post-War Record*: Charman of large Brewery Company, etc., etc.

8. *Name*: Major-General M. E. Dennis, C.B., C.B.E., D.S.O., M.C., *Principal Appointments*: Eighth Army, Major-General, R.A., 21st Army Group, *Post-War Record*: M.G.R.A. India. Retired in Eire, active in local public life.

9. *Name*: General Sir George Erskine, G.C.B., K.B.E., D.S.O., *Principal Appointments*: B.G.S., 13th Corps at Alamein; Commanded 7th Armoured Division (Desert Rats), *Post-War Record*: G.O.C.-in-C., Eastern Command, and now Governor of Jersey.

10. *Name*: Major-General Sir Miles Graham, K.B.E., C.B., M.C., *Principal Appointments*: A.Q.M.G., Eighth Army, Major-General, Administration, 21st Army Group, *Post-War Record*: Chairman of many companies including G.R.A. and director of *The Times*.

11. *Name*: Major-General Sir Randle Feilden, K.C.V.O., C.B., C.B.E., *Principal Appointments*: Deputy to Major-General Sir Miles Graham, 21st Army Group, *Post-War Record*: V.Q.M.G., War Office. Steward of Jockey Club. Head of N.A.A.F.I.

12. *Name*: Field-Marshal the Lord Harding, G.C.B., C.B.E., D.S.O., *Principal Appointments*: B.G.S., Army Corps, Eighth Army; Commanded 7th Armoured Division, *Post-War Record*: C.-in-C., B.O.A.R.; became C.I.G.S.; appointed a Field-Marshal; Governor and C.-in-C., Cyprus, created a peer. Active in industry, etc.

13. *Name*: Lieut.-General Sir Brian Horrocks, K.C.B., K.B.E., D.S.O., M.C., *Principal Appointments*: Commanded an Army Corps at Alamein; wounded and later commanded Corps in N.W. Europe, *Post-War Record*: Black Rod, House of Lords. TV personality and now an industrialist.

14. *Name*: Major Johnny Henderson, O.B.E., *Principal Appointments*: A.D.C. to Montgomery from Alamein to end of war, *Post-War Record*: Partner in large firm of stockbrokers. Lately High Sheriff of Berkshire.

15. *Name*: Major Geoffrey Keating, M.C., *Principal Appointments*: Commanded Eighth Army Film Unit and subsequently took over public relations activities in the field, *Post-War Record*: Since 1946 has worked for the British Petroleum Company both in the Middle East and the United Kingdom.

16. *Name*: Lieut.-General Sir Oliver Leese, K.C.B., C.B.E., D.S.O., *Principal Appointments*: Commanded 30th Corps at Alamein and onwards; took over Eighth Army from Montgomery and later became C.-in-C., Allied Land Forces S.E. Asia, *Post-War Record*: Retired at family estate making great success of growing cactus. Active in many public works.

17. *Name*: Rt.-Hon. Selwyn Lloyd, P.C., C.H., C.B.E., T.D., M.P., *Principal Appointments*: B.G.S., 2nd Army, in N.W. Europe, *Post-War Record*: Became M.P. and later Chancellor of Exchequer.

18. *Name*: Lieut.-Colonel Harry Llewellyn, C.B.E., *Principal Appointments*: Liaison Officer in Eighth Army and G.S.O.1 Liaison 21st Army Group, *Post-War Record*: Trained team which eventually won gold medal for show jumping at Olympic Games. Prominent industrialist.

19. *Name*: Lord Poole, C.B.E., *Principal Appointments*: Administrative Staff, Eighth Army; 'Q' Plans, 21st Army Group; took part in airborne attack across Rhine 1945, *Post-War Record*: Very active in financial, industrial and newspaper worlds. Created a peer. Chairman of the Conservative Party.

20. *Name*: General Lord Robertson, G.C.B., G.B.E., K.C.V.O., D.S.O., M.C., *Principal Appointments*: Head of Administration, Eighth Army, and later under

Eisenhower in Central Mediterranean and Italy, etc., *Post-War Record*: C.-in-C., M.E.L.F., U.K. High Commissioner in Germany and Chairman of British Transport Commission. Created a peer.

21. *Name*: Lieut.-General Sir Charles Richardson, K.C.B., C.B.E., D.S.O., *Principal Appointments*: G.S.O.1 Plans, Eighth Army; B.G.S. Plans, 21st Army Group, *Post-War Record*: G.O.C.-in-C., Singapore. Now G.O.C.-in-C., Northern Command.

22. *Name*: Major-General G. W. Richards, C.B., C.B.E., D.S.O., M.C., *Principal Appointments*: After commanding Tank Units in desert became Brig. A.F.V., Eighth Army, and Major-General, A.F.V., 21st Army Group, *Post-War Record*: Retired in Wales. Active in public life.

23. *Name*: Field-Marshal Sir Gerald Templer, K.G., G.C.B., G.C.M.G., K.B.E., D.S.O., *Principal Appointments*: Commanded Division in Italy; wounded and later Head of Military Government, Germany, *Post-War Record*: High Commissioner in Malaya during rebellion. Later created Field-Marshal and C.I.G.S. Now active in industry, etc.

24. *Name*: Brigadier Bill Williams, C.B., C.B.E., D.S.O., *Principal Appointments*: Head of Intelligence, Eighth Army, and later 21st Army Group, *Post-War Record*: Returned to life he enjoys at Oxford. Now Master of Rhodes House.

All in all, not such a bad record for this team of young men who served Montgomery during the war.

Although the war ended nearly twenty years ago many of us meet from time to time, and in particular we foregather nearly every year at a dinner-party which I give in London to these old friends in honour of our old Commander. It happened like this:

One day in the early fifties I visited, for the first time, Apsley House (No. 1, London) the former home of the Duke of Wellington. I was most impressed by the great Banqueting Hall laid out as it used to be for the Iron Duke's annual dinner to those senior members of his staff and commanders who had fought under him at Waterloo. The table was laid, the chairs in position and along the length of the long table was the great centre-piece presented to Wellington by, I think, the King of Portugal. I could vividly picture the scene. The magnificent food and wine; the colourful uniforms and the high spirits and comradeship born on the field of battle. It impressed me enormously.

A short time afterwards I happened to run into my old Chief and I described my impressions, adding, 'I think it would be an excellent idea if you emulated Wellington's practice and held an Alamein Banquet each year.' The response was not very enthusiastic, no doubt because Montgomery already took part in an Alamein Reunion which thousands attended each year. I then said, 'Well, I would like to give a dinner for you each year to meet your old team again.'

The reply was immediate. 'An excellent idea — excellent.' And so it started and the occasion is one which I enjoy immensely and most of the officers whom I have mentioned above attend. We are delighted to meet each other again and, to a man, we feel honoured to pay tribute to a Commander we loved so well.

PART FOUR: TWO GENERALS

CHAPTER TWELVE: THE 'AUK' — AN APPRECIATION

In this chapter I shall give a brief description of Auchinleck: his strength and his weaknesses as I saw them. He was one of the great Commanders under whom I served and, as I happened to have been in the unique position of working close to Wavell, Montgomery and Eisenhower, my conclusions will perhaps prove of value to those who are interested in comparing the merits of these four men.

'The Auk' inspired tremendous loyalty and affection amongst those who served close to him. This was also true of Eisenhower, Wavell, Alexander and Montgomery, and it is, of course, very necessary if a commander, his staff and senior commanders are to work as a team. Although I was more intimately associated with Montgomery than any other Commander, I was nevertheless not blind to the merits of the others, and I shall never forget that it was Auchinleck who gave me my real chance by appointing me first as Director of Military Intelligence in the Middle East and later as B.G.S. of the Eighth Army. As I have related earlier in this book, I was in the latter position when Montgomery took over command of that Army.

Like many others at G.H.Q., I was immediately impressed by Auchinleck when he arrived in Cairo. He certainly looked the part and had a warm-hearted and attractive personality. It was like a breath of fresh air after the last rather depressing few months under Wavell. He wasted little time in getting to know his staff and we liked his enthusiasm and accessibility. Here, as Monty would say, was a proper chap!

We planners had been struck by his robust attitude towards the Rashid Ali rebellion in Iraq. He was all for 'having a go', while Wavell opposed intervention and even suggested a political solution. In the end, Auchinleck's view prevailed and he successfully directed the operation. His achievements during his term of command were considerable and although he was relieved of his appointment after about a year, the British people and their Allies have much to thank him for. To start with, he was immediately responsible for producing a new spirit in the Middle East: more confidence, a feeling of expectancy, a more robust outlook and altogether a raising of morale. He was, in fact, responsible for a change of heart. Then he acted with great courage and determination during a critical phase of the 'Crusader' battle. General Cunningham lost heart when Rommel's mobile forces looked like threatening his communications. He ordered a withdrawal of the Army Headquarters back behind the wire into Egypt. It was then that Sandy Galloway, B.G.S. Eighth Army, showed great foresight and initiative, for he pretended to pack up the many vehicles, but did so with the firm intention of staying put until the Commander-in-Chief arrived. On Auchinleck's appearance he took him aside and expressed his alarm at the proposed backward move, and Auchinleck lost little time in cancelling the orders and relieving Cunningham of his command. He then proceeded to take over the army himself for a time, winning considerable successes against the Germans, including the relief of the isolated garrison of Tobruk. Having got things well under control, he then handed over the command to Ritchie and returned to Cairo. His action earned him high praise from Churchill and, I think, the thanks of Parliament.

However, his selection of Ritchie to take over the command of Eighth Army from Cunningham was hardly a wise one. Ritchie had not had the necessary experience and it was unfair to expect that he could hold down this key job. Auchinleck was influenced by the fact that Ritchie had been his B.G.S. in England and later his D.C.G.S. in Cairo. He wanted one of 'his own chaps'. This led to complications, for the Commander-in-Chief felt he could not give Ritchie his head and a pretty firm control was exercised from G.H.Q.

I have always felt that a great opportunity was lost in not inflicting a heavy defeat on Rommel during the Gazala Battle in June 1942. The attack started on 27th May, 1942, and by good fortune our Intelligence had obtained extremely reliable information as to this date and of the enemy's intentions. During the previous two months, Auchinleck had been resisting strong pressure from Churchill and the War Cabinet to start an offensive; he was quite right to delay, but it was obvious to me that the strain was beginning to tell. However, once we knew what Rommel proposed to do, a great opportunity was opened up. As D.M.I. I visited Eighth Army and warned all those I could what to expect, even to the very date. But, in spite of this, the defensive battle was fought badly, and in some cases our troops were taken by surprise. Initially, everything appeared to be going well and it really looked as if Rommel had, for once, bitten off more than he could chew, but he was too clever for us or, more accurately, we failed to take advantage of a favourable situation. He was allowed to extricate himself from a very dangerous position, while piecemeal and uncoordinated attacks were made against the 'cauldron' area which did not achieve their object. Of one thing I am certain: if Montgomery had been in command of Eighth Army at the time, Rommel would never have got away with it.

So I suppose Auchinleck must take the blame either for a bad appointment, or for not having intervened himself in time.

Auchinleck is sometimes criticized for his decision to hold Tobruk when the Gazala front was crumbling. Yet he was faced with an appallingly difficult problem. It can be argued that the garrison did not put up much of a fight, but I have always held that they didn't really have a chance and that its capture was inevitable. The Tobruk perimeter was no easy one to hold, owing to its length and the fact that there existed no strong tactical features. Unless adequate armour and air support were available, the garrison was at the mercy of the enemy who could concentrate on a narrow front at the chosen point of attack. It was quite clear that this would be the case once the Eighth Army was driven back over the Egyptian frontier. Extremely few tanks were still runners and the airfields that could be used by the Desert Air Force were too far back to enable anything but occasional fleeting air support to be given over the area. I shall always remember the momentous meeting held in the G.H.Q. war room by Auchinleck at which the decision to hold Tobruk was made. As I have already mentioned, the Commander-in-Chief kept Ritchie under strict control and on that particular night the Army Commander was calling desperately for instructions as to whether Tobruk should be held or not. As D.M.I. I was asked to give an appreciation as to how Rommel would view the holding of the fortress [sic]. I made it quite plain that he would welcome such a development but would consider the task of capturing it a reasonably easy one. It is my recollection that about midnight a signal was brought in from Churchill inquiring anxiously what decision had been taken, stressing the importance of Tobruk and the depressing effect its loss would have on the Allies, and ending with a reminder that Wavell had, in similar circumstances, left a garrison to hold it, a decision which produced rewarding dividends. I can, even today, see Auchinleck retiring to a desk situated on one side of the room, studying the signal with great concentration, and then in his own hand drafting his orders to Ritchie. Having finished, he passed them over to us to read — Tobruk was to be held — but in the event not, I'm afraid, for long.

It is fascinating to speculate on what might have happened if errors of command had not taken place during the Gazala Battle and if Tobruk had not been captured with so much transport, petrol and supplies. It enabled, in fact it tempted, Rommel to have a go at capturing Cairo and the Middle East base; but it also stretched his communications to breaking point and, at the same time, allowed the Eighth Army and Desert Air Force to fall back on their supplies to end up like a coiled spring ready to be released at Alamein. It might, however, have proved much more difficult to defeat Rommel decisively if a partial success had been achieved at Gazala. It is, I believe, a case of a failure contributing to a future victory.

When the Gazala battles began to go badly for us, Churchill did not forget Auchinleck's resolute and successful personal command of Eighth Army in the Crusader Battle in 1941. He pressed Auchinleck to go up and take over command again.

However, in this case, I think Auchinleck delayed the inevitable take-over too long, in spite of the urgings of men like Tedder. Once he had decided, however, that the time had come to relieve Ritchie he again acted with great vigour and, taking with him Dorman-Smith, his D.C.G.S., and leaving Corbett (C.G.S.) to act for him in Cairo, he played a conspicuous part in bringing order out of chaos and finally holding Rommel along the Alamein position, which he had had the foresight to prepare for defence. As I have mentioned earlier, I joined him in the desert at about this time and enjoyed those exciting days when one didn't really know what was going to happen next. Auchinleck's contribution was considerable, but one wonders whether a more experienced Army Commander than Ritchie might not have saved the really desperate situation that finally developed. No doubt 'The Auk' has his answer to this question — I know I have mine.

I hope this comment will not be taken as an attack on Ritchie because it is not meant to be. He was given a most difficult assignment without the necessary experience or background and to his undying credit he took his supersession like a man, to serve with distinction as the Commander of an Army Corps in the Northwest European Campaign. One of the difficulties in command, even before Ritchie took over, was the fact that orders were so often questioned or disregarded. It took Monty to put this right.

After Rommel had been stopped on the Alamein position in the first half of July 1942, I think Auchinleck wasted some of his resources by ordering attacks which had little chance of producing decisive results, but which proved rather costly. In one of these, for instance, a newly arrived armoured division from England, equipped only with slow-moving and obsolete infantry tanks, was thrown into battle with little or no time for preparation or training — in fact, the tanks had not even been made desert-worthy. The result was that the division lost the majority of its tanks.

If one has to make comparisons between 'The Auk' and Monty, I found Montgomery more competent and decisive — a more professional commander who had obviously devoted a lifetime in studying war and the art of high command. I would not wish in any way to belittle Auchinleck's achievements, which for the most part were obtained with resources, both human and material, inferior to those available after Montgomery's arrival. One can never stress too much the debt we all owed to those who had to fight with inadequate arms and equipment in those early days and by their efforts made possible the victory of Alamein. To my mind, it was patently unfair that the coveted symbol '8' worn on the ribbon of the Africa Star was denied to all those who fought before Alamein. I certainly know, however, of one or two distinguished officers who technically have no right to the '8', but who nevertheless wear it, and I don't blame them!

Like all of us, Auchinleck had his weaknesses. His admirable quality of accessibility, for instance, led him to listen to too many people. The principle of the 'Brains Trust' is often not the best method when applied to the art of high command in war. I also suspect that he had a bit of a chip on his shoulder because he came from the Indian Army, and there is no doubt that in a way a number of military leaders in Britain looked down on their colleagues in India and associated them with messing around in the small wars on the Indian frontier. It was this factor, I think, which resulted in his making some poor choices in filling certain appointments, for he not unnaturally wished to have those whom he knew and trusted close to him. The worst example of this trend was the appointment of Lieut.-General Corbett as C.G.S. at a most critical period in 1942. Although a very pleasant fellow, he did not measure up to the job, and I shudder to think of what might have happened if 'The Auk' had had his way and placed him in command of the Eighth Army in August 1942.

There are some who criticize Auchinleck for his selection of 'Chink' Dorman-Smith as one of his chief advisers. He was made D.C.G.S. in Cairo, 'D.C.G.S. in the field' and then, just as Auchinleck had decided to return to Cairo after having taken personal command of Eighth Army when Ritchie was removed, he was nominated for a new appointment — V.C.G.S. at G.H.Q. However, fate intervened; Auchinleck was replaced as C.-in-C. by Alexander, and Dorman-Smith was posted away from the Middle East. It was, however, a curious association. It started most successfully in India when both men were involved in the task of modernizing and mechanizing the Indian Army in the face of considerable prejudice. 'Chink' had, before the war, been Wavell's Brigade Major when he commanded an experimental motorized Brigade, and his ingenious mind had not gone unnoticed. Auchinleck welcomed his old colleague, who soon became a close confidant and adviser. Personally, I liked Dorman-Smith and enjoyed his outlook on life and the high morale he displayed under any conditions. His approach to problems was often interesting and able; sometimes unique, but, on many occasions, impracticable. Nevertheless, provided his superiors were selective in their sifting of advice given, 'Chink' could be of considerable value.

Wavell, I think, used him this way to some extent, and so did Auchinleck, although I think he was sometimes mesmerized by his brilliant mind, and the association, though undoubtedly producing some benefits, ended in near-tragedy for Dorman-Smith. Owing to official unpopularity 'Chink's' contribution during the rest of the war was not great, and a soldier with a most fertile mind was wasted. There is, in my opinion, no doubt that an unnecessary and vicious vendetta was waged against him by the Army hierarchy. From being on the point of being made a Lieut.-General and V.C.G.S. in Cairo he was demoted overnight to a Brigadier and later given a Brigade in Italy. I feel sure that it would have been wiser and more profitable to have placed him in a position better suited to his particular gifts.

After the war he settled in Ireland and took a law degree — no mean achievement at his age. He has changed his surname from Dorman-Smith to O'Gowan (Irish for Smith), but I don't know the Irish equivalent for 'Chink'!

I remarked above that Wavell made good use of Dorman-Smith while he was Commander-in-Chief, and I think it only fair that I should retail what I know. I first met 'Chink' when he took over the appointment of Commandant of the Haifa Staff College from Sandy Galloway. I happened to be one of the original members of the Directing Staff, but by the time Dorman-Smith arrived I was champing at the bit and keen on moving to other fields now that the war had in all earnestness descended upon the Middle East. 'Chink' and I became friends and I enjoyed the discussions we had together, for even his enemies had to admit that he had a stimulating mind. After I became a joint-planner in Cairo I saw quite a lot of him, for Wavell used to send him on special assignments, and I remember one in particular very well. He was asked to carry out a tour of the Western Desert and study the way operations had been conducted. He spent some time on this task and held discussions with most of the Commanders. 'Chink' was not the most tactful of men, especially with those who did not listen to his views, and so some friction resulted. But from the talks he had with me on his return I can say without any doubt that he had arrived at some extremely sound deductions. He was particularly critical of the way the Army was being handled, which, of course, reflected on some of the Commanders concerned. He disliked the piecemeal way in which the forces were being used, such as the employment of 'Jock' columns — small task-forces acting independently — and the lack of real concentration of the artillery. He was a shrewd observer, but although these views were passed on to Wavell, little change resulted. I have a feeling that, especially as far as the 'Jock' columns and private armies were concerned, Wavell was influenced by his experiences in the First World War under Allenby, when Lawrence's independent exploits became a legend. One must, however, face the fact that a critic who has not got to shoulder the responsibility is rarely popular.

During his time with Auchinleck he made his influence felt for the good in certain directions. I happen to know that he was very opposed to divisions not fighting as divisions but, as was the growing practice, of fighting in 'boxes' instead of using their mobility. He also preached greater concentration of our armour. I think it true to say that 'Chink' made a definite contribution in helping Auchinleck to stem the tide at Alamein, although in certain other directions he was apt to cause friction and disharmony. To sum up, whatever weaknesses Dorman-Smith may have had, I consider that it was hardly fair to lay at his feet many of the Eighth Army's shortcomings. He was certainly ambitious, perhaps too much so, but this is not an unusual trait amongst able men.

Dorman-Smith was always a fighter, and after the war he became involved in some controversy when certain books on the war appeared. The first occasion was in connection with Churchill's *Memoirs*. He took strong exception to some of the wartime leader's comments and the author had, in the end, to make certain amendments. I became involved in a small way. I received an invitation to lunch with the Prime Minister at No. 10 Downing Street, and the other guest was Churchill's legal adviser. I was interrogated about the events surrounding the offending passages and my evidence, no doubt, helped them to decide upon what action should be taken. As far as I was concerned it was a most enjoyable occasion, for the lawyer had to leave immediately lunch was over and I stayed on to have an intensely interesting talk with the great Englishman.

When Montgomery's *Memoirs* appeared both Auchinleck and Dorman-Smith challenged some of the Field-Marshal's observations on the situation which he found when taking over command of the Eighth Army. In particular, objection was raised over the question of what plans were in existence at that time. The inference in the *Memoirs* was that no plans for an offensive had been considered and that plans for a withdrawal to the Nile were uppermost in the minds of the High Command. The counter-attack by Auchinleck and Dorman-Smith proved successful, and Montgomery was forced to make an amendment in subsequent editions of his book. The truth is that many plans were prepared to meet certain eventualities, including that for a withdrawal to the Nile. In fact, at about the time Montgomery arrived, Miles Graham, the A.A. & Q.M.G. of the Army, was engaged in reconnoitring the withdrawal route in case this course became necessary. On the other hand, there was also a full study or appreciation of a future offensive prepared by 'Chink' Dorman-Smith, but as far as I know Montgomery never saw it.

In 1960 Corelli Barnett published his *The Desert Generals* which caused quite a controversy in certain quarters. Although I didn't agree with some of his conclusions, it was a fascinating study of some of the generals who served in the desert, and his book brings to life some of the lesser-known characters, giving credit to such men as Auchinleck and Dorman-Smith for what they contributed before Montgomery's arrival.

Then in 1962 Alexander's book was published and his comments on the genesis of the Battle of Alam Halfa caused further controversy and discussion.

Once again the question of plans for a withdrawal to the Nile was raised and of who was responsible for appreciating the importance of the Alam Halfa Ridge, which formed the keystone of the successful defensive battle of that name. As I was in an exceptional position to know the score, having been B.G.S. of the Eighth Army under Auchinleck and later, Chief of Staff under Montgomery, I can put the record straight and settle once and for all the Alam Halfa who dunnit story.

Alexander rightly stresses in his book the great tactical importance of the Alam Halfa Ridge, but he goes on to say that Auchinleck made no mention of its significance in his dispatches. I can categorically state that he was fully aware of its strength. Admittedly, when Montgomery took over command the dispositions of the Eighth Army did not adequately defend this vital feature, but this was primarily due to the paucity of the resources that existed at the time. Although, as I have stated previously, several plans had been prepared to cater for various situations that might arise, Auchinleck's intention was very definitely to defend the Alamein position to the best of his ability and he had no doubt whatever about the importance of the Alam Halfa Ridge.

After meeting Montgomery outside Alexandria and driving with him to our Tactical Headquarters established on the Ruweisat Ridge, I reported on the general situation and the condition of the Army he was about to command. Among other things I told him about the various plans which had been produced and his reactions to these were sharp and to the point. 'Burn the lot', he said, 'from now onwards there is only one plan: the troops will be ordered to stay where they are, fight where they are and, if necessary, die where they are.' He showed no interest whatsoever in any alternative plans, and to the best of my knowledge he never examined any plans or appreciations that existed at the time.

I have always considered that Montgomery's first two or three days with his Army was one of the most rewarding experiences of my life, and the way in which he put over his personality, right through the Army, was really remarkable. Besides talking to the staff and laying down what he called his 'military philosophy', he met all Commanders and their troops and, of course, examined in great detail the ground now held and that over which we would have to fight. I accompanied him during the reconnaissances which resulted in decisions as to the way he proposed to dispose his forces for the defensive battle which we all expected. It would be Rommel's last desperate attempt to reach the Delta, and failure would remove once and for all the threat to our Middle East Base.

During his examination Montgomery immediately appreciated the importance of holding the Alam Halfa Ridge in strength, thus denying it to the enemy, but by the time he had arrived back at our Headquarters it had become obvious to him that there was too little butter to spread upon so much bread. It would be impossible to organize a properly balanced defence, to secure this vital ridge, and to deny his left flank in sufficient depth, without further reinforcements. Turning to me he said 'Where can I get some more troops?' and before I had time to reply added 'What about the 44th Division and the 51st Highland Division — they're just sitting in the Delta, aren't they?'

These newly-arrived Divisions were, in fact, training and equipping, but we had previously learnt some unfortunate lessons when formations had been thrown into battle before the troops received sufficient training or their equipment had been made desert-worthy.

In answer to my words of caution he said 'I'm not going to ask them to take part in any attack. They should be perfectly capable of sitting in a defensive position using their rifles and automatics.'

After a moment's pause he looked at me with that piercing expression that I got to know so well and said: 'Get through to Dick McCreery and tell him I want the 44th and 51st Divisions, or at least parts of them, to be sent up here within the next two days.'

I had already in my brief association with Montgomery realized that one didn't dilly-dally when receiving instructions, so I went to the operations tent, or maybe it was to my caravan, and asked the signaller on duty to try and get me Alexander's Chief of Staff on the 'scrambled' line to G.H.Q. I admit I didn't feel too confident about Dick McCreery's reactions, because when he had previously held the appointment of Major-General A.F.V. under Auchinleck he had been critical of the way divisions had been given too little training and preparation before being employed in battle.

It wasn't long before I got through and at first my fears appeared to be justified, for McCreery pointed out some of the difficulties and dangers of using these troops before they were ready. Nevertheless, he was a practical soldier and grasped the importance of Montgomery's request and the reasons behind it. He told me he would discuss the matter immediately with his Chief, and within a few minutes Alexander and Montgomery were speaking to each other on the telephone. Little time was lost and the result was that orders were to be issued immediately for portions of these Divisions to be moved up forthwith.

I then got hold of David Belcham, who was then G.2 Staff Duties, told him of these developments, and instructed him to lay on the machinery for dealing with the movement and disposal of these welcome reinforcements. And, as usual, this capable officer organized things most efficiently. I retired to bed that night well pleased with the new management!

Little time was lost in disposing of these additional units and Montgomery allotted them defensive tasks which were well within their capabilities. The increase in the Army's strength now allowed the Alam Halfa Ridge to be adequately held, and we faced Rommel's coming onslaught with a growing confidence.

I was very sad when Auchinleck left the Eighth Army, having been relieved of his command by Churchill. He told me the news after he had asked me to take a stroll with him after dinner one evening on the Ruweisat Ridge — he was a disappointed man. I had so enjoyed working with him and was grateful for the opportunities he had given me. As to the future, I had few thoughts other than what was to happen to my old Chief, who had decided to turn down the offer of a new command with its headquarters in Persia. I could never have dreamt what was in store for me — nearly three years of a close association with Montgomery which brought excitement, plenty of hard work and victory in its train.

Before going to bed that night, I wrote a letter to 'The Auk' which came straight from the heart. Apparently, he kept it, for it appeared in a book written about the Field-Marshal published two or three years ago. It provides a fitting end to this chapter.

> My dear Chief,
>
> It was a very great shock to hear your news this evening. The injustice of it all is difficult to believe. As you must realize I am utterly sorry that it should have happened, and I am convinced they will regret the decision — a decision

obviously arrived at to turn aside criticism from its rightful target. I'm afraid it is also a victory for the old privileged school.

As to the 'offer' (of the Persia-Iraq command). It is of course a decision that only you can make. I don't wish to make comparisons, but my old boss Leslie H.-B. (Hore-Belisha) was offered the Board of Trade. But he refused. He felt he was right but I always felt later he was sorry.

I do fully appreciate the other point of view. You may feel you are sitting on a stool between two chairs in which at one time or another you once sat. But who knows how the wheel will spin?

You know that it was only because of the help I knew I should get from you that I did not refuse this job (B.G.S., Eighth Army) point-blank. My lack of experience in this particular line was great.

Every possible good wish for the future, and my gratitude for all your kindness to me.

You will be missed by many from this arid land.

Yours,
Freddie de Guingand.

CHAPTER THIRTEEN: 'IKE' — A TRIBUTE

Eisenhower's was an exceptional story of success. From comparatively humble beginnings he became President of the most powerful nation in the world and in the process he successfully held the post of Supreme Commander of the Allied Armed Forces during the Second World War. It is a story that every American boy will hear about and applaud in future years — a story that will inspire pride and ambition in many a youthful heart.

It is for others to record a full account of Eisenhower's life and achievements. My aim is quite a simple one; it is to give a thumbnail sketch of 'Ike' as I knew him, in the hope that I can convey some of those enviable ingredients of greatness that make up this remarkable man. I shall also trace his relationship with my old Chief, Montgomery, which — much to my sorrow — is now at an all-time low ebb. Perhaps the finest tribute that I can pay is to say that none of us who had the honour to serve under him in the Second World War was in any way surprised when he was elected to the top executive position in his own country, nor that, having laid down the reins of office, he remains one of the most loved and respected men in the United States.

There are few cases in history where a Supreme Commander was so universally esteemed and honoured by all the nations of a grand alliance, as well as by his own countrymen. This was not a case of 'a prophet is not without honour, save in his own country'.

To pin-point those of Eisenhower's many qualities that were responsible for his rapid rise to fame is not an easy task. Some men reach the top through a tremendous intellect, a ruthless disposition, a burning ambition, or an utter disregard for the feelings of others. It was not so with Eisenhower. I think his success was largely due to his great human qualities: his sense of humour, his common-sense and his essential honesty and integrity. He inspired love and unfailing loyalty; he had a magic touch when dealing with conflicting issues or clashes of personalities; and he knew how to find a solution along the lines of compromise, without surrendering a principle. He is, in fact, a great democrat in a modern world where the word is rapidly losing its true meaning, and in spite of his achievements he has remained humble and friendly and has never lost the common touch.

It was the war that produced opportunity for Eisenhower, just as it did for Churchill and Montgomery. To General Marshall must go the credit, for he nominated Eisenhower, who was then only a comparatively obscure junior officer, to be Theatre Commander in Europe in June 1942. Within the next ten years he was to become Supreme Commander of the victorious Allied Forces, Supreme Commander of the NATO Alliance and President of the United States.

The first time I met Eisenhower during the war was when he visited the Eighth Army near Gabes, after the Mareth Line had been captured. He stayed the night at our Tactical Headquarters and made an immediate impression upon us. He was still rather new to his job, while Montgomery was now a proven veteran with a number of victories to his credit. Eisenhower was prepared to listen and learn and it was most interesting to see how he grew in stature, knowledge and confidence as time went by. I gained the impression that some of the British 'top brass' never quite reconciled themselves to the idea that an American soldier, who had not previously commanded a formation in the field, could have the ability and qualities necessary to direct a major campaign. This, I thought, was a somewhat narrow and partisan attitude.

I had many contacts with Eisenhower and I never ceased to admire him. Whether it was in Algiers, when he presided at the final conference to co-ordinate the plans for Sicily; in London, when he overruled Leigh-Mallory's objection to the airborne plan for Normandy; or outside Portsmouth, at the weather conference, when he made his fateful decision which set the great Armada sailing for the shores of France; he measured up to the job.

I have mentioned these three particular occasions only because I happened to be present, but of course there were many others of equal or greater importance at which Eisenhower had to make all-important decisions or deal with complex problems involving personalities, future strategy, or matters fringing upon the political. I happened, for instance, to be visiting SHAEF at the precise moment when General de Gaulle had been summoned by the Supreme Commander in connection with his attitude to the First French Army's role in the elimination of the Colmar Pocket and the capture of Strasbourg. The dedicated leader of the Free French, for reasons of French prestige, was demanding a hold-up in Eisenhower's plans, so that top priority could be given to the fulfilment of these objectives. In the bigger picture, however, Eisenhower did not consider them of much importance and when he saw the uncompromising French General, he told him so. He went even further, and said that if his orders were not obeyed, he would have no other alternative but to cut off the French Army's supplies. This threat produced the desired results. I was in Bedell-Smith's office and saw de Gaulle enter and leave the Supreme Commander's room and there was no doubt, to judge from the expression on his face, who had won!

At the Algiers Conference before Sicily, I represented Montgomery and explained the Eighth Army's plans in detail, and the Commanders of the other forces taking part, Army, Naval, and Air Force, did the same for their commands. Eisenhower's confidence and knowledge had increased greatly since the days we first met at Gabes and he handled the various problems that arose with great wisdom and ability.

The story of Leigh-Mallory's appeal against the accepted airborne plan for 'Overlord' has been told before. He had decided that the operation, as planned, had become too hazardous because of recent movements of enemy formations and he predicted prohibitive casualties. It was no easy matter for Eisenhower to disregard the advice of his Air Force Commander, but he decided to do so and accept the consequences; he made it clear that he would take the blame if his judgement was proved wrong and Leigh-Mallory's turned out right. Having heard the arguments from both sides — I had to present Montgomery's case — Eisenhower did not hesitate in making his decision. The Supreme Commander certainly deserved the charming and generous letter that Leigh-Mallory wrote to him after the initial landings had taken place in which he expressed regret that he should, as it turned out, have added unnecessarily to his Chief's burden before D-Day.

As for the weather conference at which the final decision to launch the invasion forces was taken, few Commanders in history could have had to face such a terrible problem. An error here might have meant disaster and defeat or at least a compromised peace. Again Ike showed true greatness and I shall never forget hearing his final words: 'This is a decision which I alone must take. After all, that is what I am here for. We will sail tomorrow.'

I got to know him well during the months of preparations before D-Day, and in the Normandy Bridgehead. Later I saw him often on behalf of my Chief and he was invariably helpful and friendly. I remember once, when I had gone over to explain Montgomery's ideas as to the future conduct of the war, he interrupted our talk by saying that he had to present some medals on behalf of the President. It was quite a small impromptu affair and one of those to be honoured was an American Admiral. He asked whether I would like to attend, an invitation I readily accepted. He made an 'off-the-cuff' little speech which was quite perfect in every respect, and I have always remembered what he said.

He started by saying that the President of the United States had given him the authority to present this decoration to the Admiral. It embodied the gratitude of the American people to one who had served their cause so courageously and so well. He felt particularly humble on this occasion for fate had placed him in supreme command of this the greatest amphibious operation of all time, and it was his orders that had gone out to the Admiral and his ships to face hazards which he himself could not share. His role was to sit and wait — and hope. He went on to describe briefly the task which the recipient of the medal had so ably carried out and to say what a joy it was to him to know that his confidence had been justified. He knew, he said, that the Admiral appreciated that this honour was shared by all those who served under him and it was with real pleasure that he made the presentation. He finished up by drawing attention to my presence, emphasizing that this was a crusade for freedom in which all the Allies were taking part.

And then, with that engaging smile of his, he hung the decoration round the Admiral's neck.

Eisenhower had a really first-class Chief of Staff, Walter Bedell-Smith, and together they formed a wonderful team. They were inseparable and understood each other perfectly. Bedell and I became firm friends, which was as well since there was many a knotty problem that we had to sort out, especially when our respective masters were not hitting it off too well.

Eisenhower was somewhat critical of the way Montgomery lived alone with his A.D.C.s away from his staff. (This was a progressive development and I don't think it really caused any great harm.) He made a point of seeing his principal Staff Officers regularly and I myself was in constant touch, spending part of my time at his Tactical Headquarters. It must be remembered that the role of an Army or Army Group Commander is very different from that of a Supreme Commander. The former has to spend much of his time with his troops, besides having sufficient opportunity for reflection. It, of course, made my job more onerous and exhausting, but I appreciated Montgomery's reasons for organizing his life as he did. And, what is more, it worked. It was, however, I think, a pity that my Chief did not attend certain conferences which were called from time to time by the Supreme Commander. Admittedly, these involved long journeys and a consumption of valuable time. On the other hand, they were most necessary and a lot was to be gained by meeting the other Commanders from the three Services. It fell to my lot to answer for my Chief on these occasions. This formed a most interesting part of my duties, and after so long an association I usually knew how my Chief's mind worked, but sometimes I was unable to give a clear-cut decision on Montgomery's behalf and this, in turn, meant a delay in the normal processes.

It was quite clear to me that Montgomery disliked doing business around the conference table; he preferred to deal with one person at a time. Being faced with having to make a decision after a brief general argument was not to his liking; for his usual practice was to have all the relevant facts produced for his examination and then, only after a period for reflection, would he finally make up his mind. He would, of course, summon me and others from time to time in order to clarify a point, but it was in a quiet and solitary environment that he finally reached his decision on important issues that could mean success or failure and in which men's lives were at stake.

Unlike Montgomery, Eisenhower was at his best when discussing big issues in general conference. While the Supreme Commander welcomed his Chief of Staff and others being present when he saw important people, Montgomery, as a general rule, insisted upon seeing them alone. This resulted, of course, in more effort for both my Chief and me, for the gist of any discussions had subsequently to be relayed to me. Eisenhower's accessibility, I think, sometimes meant that he listened to too many people, which was a disadvantage at times.

I remember an occasion when Eisenhower commented quite strongly on Montgomery's practice. The Supreme Commander and Bedell-Smith were touring the front in a special train and the former had a date with Montgomery at Hassalt where he had his Tactical Headquarters at the time. I joined the train at Brussels and spent a few pleasant hours on board. There was an excellent lunch provided and we played some bridge — Eisenhower was a top-class player — and we also did some business.

On arrival at a siding we were met by Montgomery. Eisenhower indicated that he would like to get down to business right away, so he led us towards the conference coach. When we got there, Montgomery turned to me and said 'I shan't want you, Freddie,' and I, knowing the form, obediently started to withdraw. Eisenhower looked a little surprised and suggested that it would be a good thing for him to have his Chief of Staff in attendance. But Montgomery was adamant. 'I like talking alone,' was his reply. The Supreme Commander then made it quite clear that he had every intention that Bedell-Smith should be present, and so he was. Of course, I later received a full account of what transpired.

Here is another example of how differently these two great men acted. When the news came through that German plenipotentiaries were requesting discussions with the 21st Army Group with a view to surrender, I was back at our Main Headquarters at some small town in Germany. As this was to be such an historic moment — the consummation of several years of toil — I thought I must get up to Lüneburg Heath to be present at the occasion. So I phoned up my Chief, and told him *en passant* that I proposed flying up. The suggestion, however, was not very warmly received and I was in fact told that my presence was entirely unnecessary and that surely I had plenty of work to keep me occupied! Well, of course, this was all perfectly true, and so I agreed rather lamely and in deference to my Chief's wishes decided against going. I have, however, regretted it ever since. I should have flown up to witness this momentous event. I thought better of it the next day and flew up in time to meet Jodl and take him to Rheims in my aircraft where unconditional surrender to the Allies took place.

The surrender conference at SHAEF was a big affair with full Hollywood effects. Eisenhower merely saw Jodl for a moment to ascertain whether he possessed the necessary credentials, but it was Bedell-Smith who took the Chair at the meeting and accepted the German capitulation on behalf of the Allies. Eisenhower was not even present. Similarly in Italy, Alexander deputed General Morgan, his Chief of Staff, to accept the enemy's surrender on his behalf. This may all sound like a personal bellyache, but in point of fact it is not, for if I had been in Montgomery's place I am sure I should have taken the German surrender myself.

Let me now describe briefly the development of Montgomery's relationship with Eisenhower from that day when they first met near Gabes until the present time. The first phase was the period when Eisenhower was Supreme Commander of all the Allied forces operating in North Africa, Sicily and Italy during part of 1942 and the whole of 1943. Alexander, however, was Eisenhower's Deputy in charge of the land forces and therefore contact between the two men was not as frequent as later on. Nevertheless, mutual esteem was well established, the Supreme Commander admiring Montgomery's experience and ability as a successful fighting General and Monty looking upon 'Ike' as a 'very decent chap,' but who had still a lot to learn.

I think that today Montgomery would admit that he was sometimes a little unkind in his criticism of the conduct of operations under Eisenhower after the landings in North Africa in November 1942. The slowness of the 1st British Army's advance was commented upon and its Commander referred to as a 'good plain cook'! The Commander of the Eighth Army, not unnaturally, considered that he could himself finish off Rommel, provided that additional resources, both land and air, were given him. He perhaps did not appreciate fully the difficulties of terrain and climate with which Eisenhower had to contend when fighting in Algeria. This attitude, no doubt, caused harm in their relationship, but not to any great extent. It probably had more effect upon Bradley and Patton than upon the Supreme Commander himself.

By and large, however, Montgomery's advice was sought and generally accepted, and this was more particularly so when we objected to the original plan for the invasion of Sicily. Major changes were agreed to at the request of my Chief and mutual regard was strengthened accordingly. There were some occasions during the first few months in Italy when a degree of friction occurred, due mainly to criticism by Montgomery concerning the supply position, and also allocation of resources between Mark Clark's army and his own. But, nevertheless, the relationship during this period between the two men was pretty good.

When the news came through that Montgomery was to be appointed Commander of the 21st Army Group for 'Operation Overlord' under Eisenhower, a period of excellent relations commenced. It was a post Eisenhower had asked should be filled by Alexander, but the Chiefs of Staff decided to leave him in command of the Allied Forces in Italy. Therefore Montgomery was his second choice.

My Chief set about his new task with 'fire in his belly' and the Grand Alliance has much to thank him for. Without his enthusiasm, drive, experience and confidence, I doubt whether the landings would have been so successful. He was particularly pleased that Eisenhower decided to entrust him with the command of *all* the land forces — both American and British — during the initial phase. But it was this very fact which, in a way, created a strain upon the future relationship of these two men; for Montgomery increasingly became convinced that the best command solution was for Eisenhower to have an overall Land Force Commander and it was, therefore, only logical that the initial arrangement should be continued. I have enlarged in an earlier chapter upon my Chief's attitude on this problem.

Soon after Montgomery had had an opportunity of examining the existing plan for 'Overlord', he decided that certain major modifications were necessary requiring considerable additional resources, particularly with regard to aircraft and landing-craft. Eisenhower supported these requests with the utmost vigour and battled with the Combined Chiefs of Staff in Washington to ensure that his subordinate got what he desired. Relations at this time could not have been better and it was a real pleasure to see how they worked together.

And then the bridgehead was established in Normandy and a bitter period of fighting followed. To some it appeared that we had got bogged down and it was then that some murmurings regarding Montgomery's exercise of command were to be heard, particularly in certain American circles, egged on, I regret to say, by one or two British officers serving on Eisenhower's staff. There was a deplorable lack of appreciation of the problem on hand, and of Montgomery's strategy. It was not realized how important it was for the British forces to take no risk whatsoever on their left flank where they were opposed by the bulk of the enemy armour; a reverse here could have jeopardized the whole Allied position in the Cotentin Peninsula.

It is extremely interesting to see what the official historian has to say about Tedder's attitude during this period. In the first place it looks as if Eisenhower's Deputy had grave misgivings about the conduct of the operation, for at his daily meeting of the Allied air commanders on 14th June he said that the military situation 'had the makings of a dangerous crisis'. From this point onwards the official historian asserts that Tedder's fears 'developed into a positive distrust of General Montgomery's leadership and outspoken criticism of his conduct of operations'. He goes on to suggest that the criticism 'finally infected the Supreme Commander'[22] himself.

On 23rd July, two days before we broke out of the bridgehead, Tedder expressed his dissatisfaction to the Supreme Commander in writing. In this letter, a copy of which was sent to the Chief of Air Staff (Portal), he gives his reasons for his disquiet and the following are extracts from the letter which the historian says is too long to quote in full. (I would certainly like to have a glance at it!)

He was 'shocked by the satisfaction with the situation' expressed in Montgomery's directives. 'I've no grounds for satisfaction with the operations in the Eastern sector.' He also expressed 'faith in General Bradley and his commanders'. He then urged Eisenhower to set up his Tactical Headquarters in France and take over direct control and put an end to the arrangement by which Montgomery had operational control of both British and American forces in Normandy. And most significantly he assured the Supreme Commander that he would support 'any action you may consider the situation demands'. This surely can only be interpreted as support for the replacement of Montgomery. But the official historian then points out that Eisenhower 'did not think the situation demanded any such action and in the next few days General Montgomery's policy was justified (i.e. staying put on the eastern flank) and Sir Arthur Tedder's views disproved'.

Finally, in the Supreme Commander's Report to the Combined Chiefs of Staff, Eisenhower said this of the operations which preceded the break-out in Normandy: 'Field-

---

[22] All quotes from *The Battle of Normandy*: pages 265, 353-5.

Marshal Montgomery's tactical handling of the situation was masterly.'[23]

So, in spite of the difficult period, the disappointments and the pressures, Eisenhower and Montgomery still remained on excellent terms.

I can bear this out. I saw a lot of Eisenhower during this period because the major portion of our Headquarters was still positioned around Portsmouth close to the Supreme Commander's Command Post. Never once did he convey to me that he was dissatisfied with Montgomery's handling of affairs and his whole approach was what could he do to help. This does not mean that he was not a little disappointed at the slowness of our progress, but, on the other hand, he appreciated the difficulties with which we had to contend. I remember, however, that once or twice Montgomery did give Eisenhower what proved to be over-optimistic forecasts of what certain battles could achieve. When Eisenhower eventually ordered Bradley to set up the 12th Army Group to take over the American forces, the change was made easier for Montgomery because he was given the task of co-ordinating operations which, in effect, meant that he was virtually functioning as the Land Force Commander in this particular zone.

In Part Two, Chapter Six, I have described briefly the controversy that took place between my Chief and the Supreme Commander over the question of future strategy and the allocation of resources between the two Army Groups, and so will not repeat myself here.

After Arnhem, which was more or less a failure, Montgomery felt more strongly than ever that an overall Land Force Commander was necessary. He claimed, of course, that

---

[23] All quotes from *The Battle of Normandy*: pages 265, 353-5.

the reinforcements he eventually received arrived too late. He made no secret of his views and, in fact, did all in his power to obtain support for them. This attitude, not surprisingly, increased the friction which had now begun to develop between the two Commanders, Montgomery being supported by Alanbrooke and the British Chiefs of Staff, and Eisenhower acting with General Marshall's full agreement. Montgomery's isolation in his own Tactical Headquarters, which reduced personal contact with the Supreme Commander to a minimum, did not help. And so things drifted on until von Rundstedt's Ardennes offensive, when a major crisis in their relationship occurred. This crisis and its outcome I have fully described in Chapter Six.

After this, relations improved considerably right up to the day of victory and Montgomery received all he requested for the Battle of the Rhine. There was, however, still another matter upon which the two men failed to see eye to eye, and that was the question of Berlin. Montgomery, I think, rightly appreciated the importance of the capital city as a major and vital objective. Eisenhower, no doubt in agreement with the American Chiefs of Staff, considered the defeat of the enemy's forces as the paramount aim. Whether an Allied occupation of Berlin before the Russians would have changed post-war history is arguable, for it must be remembered that the politicians made certain decisions at Yalta concerning Berlin and the division of Germany, and it is difficult to see how these agreements could in the end have been disregarded. I understand a book dealing with this intriguing question is in the course of preparation and it would be quite impossible to do justice to the subject in this brief survey.

And so the war was won, and the two men took over Command of their countries' respective zones in Germany.

There are some interesting letters that passed between them about this time, showing the high esteem in which they regarded each other.

On 5th June, 1945, the Allied declaration regarding the defeat and unconditional surrender of Germany was signed in Berlin and two days later Montgomery sent a very revealing and even humble letter to Eisenhower. Here it is:

7th June, 1945.

Dear Ike,

Now that we have all signed in Berlin I suppose we shall soon begin to run our own affairs. I would like, before this happens, to say what a privilege and an honour it has been to serve under you. I owe much to your wise guidance and kindly forbearance. I know my own faults very well and I do not suppose I am an easy subordinate; I like to go my own way.

But you have kept me on the rails in difficult and stormy times, and have taught me much.

For all this I am very grateful. And I thank you for all you have done for me.

Your very devoted friend,
Monty.

This letter deservedly received this reply:

8th June, 1945.

Dear Monty,

Your letter is one of the nicest I have ever received. Your own high place among military leaders of your country is firmly fixed, and it has never been easy for me to disagree with what I knew to be your real convictions. But it will always be a great privilege to bear evidence of the fact that whenever decision was made, regardless of your personal opinion, your loyalty and efficiency in execution were to be counted upon with certainty.

Yours always,
Ike.

Not long after this SHAEF was disbanded and Eisenhower no longer retained the appointment of Supreme Commander. He considered it an occasion to write once again to his old subordinate.

Dear Monty,

Combined Command terminates at midnight tonight, 13th July, 1945, and brings to a close one of the greatest and most successful campaigns ever fought.

History alone will judge the Allied Expeditionary Force in its true perspective, but we, who have worked and struggled, can feel nothing but pride in the achievements of the men we have been honoured to command, and sadness at having to be parted now.

Whatever history may relate about the exploits of this Allied force, and the memory of man is short and fickle, it is only we, at this time, who can fully appreciate the merit and due worth of the accomplishments of this great Allied team.

These accomplishments are not limited to the defeat of the Nazi hordes in battle — a continent has been liberated from all that is an antipathy to the ideal of democracy which is our common heritage. Above all, we have proved to the whole world that the British and American peoples can for ever be united in purpose, in deed and death for the cause of liberty.

This great experiment of integrated command whose venture was cavilled at by some and doubted by many, has achieved unqualified success, and this has only been made possible by the sympathetic, unselfish and unwavering support which you and all other commanders have wholeheartedly given me. Your own brilliant performance is already a matter of history.

My gratitude to you is a small token for the magnificent service which you have rendered. Time and opportunity prohibit the chance I should like to shake you and your men by the hand, and thank each of you personally for all you have done. I can do nothing more than assure you of my lasting appreciation, which I would ask you to convey to all those under your command for their exemplary devotion to duty and for the most magnificent loyalty which has ever been shown to a commander.

As ever,
Ike.

Here is high praise and warmly expressed, and I'm sure that Montgomery must have replied in equally charming terms. Unfortunately I cannot trace the letter. Perhaps Eisenhower has it among his papers. One is certainly justified in concluding that any disagreement or friction of the past was now buried and forgotten.

As was expected, Montgomery soon afterwards became Chief of the Imperial General Staff and Eisenhower was made Chief of Staff in Washington. As respective heads of their national armies contact was maintained and their relationship was friendly and of great value. Montgomery, for instance, stayed with his old Chief at his home in Washington. It was not long, however, before they found themselves once again in close association. Eisenhower was appointed Supreme Commander of the NATO Forces and Montgomery became his Deputy. So an old partnership was revived and it worked extremely well. Eisenhower made full use of Montgomery's great qualities and he was permitted to play a large part in training the forces, drawn from the Allied nations, for war. It is no exaggeration to say that both men, during this period, became firm friends as well as comrades in arms. Eisenhower, like many famous soldiers, e.g. Alexander and Auchinleck, took up painting as a form of relaxation and, unbeknown to Montgomery, painted his portrait. This little story throws light on the relationship that then existed between the two.

Montgomery had occasion to discuss some important matter with Eisenhower and arrived in his office for the appointment. As he was engaged in explaining some of the salient features of a certain plan, he noticed that the Supreme Commander was staring at him with great concentration. Montgomery began to feel quite uncomfortable and wondered whether his Chief was really taking in what he was saying.

Eventually he said, 'Well, do you agree that we should work on these lines?' — or words to that effect.

Eisenhower's unexpected reply was, 'Yes, Monty, I think I've got them!'

He then went on to explain that he had been painting a portrait of him from memory and that he had not been very happy about the eyes. No wonder, for they are probably the salient feature of Montgomery's face and not easy to reproduce. He was then taken next door and shown the portrait which Eisenhower eventually gave him. It is really a very good likeness and is to be found at Monty's house near Alton.

I have since learnt that when Eisenhower was appointed Supreme Commander to the NATO forces there was quite a chance of my being recalled from retirement. My name was suggested as Chief of Staff; I suppose the idea was to have an internationally integrated staff. But rightly, I think, it was finally decided that an American Commander should have an American Chief of Staff. It might have been vastly interesting at that time, but it would have certainly interfered with my endeavours to get established in the world of industry.

Then Eisenhower became President of the United States and Montgomery continued to serve as Deputy Supreme Commander under Ridgeway, Al Grunther and Lorrie Norstad. On several occasions he stayed with the President; they were seen together in public and by and large they appeared to be on very friendly terms. But then the bomb burst — Montgomery's *Memoirs* were published, followed closely by the second volume of Alanbrooke's *Diaries*. Each criticized Eisenhower for some of his decisions and for his ability as a soldier. In particular, he was attacked for his strategy after the break-out from the Normandy Bridgehead. Montgomery sent his old colleague a copy of his book, but Eisenhower never read it, although no doubt much of its contents was passed on to him and the newspapers, of course, gave it the full treatment.

It was either in 1959 or 1960 that I spent a day at the White House and we had lunch quietly alone together. Eisenhower was his usual delightful self and in spite of his recent illness I found him very alert, with a real grip on affairs. He conducted me around his offices and private quarters. We talked of the war, of course, and I realized how hurt he was feeling about Montgomery's book.

I have to admit that I have every sympathy with Eisenhower for feeling as he did. For a highly successful Supreme Commander to be told he did not know very much about the land battle and, in addition, that by following a certain line of strategy he had prolonged the war, could not have been very palatable — nor was it acceptable. In its simplest form the latter conclusion reached by Montgomery in his *Memoirs* was tantamount to saying that Eisenhower had been responsible for many thousands of unnecessary lives lost and other casualties. Personally, I consider it highly dangerous to speculate in this way. The unexpected so often happens in war. Under Hitler, the armed forces, as well as the civilian front, often showed amazing powers of recuperation.

Not unnaturally I discussed with Montgomery his criticism of Eisenhower in his book, stressing that he would obviously dislike some of the statements made.

'Why should he?' came the reply. 'I said lots of very nice things about him.'

I then explained that having accused a Commander of making all sorts of errors, and major ones at that, you could not merely erase the harm done by enumerating all his good qualities and concluding that he was really 'a wonderful guy'! It was oversimplification at its worst!

But, to be quite fair, the boot was not only on one foot. Eisenhower wrote a book called *Crusade in Europe* which was published in 1948, a long time before Montgomery's *Memoirs* saw the light of day. Some of the Supreme Commander's views about my Chief were hardly to his liking. For instance, the stressing of his tactical ability in the 'prepared' battle left the reader with the impression that he wasn't so skilful with other kinds of battles, nor in the realms of strategy. Then there were comments regarding his caution and the difficulties which were caused because of the way he had of 'living by himself, divorced from his staff'. So, in one way or another, both of these men felt that they had been attacked.

Here, certainly, was a case where, in the disruption of friendship, that the pen proved mightier than the sword! The effect of Montgomery's *Memoirs* upon the relationship between the two men was brought out in clear relief at a dinner-party given by Ambassador Jock Whitney at his residence in Regent's

Park in 1959 during Eisenhower's visit to England. He was given a tremendous reception by all sections of the people. There were unforgettable scenes of welcome and it was good to find that the British Nation had not forgotten his great services during the war and after. I was holidaying at the time at Evian in the Haute Savoie and, much to my surprise, I was rung up from the American Embassy in London and asked to attend the dinner. Apparently, I was on the President's list and I must admit I felt extremely flattered at being remembered. He wanted once again to meet his wartime comrades. It was one of those memorable affairs. Churchill, although none too well, came along and so did many others. There were Alanbrooke, Ismay, 'Bomber' Harris, Portal, Tedder, Alexander, Montgomery and a number of others. I think there were between twenty and thirty in all.

It was really just like old times. And, if ever a man was to experience the esteem of his fellow-men, 'Ike' enjoyed it on that summer evening in September 1959.

As I have already mentioned, Montgomery was one of the guests and unfortunately the relations between the two men were at that moment not at their best, because of the recent publication of the *Memoirs*. I think Montgomery felt a little apprehensive for he rang me up at my London Club and suggested we should go along together. I explained to him that I was catching the night train to Scotland as I was going shooting.

'That's all right,' he replied, 'I'll call for you at 7.30 and you can put your kit in the back of the car, and if necessary Parker will drive you to King's Cross.'

As it happened the boot wouldn't close, as I was travelling with rather a lot of luggage. When we arrived at the Ambassador's house the inevitable photographers were there to catch Monty as he alighted from his car. One of the reporters, having noticed the loaded boot said 'Is the Field-Marshal distributing copies of his *Memoirs* amongst the guests?'

I assured him that this was not the case and I don't think that such a gesture would have proved very popular; for besides Eisenhower, Tedder and Freddy Morgan were also in the party, neither of whom could have been very pleased with some of the things said about them in Montgomery's book!

Montgomery's reception by Eisenhower was anything but warm. In fact, I felt uncomfortable and sad, for I hated to see these two men, whom I admired greatly, feeling as they did towards each other. The atmosphere, however, improved slightly after dinner.

So much for the relationship between the two men.

After the war ended, Eisenhower was given the Freedom of the City of London and I am sure that no one who was present on that occasion will have forgotten the speech he made. It was quite simple, utterly sincere and so generous. He accepted this high honour for those who had served him so well, claiming nothing for himself. I was deeply touched by his kindness in ensuring that I received an invitation to sit on the dais. After the luncheon, he appeared on the balcony of the Mansion House and spoke to the enormous crowd that was gathered beneath.

Thunderous cheers greeted his: 'I've now got just as much right to be down there as you guys!'

In 1947 I visited the United States on business and Eisenhower asked me to stay with him at his home outside Washington; he was then Chief of Staff. One afternoon, he took me up to Mount Vernon and gave me a personally conducted tour. It was wonderful to see the reception he received wherever he went. Crowds gathered as we walked along and old women knelt down and grabbed his hand or kissed his coat, saying, 'God Bless you, sir.' There was no doubt that the nation was grateful for what he had achieved.

About this time, there was a lot of talk of 'Eisenhower for President', and he had been reported as saying that he was 'not interested'. One evening, when sitting with him drinking a whisky and soda, I asked whether he was quite determined to refuse nomination if the chance came his way.

I finally said 'Surely, if you felt that the American people really wanted you as their President, would you refuse them their wish?'

He took some time to answer and then replied 'Well, if you put it that way, perhaps I might change my mind, but I would have to agree with the party platform.'

I had occasion to visit America in September 1954, and I wrote to the President asking whether I could see him. But unbeknown to me he was just setting off to Denver, Colorado, on holiday. I received, however, a very warm and friendly invitation to spend a couple of days with him in that city, so I flew there after carrying out my business in New York. The President and Mamie, his wife, were staying very simply with his mother-in-law, in one of those neat little villas situated in a residential boulevard. No pomp or ceremony — he was living like any ordinary American on holiday. He did, however, have a large suite reserved for him at the Brown Castle Hotel, and it was here that I was to stay as his guest.

We dined together the first night at the hotel and it was an unforgettable evening. I cannot remember what time I got to bed, but I know it was very late. We had a great 'natter' about the war and argued about some of the 'ifs' and 'buts' and 'might-have-beens'. It was all great fun. We then looked at the changing world. The President was fully alive to the pattern that was to come in respect of the colonies and the young emerging states. He predicted very accurately what has recently taken place. He was, for instance, dead right about the future of Cyprus and the increasing influence of the African-American vote in the United States and the potential power of the Afro-Asian Bloc. He saw the dangers as well as the benefits. We discussed Western Defence, Red China and Formosa, Cyprus and many other current problems and I soon realized how ignorant I was about existing American feelings and public opinion in general.

The next day I suggested to the President that something might be done to get the two English-speaking nations closer together by way of more personal contact. I pointed out that, owing to the scarcity of foreign exchange, few British people could visit the United States; while, on the other hand, Americans, both servicemen and civilians, visited England in their thousands each year. I then outlined an idea I had to raise funds to help send a cross-section of our people to America to stay with families so that they could get to understand their 'cousins" point of view. Eisenhower was enthusiastic and agreed to help where he could.

Flying back across the Atlantic I drafted out an article based upon what I had learnt in America, particularly as a result of my talks with the President. I called it 'Understanding America'.

I started by drawing attention to the criticism and friction that arose and said how so much was due to lack of understanding of the other man's point of view. I then made the point about the effect foreign exchange difficulties had on people from Great Britain visiting America. I proceeded to deal with some of the existing criticisms that one heard in the United Kingdom regarding current United States policies, and how dangerous it was for the two most powerful countries in the anti-Communist alliance not to march forward hand-in-hand. I discussed three main issues in particular — Western Defence; the American attitude to Red China and Formosa, and their approach to the Colonial question including Cyprus. Briefly the points I made were:

(a) Western Defence

I criticized those who attacked America's attitude to Western Defence and those who said that she was only interested in her own security and was being drawn towards Germany. I mentioned the tremendous contribution the United States had made towards Western Defence in respect of arms, troops, etc. I also stressed the very genuine sympathy that existed in the hearts of all Americans for the oppressed and those less fortunate than themselves. As for America's changing attitude towards Germany, the sudden failure of previously accepted plans, caused by France's refusal to ratify E.D.C., made this development understandable.

(b) Communist China and Formosa

Those who considered that America was being pig-headed in refusing to agree to Red China joining the United Nations just had no idea of the very deep feelings that existed against this Communist country on account of her support for North Korea's aggression and her disregard of the promises made for the return of prisoners. Red China had done nothing to show a change of heart and Great Britain's precipitate action in recognizing this regime was anything but popular. There were few American families who had not suffered from the results of their country's major contribution in the Korean War, which fact hardened their attitude.

As for Formosa, whatever were the defects of the Chiang Kai-shek's régime, these people were America's friends and she was not prepared to let them down and accept the unfortunate impression such action would create elsewhere.

(c) The Colonial Question and Cyprus

Although I was often critical of America's attitude towards our colonial policy, nevertheless one had to meet Americans to appreciate how deep-rooted was their almost fanatical dislike of the colonial system, dating back from the War of Independence. I found that most people at that time differentiated between the backward peoples of Africa and such Colonies as Cyprus and West Africa. Great pressure was being exerted upon America by Greece and other members of the United Nations regarding Cyprus. Whilst appreciating the problems of economics, defence and prestige that faced Britain, Americans nevertheless, as a whole, felt little sympathy for the British attitude.

I concluded by advocating an increase in the opportunities for our two peoples to get to know each other and suggested that an answer should be found for ending this virtual one-way traffic. Funds would be needed and here the Americans must help. A scheme must be devised whereby a large number of British men and women could visit the United States each year.

They should be chosen from a cross-section of the community — M.P.s, Trade Unionists, Teachers, Scholars, Factory Workers, and the Press. I hoped that powerful Foundations such as the Ford might help.

This article was published in *The Sunday Times*, and it was supported by this leader:

A BOLD PLAN

In his striking article today, General de Guingand — an old friend and colleague of President Eisenhower in SHAEF — draws attention to certain points on which American opinion differs, sometimes sharply, from predominant opinion in this country. We may well feel that there are powerful arguments on our side, to counter the popular American case; but we are not asked to agree, we are asked to know and try to understand. The point is vital. Any break between the United States and ourselves, which prolonged misunderstanding could cause, would be a disaster.

The dollar shortage, with its virtual ban on private British travel across the Atlantic, has been an enemy to understanding — both ways, for each traveller is not only a learner, he is also an ambassador for his country's point of view. General de Guingand, to help remedy this, advances a bold plan; to send to North America each year a thousand British people from all walks of life. It is to be hoped that one of the great American foundations would meet the dollar cost, and surely the sterling cost would not be beyond our resources. Business firms and associations, trade unions and the like, might meet the expenses of their own nominees. The plan is imaginative, yet it is simple, and it accords with a vital need.

I received a great number of letters supporting my views and I obtained promises of financial help from some important and influential people and industrial groups. But, as I had to return to South Africa, I couldn't give sufficient time to the project. In the end, the English Speaking Union became interested and, if my memory serves me right, they benefited from contributions donated by certain American foundations, through the President's influence, to help them to increase the visiting schemes that they already sponsored.

Before I left, the President insisted on my being taken for a drive up into the mountains to the west of Denver City. I was driven through beautiful country and we visited the skeleton towns which once were booming when gold was plentiful. Now the deposits had petered out and there was nothing to take their place. I think the President sent me on this journey with his tongue in his cheek, for he well knew that I was living in Johannesburg, which is the centre of the gold-mining industry, and which forms the basis of South Africa's economy. It was perhaps a friendly warning, but fortunately the Republic is rich in other things and both primary and secondary industries are well established. So one hopes that the Colorado lesson will not be applicable to South Africa when the gold deposits become exhausted.

Although not an American, nothing used to make me more furious than to read and hear criticism of Eisenhower, when he was President, because he played golf or fished. It should never be forgotten that he held office during a period of appalling crises, during which he suffered two very serious set-backs in health.

In such a demanding job there are few men who would have been able to carry on as Eisenhower did after his illnesses. He showed remarkable courage and resolution. By the constitution he could not just retire and live a life of ease; he had to carry on and try and follow his doctor's orders which specifically recommended exercise and a certain amount of relaxation. And yet he was attacked on this account. But I doubt whether these attacks reflected the real feelings of the nation; the attitude of the man in the street during the time of his operation and heart attack showed most clearly the love and respect they felt for their President. The relationship between the people and the man was akin to that of Churchill and the British people.

In spite of the negative results of some of his policies — mostly through no fault of his own — he was looked up to by those who directed the affairs of other Western Nations. I remember talking to a well-known British political leader during the presidential campaign which preceded Eisenhower's second term of office. I asked him whom he hoped would be elected. His answer was clear and definite:

'Ike — give me Ike every time, you can trust him.'

Now, at long last, Eisenhower is enjoying a well-earned rest from public service, although he is not left alone by politicians and others. He is still alert and active, and loves his farm and his golf. I visited him at Gettysburg in 1962 and found the magic of his personality as strong as ever. He is writing up his records and his office is a hive of activity. I controlled my curiosity and never asked whether another book was in the making.[24] I enjoyed our talk, as always, and left with the hope that he will be spared for many years to come.

It is certain that the memory of this lovable man will be permanently enshrined in the hearts of all those who served under him, and also in those of the British and American people.

To me it is a thousand pities that the once happy relationship between Ike and Monty should have deteriorated so greatly, for both are men who have deserved much of their respective countries. Perhaps it has reached the point of no return, but I hope not. As both men have now reached the evening of life, it still remains my deepest and sincerest wish that a reconciliation might still be possible. I would like to think that this might be an extra-mural effort of mine; a reincarnation of similar problems with which I was faced during the war. If I could bring about a healing of these wounds, I would be very happy and content.

---

[24] Now published.

PART FIVE: REWARD AT THE SUMMIT

CHAPTER FOURTEEN: LE TOUQUET IN THE RAIN

The sun was streaming through my office window, lighting up a large-scale map of Normandy that hung on the wall. I had just finished a good breakfast and was staring at the outline of that part of France which would see victory or disaster when we launched the Second Front against Germany. D-Day was only about three weeks ahead and my mind was drifting rather aimlessly, building castles of hope for 'Operation Overlord', when I was brought back to reality by a sharp rap on the door. It opened and David Belchem, my Chief of Operations, poked his head in.

'Are you ready, sir?' he said.

Automatically I said 'Yes', though for the moment I could not for the life of me remember what particular meeting had been arranged at 8.30 on that lovely May morning. There were so many each day that it was quite a business to keep track of them.

My expression must have betrayed me, for David followed up his query by adding:

'It's the Cover Plan bombing conference, General.'

After arriving back from the Eighth Army with Montgomery at the end of 1943, the main Headquarters of the 21st Army Group was located at St. Paul's School in London. At the close of the following April, however, it was with a sense of relief and expectation that its advanced Echelon moved to the vicinity of Portsmouth. A delightful old country mansion — Southwell Park — which up till then had been the home of the Naval School of Navigation, had been taken over so that the three services could live and work together during these important days before the landings were due to take place. At this period, Montgomery, Admiral Ramsay, the Allied Naval C.-in-C., Coningham, who commanded the Tactical Air Forces, and their Chiefs of Staff, were to be found in close proximity. Besides the house there were many acres of beautiful parkland studded with a great number of majestic trees. Under their shade and cover our various caravans and other vehicles began to collect. Many of us who had arrived from the Desert Army felt more at home living in these conditions, although of course these sylvan surroundings could hardly be compared with the drabness and barrenness of North Africa.

Most of the various offices, signal, intelligence, etc., were now on a lorry basis, but a few fortunate ones like mine were allocated rooms in the manor house itself. Downstairs was to be found a charming old library where Eisenhower held his fateful weather conferences on the eve of D-Day. This was in every sense of the word the calm before the storm.

There was, of course, still a great deal to be done, particularly in respect of tying up innumerable matters between the three services. But the main orders and plans had been issued for better or for worse — and the various subordinate headquarters throughout the British Isles were busy implementing these instructions. All the machinery for the greatest amphibious operation in history was now being geared for action.

One of the most important matters that required continual attention was the question of security: preventing the enemy from gaining knowledge of our intentions and deluding him to the maximum extent about the real purpose of our plans. The way in which these great problems were handled might well mean success or failure of the whole operation. And perhaps the greatest contributing element in this sphere of planning was what was termed the 'Cover Plan'.

This deception plan was a very complicated affair requiring a high degree of thought and ingenuity. It was vital that we obtained the maximum amount of surprise both as regards the area chosen for our landings and the date when the expedition sailed from the United Kingdom. In the event it proved remarkably successful and there is no doubt whatever that it contributed very largely to 'Overlord's' success.

I have not read any complete account of our 'Cover Plan', which had a code-name of its own. I should have thought that there was sufficient material available to make a really exciting book. Someone should attempt the task, provided, of course, that the Official Secrets Act would not make such an undertaking impossible. I will, however, try to give the reader some idea of the various ingredients which went to make up the 'Cover Plan'.

With the colossal scale of preparations that were taking place, it was clearly impossible to hide from the enemy our intention to land on the Continent. The concentration of shipping and landing-craft in the various ports alone gave this indication, and we received plots of the enemy's photo-reconnaissance sorties which demonstrated his curiosity and indeed his anxiety as to the future.

The first and main phase of the plan was to persuade the enemy that the assault was to be delivered in the Pas de Calais area astride Cap Gris Nez. After D-Day, however, when the landings had once taken place in Normandy, the idea was to suggest that these were preliminary and diversionary operations aimed at drawing the German reserves from the Pas de Calais and the Low Countries, so as to facilitate the main attack when launched against that area. In conjunction with all this, we schemed to convince the enemy that the assault would not be launched until some time after our chosen D-Day.

It would have been of little use merely to concentrate on the Calais sector, for the area of the actual landings had to be softened as well. For a long period, therefore, the enemy's defences all along the wide stretch of coastline were given attention by our Bomber Forces. This resulted in a considerable, yet necessary, dispersion of effort, and as time drew on the Pas de Calais sector, with its defences, were subjected to at least an equal weight of attack as that which was delivered against the real assault area of the Cotentin Peninsula.

We had other means besides bombing for making the enemy think the Pas de Calais was the selected target for 'Operation Overlord'. For a long period steps were taken to persuade the enemy that a group of armies was concentrating in South-east England. A bogus Headquarters was set up and all wireless traffic from our real command post near Portsmouth was sent by land-line as far as Dover. Large numbers of dummy landing-craft were assembled in south-east coast ports where artificial hard standings had been prepared. Many other indications of preparation were made obvious to those who were interested. In addition Canadian and American troops were moved into the Dover-Folkestone area and embarkation and other exercises were practised.

In order to delude the enemy as long as possible during the time our forces were crossing over, two diversions were carried out by specially equipped naval craft and aeroplanes: one in the Straits of Dover and the other near Cap d'Antifa. In conjunction with these operations radio counter-measures were employed to convince the enemy radar that these were indeed the real thing. Ample evidence eventually came into our hands to show that these diversions were most successful in attaining their object.

At some point during the pre-D-Day period it was suddenly realized that the various diplomats in London still enjoyed diplomatic privilege and could, therefore, send correspondence by diplomatic bag to their Governments without it passing through the censor. There was no doubt that leakages were occurring and it took considerable pressure from Eisenhower and his Commanders-in-Chief to convince the Foreign Office that these privileges must be rescinded — not, however, before certain diplomats were conveniently allowed to see the very activities that we wished them to report upon in South-east England.

The British counter-intelligence was first-rate, and it had rounded up all enemy agents before D-Day — except one. I believe, however, that by this time this one was under our 'control'. He was our trump-card and was fed with true information in order to establish his reliability. But at the right moment, when the armada sailed, he was sold the 'dummy' which was passed on to the enemy High Command.

It fell to the Chiefs-of-Staff to confer together from time to time with the experts who were controlling the 'Cover Plan' operations. As a result one of my jobs was to recommend where bombs should be dropped along the coast. As far as possible, however, these bombing attacks had to be realistic, although they were often made against sectors that we had no intention of assaulting.

We had been working to a D-Day about 1st May, but later found that this was too early and, somewhat to our surprise, Stalin accepted a delay of a month without any apparent 'belly-aching'. And this change was instrumental in causing me a particular personal problem. I will explain.

The beaches around the mouth of the Conche which lay adjacent to the French resorts of Le Touquet and Paris Plage would obviously play an important part in any invasion plan in the Pas de Calais sector, i.e. the 'Cover Plan' sector. The defences and gun emplacements in this vicinity had, therefore, to receive a considerable amount of attention from the Allied bombers.

Over the years, ever since I had joined my regiment I had always cherished a great love for Le Touquet. Everything about it delighted me. Its golf-courses, its Casino with those typically continental smells; its food and its villas and, of course, *le forêt*. I enjoyed the friendship of many French and English Le Touquet *habituées*, and I looked back with pleasure upon the many weekends and holidays which I had spent there. I could never have afforded such frequent visits but for the fact that I had one or two very close friends at whose villas I used to stay. It was, therefore, with the greatest care that I now selected the target areas for bombing so that the villas were, as far as possible, saved destruction from our bombs. As time drew on this policy of selectivity became more and more difficult to carry out. And when D-Day was put back by at least a month it became impossible. Air photographs and Intelligence reports showed that many of these buildings were either being used by the enemy as living quarters or formed part of some defensive locality. It was conferences such as the one on which this story opens, that I attended with a heavy heart. Taking the special lenses, I would examine the aerial photos, check up upon previous damage and finally ring round the target for tonight. It seemed a sacrilege — almost like murdering my best friend — for, as I looked, old scenes and happy memories would intrude upon my thoughts and would spotlight the hatefulness of war. But it was a task that had to be done and I would rapidly withdraw to tackle the many other problems awaiting me, and so forget it all.

At long last 'Operation Overlord' was launched, and the great battles of the Bridgehead began. This was to be followed by the victory of Falaise, the thrust to the Seine, its crossing, the liberation of Paris and the hectic 'gallop' across the Plains of France until Brussels was safely in our hands. In these operations the 2nd British Army was the lucky one, for it fell to its formations to carry out this unprecedented advance with all its thrills and excitements. The Canadian Army, however, was allocated the slower and more exacting task. They had the job of reducing the various pockets of resistance along the coastal sector such as Le Havre, Dieppe and Boulogne; all of which lay in their path. It was a slow business and involved a great deal of solid fighting, but to have speeded up these operations would have meant a mounting and unnecessary scale of casualties.

At the time when the main battle was being fought along the great canals of Holland, the Canadian Army was engaged in liquidating a stubborn defensive zone around Le Touquet and Boulogne. And there was still the complicated and troublesome area of the Estuary of the Scheldt lying before them, with its intricate problems of inundations and other water obstacles.

It was about this time that I received several letters from old Le Touquet friends, all asking the same question. Would I let them know whether their villa had survived or been destroyed? I was grateful that I had never possessed the means to own a villa of my own, but in spite of this I shared their apprehensions and understood their love for these happy homes of yesterday. As I read these letters my thoughts would turn to some quiet room with the sun cascading through its windows on to a table, or some veranda, with the shadows of the pine-trees making changing patterns on the white table-cloth, and a number of happy smiling people enjoying a typical Le Touquet luncheon served after a strenuous morning's golf. I resolved, therefore, to take the necessary steps to find out the truth. This necessitated a personal reconnaissance. It was therefore only natural that each morning, when the operation reports came in, I eagerly sought for information about this particular sector, in spite of the fact that more exciting events were usually taking place elsewhere.

Finally the news which I awaited came through. The enemy in the Le Touquet-Boulogne sector had capitulated and the war was rapidly moving northwards. I therefore put my plan into effect. Harry Llewellyn, our Chief Liaison Officer, started off with two Jeeps. He took with him a wireless set and some sappers with mine detectors. His instructions were to locate a suitable air strip as near as possible to Le Touquet; check for any mines and, if necessary, remove them and signal back to Headquarters its map reference. Within twenty-four hours the message arrived indicating a point some fifteen miles or so from our objective.

I decided to make this a gala occasion and so invited Miles Graham — an old Le Touquet fan — David Belchem, Bill Bovill and Bill Culver to come along with me. I left the catering arrangements to David, who had a flair for that sort of thing, and the next morning, after my usual Staff Conference, we assembled at about 10 a.m. at the air-base near Brussels where my Dakota was waiting, ready to take off. We were in a happy mood at the thought of getting away for a few hours from the more serious side of the 21st Army Group's activities.

Jack Race, my pilot, had made his flight plan and, having obtained the necessary clearance, we took off into a rather dismal overcast sky and pointed in a westerly direction.

The time passed quickly until we were interrupted by Jack Race phoning through to say that we were now nearing the airstrip and should fasten our seat-belts. The weather was still dull and uninviting, but it was not long before we spotted a very desolate and lonely runway through the windows. It was obviously an emergency landing-ground which the Germans had used to help lame ducks on their return from raids on England and elsewhere. As we circled over, we could see Harry Llewellyn standing beside a Jeep at the edge of the runway, where a smoke-candle had been lit to show us the direction of the wind. Race was in touch with the Jeep by R/T and was satisfying himself that everything was in order. But before he made his final approach he wisely decided to fly very low over the strip to check up on the state of the surface. It did not look very reassuring, for there were a number of scars along it which had been caused either by Allied bombs or the digging-in of mines. In spite of Harry's assurances that everything was O.K., we could not help sharing some doubts as to the correctness of the clearance he had given us. Race appeared satisfied, however, and we were soon gliding in to make our landing, during which I held my breath as the wheels ran over those tell-tale scars. One is never at one's bravest in an aircraft.

The touch-down proved to be a perfect one, and Race, braking fairly sharply, swung the aircraft round and taxied back along our tracks to where the Jeep party was assembled. We were all feeling very cheerful and a buffet bar was opened in the aircraft so that the advance party could enjoy some of the delicacies that we had brought with us. Sufficiently reinforced, we then divided ourselves up between the two Jeeps and set out for Le Touquet.

It was a chilly and cheerless drive, for it had started to drizzle and the countryside appeared to be devoid of inhabitants. Fortunately there were few signs of war other than the usual blown up river or railway bridge. We saw the occasional burnt-out vehicle or tank — no doubt the victims of our fighter-bomber aircraft. As we approached Staples, however, the signs of war and destruction were considerable, for not only had a battle raged in this area but the Allied bombers had given it plenty of attention.

We drove along the north bank of the Conche with the idea of crossing by the bridge that joined Staples with Le Touquet. This bridge had defied attack during the First World War, but it had sustained considerable damage this time — whether by demolition or bomb we did not know. This meant that we had to about-turn and cross the river by another bridge farther up which, although having suffered damage, had been repaired sufficiently to allow a vehicle to pass.

As we arrived at the other side I felt a measure of excitement and expectation and my mind went back to those days at Southwell Park when I used to help select the targets for the 'Cover Plan' bombing operations. What would I find — total destruction and desolation? Or had many of the buildings and villas that I knew so well escaped the effects of bombing after all? The forest looked badly mauled, many trees had been cut down, and there were numerous signs of bomb damage. The old airfield was covered with anti-paratroop obstacles and there were minefields indicated by the usual wire and warning notices. There were trenches and solid concrete pill-boxes camouflaged as far as possible to blend with the trees. What we found upon entering this one-time famous holiday resort was sad, although not unexpected. As we drove slowly along the main road that led to the Hermitage Hotel and the Casino, I looked eagerly around me to pick out those well-remembered villas that used to nestle in the trees on either side. Some were standing apparently unhurt, others were just a mass of rubble, while here and there one appeared to have been converted into some sort of defensive strong-point. We arrived at the hub of pre-war Le Touquet and I left the Jeep to look around. Everything was quiet and peaceful. Not a living soul was to be seen, and the gentle patter of the rain seemed to caress this deserted little town which had lost all its gaiety and laughter.

After looking at the hollow shell of the Hôtel Picardy, and the only slightly damaged Hermitage and Westminster, we drove off to investigate the area around the golf-course and those particular villas that held such vivid memories for me. But here we were to be brought face to face with total devastation. The Golf Hotel had ceased to exist and in its place was a mass of rubble. The golf-course itself was quite unrecognizable, for the magnificent club house had been smashed to pieces and the whole area of the course looked like Kentish hopfields during August. As far as the eye could see, spiked poles had been dug into the ground with wire and booby-traps festooned between them. The poles had, of course, been cut from the beautiful *forêt* and the unnatural clearings were there to see — wounds that would take years to heal. An attack by paratroops would certainly have received a very unpleasant welcome, but in the event none was made. In addition, extensive minefields had been prepared, and I pictured the task that would eventually fall to the lot of the German prisoners-of-war. Let them clear up this foul mess. I felt no sympathy for the casualties that would probably result from these operations.

I then turned to that corner of the *forêt* that particularly interested me. Here the four villas used to stand whose owners had written to me. One had more or less escaped, but two others had been badly smashed up. I paused a few minutes to examine the damage and then drove along until I reached the Allée des Amazons. At the end of this little lane was to be found the fourth villa, Dormey Two, which held such special recollections. I hardly dared proceed. I reached the cul de sac but found myself puzzled and unable to orient myself. It was then that I realized that many of the fir-trees had been cut down; what once had been a delightful garden was now nothing but an untidy and overgrown patch with the entrance to a German dug-out just showing above the long grass. Having got my bearings, I spotted the villa — or what remained of it. One side had been badly blown in, but the roof appeared to be intact. I walked gingerly forward, conscious that there might be mines around, and found things worse than I had at first expected. It soon became obvious that this home had been damaged beyond repair. Great holes in the walls told of near-misses by H.E. bombs. The stairs leading to what was left of the upper storey were held precariously in position by a single prop of wood. Most of the furniture — once so gay and bright — had been looted, but there still remained one or two pieces that were too badly damaged to be worth taking away. The gales and rain had played havoc, and lying in a corner of the lounge were a few books which were mostly torn and wet. Kicking some of the debris aside, I recognized a volume on which my eyes came to rest. It was a book on elephant hunting which had been my bible when I first served with the K.A.R. in Central Africa. When I picked it up I found it intact, though badly soiled by rain. I decided to take it away, and send it back to my old friends as a last offering from their beloved villa.

I felt desperately sad as I looked around and my thoughts revived the past. The owner of the villa and I had served together in Nyasaland and had, during those wonderful leaves from Africa, spent many carefree weeks in this very house. Here one used to find a warmth of friendliness that would be difficult to recapture. I had last stayed here in August 1939, when I was Military Assistant to the Secretary of State for War. The war clouds were building up and I knew that we might be seeing the end of an era, and that disaster was just around the corner. I returned sorrowfully to my Jeep with a lump in my throat, and with misty eyes drove back along the little tree-flanked avenue, bound for Paris-Plage.

We drove along the Rue Saint Jean — the once-gay shopping centre with its smart little *magazins*, its restaurants and its cafés. But here again, all was quiet and no one was to be seen. There were road-blocks at the entrance of each side-road, combined with the inevitable minefields. We walked down to the *plage* which was, of course, covered with beach obstacles, booby-traps and minefields, with pill-boxes sited to command the beaches. I thought of the 'Cover Plan' and how successful it had been, and conjured up a picture of Rommel standing in that very place, expressing satisfaction at the way in which his orders had been carried out.

Turning from the bleak English Channel we retraced our steps up the Rue Saint Jean, and it was just as we had passed a little café, with all its windows boarded up, that we heard a sound and, looking round, saw a door open and a very old lady in a black bombasine dress look out fearfully into the street. She must have been nearer eighty than seventy years of age. With a joyous cry she moved towards us shouting '*les Anglais — les Anglais — les braves Anglais*', and then proceeded to embrace us. This demonstration of goodwill was then followed by a highly seasoned description of what she thought of '*les Sales Boches*' and what wonderful chaps we all were.

We asked her what had happened to the other inhabitants and were told that the Germans had removed everyone. But she had returned from an outlying farm the day before and she expected many others would follow her within a short space of time. Running true to type she asked us whether we had eaten, and we replied that we had not as yet, but would do so on our return to the aircraft. This would never do, she said, and insisted that we follow her into her battered little café.

Because of the blocked windows, candles had to be lit and we were made to sit down round an old and dirty wooden table. With many apologies the old lady explained that she could only give us an omelette, but she had something that was very dear to all Englishmen and which she had hidden from the Germans. She then asked us to help her lift up the soiled linoleum which covered the floor, and when this was done a trap-door with an iron ring was exposed. With some difficulty we prised it open and, in spite of our offers of help, the sturdy old lady insisted on going down the steps herself into the darkness below. We handed her a candle and heard her moving things about as she ferreted around for this very special thing that was loved by all Englishmen. Eventually she reappeared; we helped her up the stairs and closed the trap-door behind her. We now saw the object of her search. It was a bottle — but owing to the dirt and dust it was impossible to recognize the particular liquor it contained. Taking down an old apron which was hanging upon a hook on the wall, she proceeded to wipe away the years of grime and there before us was a bottle of Johnny Walker Black Label Scotch Whisky. She explained that she had kept this hidden from the enemy for such an occasion as this. We must now drink it while she lit her little oil-stove and got busy cooking us the omelette made with some eggs which she had brought from the farm. We naturally protested about making such an inroad upon her food supply, but it was clear that the old lady would be very hurt if we did not accept her hospitality. So we sat down at the table, opened the bottle of whisky and began to drink it neat out of a cracked old cup which she had produced for the purpose. We felt that she would have been grieved if we had suggested adding water to this very special gift.

As she cooked, our spirits rose with the warming effects of this excellent whisky, we were told her story — how her husband and two sons left her when the war broke out and how she had received no word from them ever since. She lived in hopes of their turning up one day, but she appeared quite philosophical about the whole business. She made one thing abundantly clear, and that was her great hatred and loathing of the Germans.

The omelette was enormous and we ate it with chunks of rather stale bread, but we were grateful for the meal and also for the privilege of meeting this brave old Frenchwoman — one of a type which represented the backbone of France.

The time had now arrived to leave and with expressions of gratitude and fond embraces we said our farewells and raised our new-found friend's morale with predictions of an early victory. Glancing at the near-empty bottle on the table, we felt we had better try to pay for what we had received. After a short conference we collected together the few francs which we had between us and decided to offer them to her, hoping that she would not consider such a gesture on our part insulting. We need, however, have had no qualms on this score, for she immediately grabbed the notes and stuffed them into the pockets of her skirt.

So our visit to Le Touquet drew to a close. I had carried out a promise to my friends. It was a sad and depressing day, for it was almost impossible to imagine that Le Touquet would ever be the same again. But the world is resilient and its people soon forget the horrors of the past in their endeavour to build afresh. Today Le Touquet has returned to much what it used to be.

That evening in Brussels I sent off four letters to my friends reporting on my mission.

CHAPTER FIFTEEN: REWARD AT THE SUMMIT

It was after the war. I was enjoying a very pleasant week-end at Le Touquet and, after a round of golf in the early afternoon on a glorious July day, I strolled over to the Casino to while away an hour or so before changing for dinner. It was a Friday evening; a fair number of people had already arrived, and the gamblers appeared to be pretty busy. The *chemin de fer* tables in use were all complete with their nine players so, after asking one of the Casino staff to let me know when there was a vacant seat, I walked into the bar and ordered myself a whisky-and-soda.

I had hardly swallowed my drink before one of the attendants came up and reported that there was a seat available at No. 3 table. I got up and followed him out and sat at No. 6 place. The shoe had reached No. 8 so it looked as if I should have a little time to wait until my turn for the bank came round. I glanced around to see if I knew any of the players. Opposite me was a Greek whom we all called 'the Professor', because he kept a complicated sheet of statistics and played to some system that none of us quite understood. It didn't appear, however, to bring great fortune in its wake, but he used to keep everyone amused. On my left, in No. 5 seat, was a pleasant-looking man: he was stocky in stature, had a strong face and a mop of curly brown hair that was beginning to go grey. His blue eyes were clear and arresting. I tried to guess his nationality, for he was speaking perfect French, and later changed to German with equal fluency. His turn now came for the bank and I went banco and won the coup. My bank came next, but the shoe was on the run and I was defeated at the first deal of the cards.

My next-door neighbour turned and said 'Bad luck', and following this up with 'Are you not General de Guingand?' I admitted that I was and he explained that we had met once or twice during the war. I now realized that he was an American General and I remembered envying him his gift for languages.

The game went on and we chatted quietly until the shoe once again arrived in front of No. 5. I went banco as before, but this time I lost and the red card had appeared indicating the end of that particular shoe. I, therefore, asked this American General to come and have a drink while the croupier shuffled the cards in preparation for the next *partie*.

We made for the bar and perched ourselves on a couple of stools, and I ordered two White Horse whiskies and Perrier, which were quickly produced by our smiling friend the barman. We lifted our glasses and drank to 'happy days' and it was then that the General took out a fine-looking gold case and offered me a cigarette. As he pressed the catch and the case flew open, I noticed a large crest engraved inside the lid. Although not a cigarette smoker at the time I asked him if I could have a look, and was very surprised to find that the engraving was King George VI's Royal Coat-of-Arms. My interest was aroused and I asked him where it came from.

'It was presented to me by your King. It's quite a story,' was his reply, and he followed this up with, 'It is my most treasured possession.'

'I must hear about it.' I said, but just at that moment a flunkey came up and informed us that it was '*Numero cinq pour la main*' — it was the General's bank, and this meant that we should have to go and that I would have to wait for another occasion to hear his story.

I was determined to hear it and so made quite a nuisance of myself until the owner of the case realized that he would have to come clean. With commendable modesty and a little unwillingness, he recounted to me what I consider to be a really exciting and charming story — one of courage and of high adventure — with a delightful ending.

There were some parts that he could not tell me and others that I feel might prove embarrassing if I were to repeat them, but as far as possible I will narrate the tale as told to me during talks which we managed to have that week-end.

It was the autumn of 1939 and Great Britain was at war, while America had embarked upon an era of benevolent neutrality. My neighbour of the *chemy* table was then a successful businessman connected with the steel industry — he was also an officer on the United States Army Reserve. He was married to a Canadian and his sympathies were one hundred per cent with the Allies in their war against Germany. From the very start he experienced an intense desire to play a part and get into the fight if he could. As he was an admirer of Great Britain he volunteered to join the British Army, for it appeared to him that before long there might be some chance of fighting in Finland. However, his hopes were soon dashed to the ground: the British authorities were reluctant to commission a United States Army officer because of the obvious diplomatic complications. So that was that, and for the time being, this militant American found no opportunity of playing a part in the war against Hitler.

The much-maligned War Office, no doubt impressed by his capabilities, tipped off Intelligence about this promising material. It was not long before he was approached and asked whether he would be prepared to work with this particular organization, and on his next visit to Europe it was suggested that he call at one of those 'cover' offices in London, where he met a leading figure in the British Secret Service. It was immediately recognized that here was an ideal operator. An American citizen, who would have a reasonable entrée into enemy territory — an industrialist, who was connected with the enormously important field of steel production. He had many contacts with the steel men in Germany; was an exceptional linguist who spoke French, German and Russian fluently; and on top of all this, he possessed a soldier's training and outlook. It was not surprising, therefore, that great keenness was shown to enlist his services, and so by about the end of the year the American had agreed to help.

The sort of work and assignments that might now come his way required a special type of courage; the risks involved and the penalties of detection were made quite plain, but were accepted cheerfully. It was understood, however, that if the United States should require his services at a later date, particularly if they entered the war, he would have to terminate his connection with British Intelligence.

During our talks I found it difficult to get any information on his activities during the winter of 1939-40, but I didn't press him, for I appreciated that it is more often than not impossible for a secret agent ever to disclose details of his work and associations. There is a high code of honour which limits what can be divulged, particularly where any indiscretion might jeopardize someone else's security. He therefore restricted his narrative to the events that led up to the gold cigarette-case.

Sometime towards the end of March 1940 he was informed of a proposed mission to Germany. The British Admiralty was apparently very worried at reports concerning the construction for the German Navy of small 200-ton two-man submarines, and it was considered of the utmost importance that some reliable and detailed information should be obtained concerning them. The American was asked whether he was prepared to volunteer, and he agreed to accept the assignment. At his final briefing he was told that any information as to the general state of military preparedness in Germany would also be welcome. Then, just as he was taking his leave, another request was added to his already formidable task.

'We are piecing together a pattern of reports which suggest that the German Army may be preparing to invade Western Europe somewhere around the first week in May. Naturally any confirmation would be of vital significance and must be got back to us with the minimum of delay.'

This was about as far as he got with his story on that first evening we met, for the Casino had more or less cleared, due to the approaching dinner-hour, and only about half a dozen people remained sitting round the bar.

My American friend looked at his watch and said 'Well, I must get going, but will see you tomorrow, no doubt. It was nice meeting you.' And so we left, but he had told me enough to whet my appetite for more, and I was determined to pounce upon him at the first available opportunity to hear the end of this fascinating story.

I was lucky enough to bump into him again the very next day at the Westminster Hotel. I had just returned from a swim in the *piscine*, for it was a very hot morning. He was dressed in riding clothes, and had been out with his family in the *forêt*.

I asked him to give me half an hour and he appeared willing. I led him to two comfortable chairs placed in rather an isolated position under a gaily coloured umbrella. A waiter came up and I ordered our drinks; when these arrived he started off as if we were still sitting in the Casino Bar.

'Well, it was early April when I left for Germany — a respectable American citizen bent upon doing what business I could with some of the German steel barons. That part was fairly easy,' he added, 'For I had the perfect cover — as representative of my company — meeting a number of people whom I already knew quite well.'

Very soon after his arrival he made for the Ruhr and visited several steelworks with which his company had been in business relations for a number of years. By good fortune, one of these was engaged in rolling the very wide ship plates which were used in building these two-man submarines. This fact he had known before leaving England and had, therefore, worked out a very carefully prepared story which would result in his obtaining interviews with certain of the leading men concerned.

'It was really remarkably easy for me, being a steel man, to get fairly accurate information about the German steel production and its war uses. This all happened quite normally,' he explained. 'But the really difficult tasks lay ahead. I did, however, learn sufficient to enable me to plan the next step in my quest to obtain detailed information regarding these little submarines. As often happens in life, something unexpected turned up and I had the most extraordinary bit of luck. I came upon the exact date of the German invasion of France and the Lowlands — quite by accident!' This was enthralling; I could hardly wait to hear the next part of his adventures.

He had arranged a meeting with the Managing Director of this particular plate-works who had been a friend of his in peacetime. This, in itself, was not a particularly easy business, for in those days all the steel and munition works in Germany were under very strict military control and surveillance, and officers of high rank were constantly visiting the factories.

I think it better if I narrate this eventful morning in his own words:

'I turned up at the company's general offices at about nine o'clock and handed in my card, and I was shown into the Managing Director's office. As I entered he got up with a friendly smile and appeared genuinely pleased to see me. He indicated a comfortable brown leather chair, sat down himself in another close beside me, and we started chatting. He asked me about America. Would she come into the war? I replied that it would take a lot to bring her in, and that I hoped Germany would not do anything to precipitate matters.

"If you only knew what I was really up to," I thought, and thanked God my looks did not betray what I was thinking.

"Oh, I don't think you need worry much on that score," he replied, "I doubt whether the war is going to last all that long; France and Great Britain are both pretty rotten and we don't believe their hearts are really in the fight. We've seen enough of Mr. Chamberlain to know that Great Britain won't get very tough under his leadership."

We then got round to steel, a subject that steel men anywhere find it hard to be reticent about. My friend wanted to know about production in America, and it was comparatively simple to ply him with some carefully worded questions concerning German output and production plans. The answers I received were of great interest and not a little frightening. Germany was certainly organizing on a gigantic scale. At the right moment I was able to ascertain where these wide ship plates were being sent. The submarines were being constructed at Kiel and I learned enough to know that I must go there to obtain the information I had been told to get.

After we had been chatting for well over an hour, the Managing Director's secretary came in unobtrusively and announced that Lieutenant-General —— of the General Staff, was there to see him. I immediately recognized the name, for he was a soldier of considerable reputation and prestige in Nazi circles.

My host appeared to be very impressed and not a little excited at this news, so I got up and said I should have to be getting along. He saw me into his secretary's office, bowed obsequiously to the General and turning to the girl, said "Please see that this gentleman's car is here to take him back to his hotel." He shook hands as if he was rather glad to see me go and didn't make any attempt to introduce me to his visitor. In the meantime the General had strolled into the main office, looking as if he was in a hurry to get done with whatever business he had come to discuss.

I followed the secretary to the outer room and my friend returned to his office, but I noticed that his door was not quite closed. Just as I was following the secretary into the passage, she turned round and said, "Don't trouble to come, sir, the car may have been parked a little way away, and I shall have it sent round to pick you up at this entrance."

I thanked her and, turning away, made for a chair on which to sit until she returned. I could hear voices talking, but they were not clear enough for me to follow the conversation. I moved a bit nearer the door, feeling not a little frightened, and after a minute or more the voices became much louder; obviously this talk was not being conducted on such a friendly basis as the one I had just terminated with the Managing Director.

And then I heard the General say in a loud and rasping voice "*Das wird zu spät sein; es geht los am 10 Mai*" — "This will be too late; it starts on 10th May!" My heart must have missed a couple of beats and I had difficulty in maintaining a calm demeanour, especially as the private secretary returned almost at the same moment and told me that my car was waiting outside. Gratefully I picked up my hat and followed her out, but I was thinking hard as I went. Could this 10th May be their D-Day? In view of the indications already received by the British Intelligence Service, this date and the context surrounding it were surely too much of a coincidence. I decided that it was certainly worth passing back.'

The next few days were glossed over in one or two sentences. The American returned to his hotel feeling a little worried. Might the General have asked who he was and have arranged to have him watched? After twenty-four hours everything appeared to be quite normal — this gave him time to work out a plan for getting to Kiel and to be employed where the information that he was after would be available. From what he said, or perhaps from what he left unsaid, it was pretty clear that he had made contact with someone in our Secret Service. In the first place he wanted these all-important words spoken by the German General transmitted to England and it was also necessary to obtain additional papers, identity cards, clothes, etc., that would allow him to carry out the next phase of his assignment.

During his journey from the Ruhr northwards towards the Baltic States, he noted signs that fitted in with the pattern, if D-Day was going to be the 10th May. For instance, there appeared to be feverish activity in the Ruhr and this extended through the Rhineland. But what was more significant was the traffic — military traffic particularly — that was moving from Cologne towards Maastricht and Aachen.

Then there was a short period when he disappeared from view, but emerged on the Baltic as a refugee from Riga. This proved to be excellent 'cover', for it gave him a plausible excuse for his slight foreign accent when speaking German. It also made entry into Kiel a comparatively easy matter, for at that time all those who claimed German origin, and yet were domiciled outside Germany, were called '*volksdeutsche*' and were admitted into the German Army and labour ranks.

On arrival at Kiel he had no difficulty whatever in obtaining employment at the factory where these heavy ship plates were being used in the construction of the small submarines. In all he remained about two weeks in Kiel. I asked him how he felt during this time as a spy.

'At first I was rather frightened', he said 'but as the days wore on I became quite confident. I suppose this was due to the fact that things were a bit easier than I had anticipated. I should say that this reaction of confidence is one to be most careful of, if one becomes a professional spy. It could so easily lead to an indiscretion and eventual detection.'

He began work as a labourer, but it was soon realized that he possessed qualifications well above those required by an ordinary artisan so he was taken on as an interpreter in the administrative office. Coming from Riga, it was quite natural that he should speak Russian as well as German; because of these languages he was put to work on some documents which the German admiralty had obtained from France and Russia.

During this stage he had numerous opportunities of getting the information that he was after. The difficulty, however, was to commit everything to memory as he was unable to put anything on paper — this would have been far too dangerous, for he never knew when he might not be subjected to a search. He had been given a lot of the gadgets that were part and parcel of a spy's equipment, such as invisible ink, pencils with hidden chambers for hiding notes, linings to suits that could be written on, etc. He decided, however, not to use these aids to memory, in order to minimize the risk. The stakes were high, the penalty, if he was detected, was summary execution by the German security troops or the Gestapo.

'On one occasion when I was working at Kiel,' he told me, 'I was sent on a trip by train and was travelling between

Hamburg and Cologne when the passengers were thoroughly searched by the German S.S. Security Police. This was one of my worst experiences, and it required the most rigid self-control not to convey a guilty impression. I was extremely glad that man is not made in the same way as those animals which emit a pungent odour from a certain gland when really frightened!'

I could so well picture the scene he described to me. The jack-booted police coming nearer and nearer. Were they after him? Was this only a routine check? Could he disguise his acute anxiety? These were the sort of questions that must have coursed through his brain.

Finishing this part of his tale he said 'Had there been the slightest doubt about the story I told them, and had they found anything on my body in the way of memos and sketches, my fate would, of course, have been sealed.'

At this stage I ordered two more drinks.

'I'm afraid I can't tell you much about how I got out of Germany except that it was by British submarine,' he added.

Apparently, having obtained the information required, he contacted a British Secret Service agent and applied for his return passage. He was later given his instructions and assisted to the rendezvous on a windy and desolate part of the Baltic shore. This was, of course, a very anxious time, for one little slip would spell the failure of his mission. Imagine his feelings when waiting for the rubber dinghy to come ashore. There was always the unpleasant thought that this might be a frame-up and that he was being used as the bait for a British submarine.

But all went well and my friend is generous in his praises of the British Intelligence organization, its meticulous planning and its incredible resourcefulness. Even in the submarine his troubles were not entirely over, for somewhere in the vicinity of the Kattegat they were subjected to a depth-charge attack and had to lie submerged deep down for many hours.

'Unless one has done a job like this before' he told me, 'it is quite impossible to appreciate what it means to step ashore in a friendly country. One never realizes at just what terrific tension one has been living over a long period. You don't know whether you want to cry or sing, or to go to sleep for forty-eight hours!'

On arrival in London, which was about 16th May, he reported to his headquarters and handed over all the information he had been able to collect. The message regarding the probable date of the German Western Offensive had got through all right, and had of course proved to be entirely accurate. That the British authorities were pleased with the work of this 'neutral volunteer', there can be no doubt. Being a modest man he said very little about this part of the business. He did let it slip, however, that he had been put in for a British decoration — I believe it was a D.S.O.

After a short rest he was ordered by the War Department in Washington to Paris, which was now under German occupation, with instructions to stay there as long as possible and to observe as much as he could. He managed to remain in the French capital until October 1940, during which period he paid several visits to London in aircraft provided by the British Intelligence. After that he was ordered to report for duty with G.2 (Intelligence) of the General Staff in Washington.

This was really only the first phase of this remarkable man's wartime activities. There must be at least another chapter or two to be told, and I hope sincerely that our mutual love of Le Touquet will mean that we can meet again in those pleasant surroundings, and that he will be prepared to tell me some more, in between the games of *chemin de fer*, or sitting peacefully on a veranda of a villa or hotel.

Now let me describe the really delightful sequel to this very gallant adventure. As I have already said, this American was put up for a British decoration, which he richly deserved. He was, however, a reserve officer of the United States Army who was about to be called up for active service, and therefore permission had to be obtained from the War Department in Washington. But, sad to relate, that permission was not forthcoming, because the United States was not at war. This ruling naturally came as a disappointment, but, in keeping with his character, he put the matter behind him and forgot about it.

He returned to England in 1941 with the mission of taking part in observing the British Special Operations (S.O.E.) and Commando organizations which were then being formed in the United Kingdom.

One morning his Chief asked the American — he was now a Colonel — to come and see him. After an exchange of civilities he said 'The King would like to see you, and has asked you to come along to Buckingham Palace next Thursday evening. The Queen will also be there. You've never met them, have you?' he asked. 'I will take you along, so meet me here at about 5.30 — uniform, of course.'

The American was naturally very eager for this meeting, not only because he possessed his countrymen's usual curiosity concerning British Royalty, but also because he had an immense admiration for the way they served the British people during such a difficult period of the war.

At the appointed hour they arrived at Buckingham Palace. The car drove through one of the great gates and then under the arch that led to the entrance to the private apartments. In accordance with the usual machine-line precision connected with events in the Royal Household, a member of the staff was waiting to take them up in the lift, and upon getting out, Tommy Lascelles[25] was standing there ready to conduct them into Their Majesties' presence.

In common with most people who were summoned by the late King to meet him informally, the Colonel was struck by the simplicity of the occasion and also by Their Majesties' charm and ease of manner. He was made to feel at home immediately, and the whole visit went off most pleasantly.

The time had arrived to leave and after he had made his bow, the King took him by the arm and accompanied him to the door.

It was then that His Majesty said, 'Do you smoke, Colonel?'

'Yes I do, Sir,' came the reply.

The King then put his hand into the side-pocket of his naval jacket and pulled out a beautiful gold cigarette-case. Slipping it into the American's hands, he said:

'Well, you might find this useful. It will also remind you of my gratitude for what you did for us.'

It all happened so quietly and informally that the American was altogether bewildered. In fact, he told me that he hardly appreciated what had really taken place. Spluttering some quite inadequate words of thanks, he left this understanding monarch and was carried down in the lift. It had been most beautifully done.

The time had slipped quickly by and he glanced at his watch, saying, 'Well, that's about the long and the short of it, and you can no doubt understand how I value that gift.'

Automatically, his hand went to his hip pocket and out came the gold cigarette-case, which he snapped open and held towards me.

---

[25] H.M.'s Private Secretary.

'Oh, of course, you don't smoke them — sorry!'

But once again I was able to see the Royal Coat-of-arms, and I also noticed something that I had missed before: underneath were engraved these words:

'Colonel ———, 10th May, 1940.'

Having heard the whole story I appreciated the significance of this date.

It was a 'kingly gift' in every sense of the word.

It was only recently that I again met my American friend and I showed him the manuscript of this story, asking him to make any corrections where necessary. He returned it and there was only one alteration — I had described his eyes as being brown when they are really blue... You see, I happen to be colour-blind!

CHAPTER SIXTEEN: ROYAL OCCASIONS

It has been my pleasure and privilege to meet both the late King George VI and his elder brother, the Duke of Windsor, on several occasions. George VI visited our Headquarters in the Middle East and Europe during the war. It was not until after the war, however, that my wife and I met the Windsors.

In 1946, soon after our arrival in Cannes on holiday, we received an invitation to dine with them. I had met the Duke when he was Prince of Wales on one or two official occasions, and again when we had been drawn against each other in the Army Squash Racquets Championships — I lost the encounter. I was, however, very keen to meet the Duchess.

I found the Duke rather a sad figure, for he had obviously felt his isolation in the West Indies during most of the war, and he used to talk to me for hours about the great events of those years on which he was not fully briefed. He was writing his book *A King's Story*, and used to return to his study at fixed times to work on it. As I was writing my *War Memoirs* at the same time, it gave us something in common, and we also used to play the odd game of golf. Whatever views one might hold as to whether King Edward VIII should have given up the throne, I have always felt sad that such an intelligent member of the Royal Family, possessing so marked a personality, should not have been available to the British people, especially during time of war. But perhaps he was too discerning and had too much a mind of his own ever to have made a success of constitutional monarchy. He is an excellent conversationalist and very well informed on a wide range of subjects.

The Duchess is an intriguing character. She can be most entertaining and charming, but can, with sufficient provocation, let her hair down! She has been called the best housekeeper in Europe, and if this means that she runs her house well, it is certainly no exaggeration. The food, drink and service at her luncheons and dinner-parties are of the very highest order. I have always felt that she must have made a vow after the abdication that the standard must never be allowed to drop below that to which the Duke had been accustomed when he was King. The servants were perfectly drilled, and most of the glass, cutlery and linen on her table came from the Royal household. They bore the Royal Cypher 'Edward VIII', and were, therefore, of no use to his brother who succeeded him. During a meal I was fascinated by the way in which the Duchess could carry on an animated conversation with her neighbours, and at the same time maintain a strict watch on the way the meal was being served. Her servants were netted on to her own wave-length, and would at an almost imperceptible sign from their mistress attend to a guest's requirements or perform some other function.

The attitude of certain English visitors to the Riviera used to amuse me. They would become most vocal in their criticism of our being friendly with the Windsors.

'I wouldn't go near that woman, let alone dine at her table,' they would declare.

'We shall see' I used to say under my breath.

And time out of number, those very people, if an invitation turned up, would accept with alacrity. They would, however, be honest enough in most cases to admit that they had changed their views about the Duchess, acknowledging her magnetic personality.

I had a similar experience with Hore-Belisha when I was serving him at the War Office. Friends would say, 'How can you work with that man? It must be frightful.' I would often arrange for these critics to meet my Chief, and it was amusing to see how they fell for his charm and wit. The world would be a happier place if people would reserve judgement until they have personal knowledge of one another.

Our nurse, for example, adopted from the start the general English outlook towards the Windsors. 'How the General can go and play golf with the Duke or dine with the Duchess, I really can't understand,' was heard on a number of occasions. 'I know what I would like to do to her,' she would add, and then mumble something with her lips tightly closed. I never found out, however, what she had conjured up in her mind as a fitting punishment for this American lady whom she regarded as having removed a King from his throne.

One evening we gave a small drinks party to which the Windsors were invited, and it was extremely amusing to observe the steps taken by Nannie to prepare herself for the occasion. A flashy but unbecoming dress was purchased of the type that could only be sold to an English tourist. My daughter was titivated up ready for the formal presentation and as the time of the party approached, Nannie became nearly hysterical in her excitement. Everything went off quite well and forever afterwards Nannie was unstinting in her praise of the Windsors, and would never lose an opportunity of informing her friends how she had spoken to them. I had to twit her about this '*volte-face*', but she denied indignantly that she had ever expressed antagonistic sentiments about them!

An evening as the Windsors' guest during another stay in Cannes ended in a social fiasco from my point of view.

The Windsors were staying once again at their Château at Antibes and very kindly, on hearing of my arrival, asked me to dinner — an invitation which I gladly accepted. It was a very large party and there were several interesting guests including Elsa Maxwell, whom I had never met but knew, of course, by reputation.

It was a gloriously warm night and we foregathered for cocktails on a charming veranda, well provided with a selection of colourful and comfortable garden furniture. The dinner was perfect as usual and the Duchess's active eye was still directing the footmen and other servants whenever any little matter required attention. There was one little mopping-up operation that had to be performed every now and then. The Duke has a peculiar and nervous habit of breaking up his bread or roll into small pieces and by the time he has finished with it remnants are scattered all over the table and the floor. A little tray and brush are then produced to clear the decks before he is allowed to start disintegrating another piece.

It had been rumoured that after dinner there would be bridge and canasta for those who played these games — otherwise one could relax in the chaises-longues on the terrace. As this sort of party generally went on rather late, I was a bit worried lest I should not have time to pay my intended visit to the Casino. My stay in Cannes was of such short duration that I did not wish to miss even one night's gambling. One of my fellow-guests was a peer, who had something to do with one of the big insurance companies. Chatting after dinner, we found that our thoughts were concentrating on the same problem, and so we made a plan.

Although I had a car and chauffeur awaiting me outside, I agreed to explain to the Duke and the Duchess that I was being given a lift back to Cannes by my newly-found friend.

We then arranged that as soon after midnight as possible, when one or other of us had come to the end of a rubber of bridge or a game of canasta, he would get up and ask permission to go.

Initially I cut out at bridge and lay back contentedly in one of the chairs, talking a lot of nonsense to some other guests. Under the beautiful evening sky, and after the extremely good food and drink we had consumed, we became a bit drowsy and conversation rather sporadic. Eventually my turn came to play bridge, and I pulled myself together and got started. At about 12.30 his lordship finished a rubber and our table followed suit, so the opportunity arrived for which we had been waiting. My partner in deception skilfully made his excuses; I added mine, and explained that as I had just had an exhausting flight from Australia and was badly in need of sleep, I should like to accept a lift and go back to bed at my hotel in Cannes. I was pressed to stay, but I made it clear that an early night was so essential that I must tear myself away. After saying good-bye I joined my friend in his car, and on the way down the drive popped my head out of the window and told my own driver to follow us to the Palm Beach Casino.

As we walked together into the gaming-rooms, I said to my companion, 'I shall go banco for the first bank that is going after entering the rooms.'

He nodded his head and we were ushered through the revolving doors by two attendants. The first table I came to had no bank worth while or which could not be dealt with by those already playing. To my right, however, I heard that well-known cry, '*Une banque de soixante milles.*'

I stepped smartly over and shouted '*Banco.*'

The bored croupier looked up and, as no one at the table appeared to claim priority, the cards were dealt. The croupier passed two over in my direction and I picked them up and fanned them out close to my eyes, ensuring that my companion could see them. My heart missed a beat, for they were a king and an eight. I gave a smug smile, thinking how clever I had been, and threw the cards face upwards on the table, saying '*Le huit*' Slowly my opponent, the banker, drew his cards towards him, and equally slowly turned up the nearest one. It was a five — so far so good. He then proceeded to turn up the edge of the other card, so that only he could see its value. Suddenly I felt less confident, as this very fat and greasy-looking gentleman started turning the card over. The expression on his face never changed, but I'm afraid that mine did, for it was the four of spades. He had dealt himself a 'natural nine' which beat my eight.

Ah well, I thought, one can't be lucky every time, and put my hand into my breast pocket to bring out my wallet. But, horror of horrors! it wasn't there. I began to go cold all over and beads of sweat broke out on my forehead. In the first place a croupier should not accept a *banco* unless he sees the money to cover the bet. This, of course, particularly applies to itinerant punters. He looked up expectantly and with scarcely veiled hostility. '*Soixante milles francs*' he repeated in a metallic voice, as if I didn't know. I glanced across at the banker who was staring at me with an unpleasant sneer on his face. There was complete silence all round me, and then the croupier started making those nasty little sucking noises with his lips that brings a Casino official to the scene of trouble. I began to feel more and more embarrassed, especially as my wallet contained nearly 300,000 francs, and foreign exchange was not easy to come by in those days. I knew that I had arrived at the Windsor's Chateau with my wallet, for I had extracted it from my pocket to give my chauffeur a mille note so that he might have some dinner. It was then that I heard a whisper to my left — it was my fellow-guest, asking whether he could be of any help. This was, of course, music in my ears, but nevertheless horribly embarrassing, for until that night he had not known me from Adam, and it was a situation that might well appear most suspicious. I must have an honest face.

'I've lost my wallet,' I explained 'and must have sixty thousand francs to pay into the bank.'

Without a murmur, he drew from his pocket a roll of notes, and peeled off six of ten thousand denomination. He handed them over to me and I threw them on the table with a feeling of intense relief. I hastily pulled my trusting friend away and explained about my lost note-case and when I had last seen it.

'It must have fallen out in my car' he suggested, and we made for the Casino entrance. But, in spite of a thorough search, the missing wallet was nowhere to be found. I went over to my car, knowing full well that it could not be there, but nevertheless I had a good look inside without success. He suggested that it might have fallen out at the Windsor's party, but it was very difficult to imagine how this could have happened in view of the fact that I always kept it in the inside breast pocket of my dinner-jacket. But I had to search everywhere, so I returned to the Casino, made for the telephone boxes and asked the glamorous blonde operator to put a call through to the Windsors. Before long she nodded to me. I picked up the receiver and heard the Windsors' butler at the other end.

'Who is that speaking?' he asked.

I gave my name, and — glory be — even before I had a chance of explaining what I was ringing up about, he said:

'Oh, yes, Sir Francis, no doubt you are telephoning about your wallet — well, it has been found and we have it here.'

With a sigh of relief I expressed my gratitude, and was on the point of explaining that I would send my chauffeur to collect it when the butler cut in saying, 'Just a moment, sir,' and a couple of seconds later the Duke was speaking to me.

'It that you, Freddie? I am glad we've found your wallet. It must have slipped out when you were lying stretched out on the veranda after dinner.' And then he added 'The Duchess and I are very amused to hear where you are, for we understood that you were so tired that you were rushing back to bed. We thought that by now you would already be tucked up between the sheets!'

There was a slight pause which made me realize what an unfortunate predicament I was in. I felt myself getting red in the face. However, the Duke has a keen sense of humour; he roared with laughter and then handed the telephone over to the Duchess, who was quite charming and suggested that I had been badly caught out — and so I had.

When my chauffeur got back with the wallet, I tipped the telephone girl a ridiculous amount, paid my debt and hastened back to the *salle privée*. As I passed through the doors once again, I heard the croupier's plaintive cry, '*Une banque de soixante-cinq milles*.' I moved over and, lo and behold, there was my old adversary running another bank. Someone at the table said, '*Avec la table*,' but I pounced into the fray and shouted *banco*, and this time flourished a fat wad of notes for the croupier and all to see.

The cards were dealt and mine added up to five. I said, '*Pas de carte*,' a thing I rarely do when holding a five, for I usually draw. Slowly the banker turned up his cards — a nine and a six were exposed on the table. I kept a straight face and, after a moment's pause, he drew another card from the shoe. He turned it over and I was thrilled to see that it was an eight. So I had beaten him. I placed my cards on the table, and the croupier examined them as if he did not credit it. He then passed over the chips without great enthusiasm and I had made good my unfortunate coup with interest.

During the Royal Tour of South Africa, when I was living in Southern Rhodesia, I received an invitation — a Royal Command I think it's called — for my wife and me to spend the following Sunday with King George VI and the Royal Family in Pretoria — an invitation which we gladly accepted.

It was a beautiful autumn morning and the Government House gardens were looking their loveliest. We were expecting to find a large number of guests but, on the contrary, we were the only two invited. It was quite a simple family affair and all the more enjoyable for that.

I had met the King on a number of occasions during the war for, as I have already mentioned, he had visited both the Eighth Army and the 21st Army Groups in the field, and like all Englishmen I admired the way he carried out his Royal duties under the testing conditions of war. He set a real example to his people throughout the Commonwealth in a role that was unexpectedly thrust upon him.

He spent a day or two with us in Holland not long after the bitter failure of Arnhem and it was obvious that he really enjoyed getting away from the restricted life he was forced to lead in England and to have a chance of mingling with his troops. He lived with us at Montgomery's Tactical Headquarters which was then situated just outside Eindhoven, and he couldn't have been more cheerful or friendly. It was as if he were a schoolboy playing truant! We all slept in caravans and the first evening, as we were getting ready for dinner in the Mess tent, one of his equerries came over to my caravan and asked me in a very confidential manner whether by any chance

I had a bottle of whisky. Apparently the King felt like a sundowner and knowing Montgomery's abstemious habits was not certain that drinks would be available at dinner.

I quickly assured my visitor that the Mess was well stocked and that my Chief was very broad-minded so far as other people were concerned. Nevertheless, I quickly handed over a bottle of whisky and felt privileged to be able to honour so promptly a Royal command.

Montgomery is a great showman and he excelled himself on this occasion. He had asked the King whether he would be willing to present a number of decorations during his visit, and in addition to bestow the accolade on General Dempsey and myself as we had recently been knighted. It turned out to be quite an historic occasion, for Montgomery told me that no reigning monarch had knighted a soldier in the field since Agincourt. I felt very proud and humble and the moving little ceremony took place within sound of the guns.

After the King left, Montgomery told me an amusing story about his batman. During the visit the batman asked His Majesty's valet what the King did when he went to bed.

'Oh, he washes his socks of course!' came the reply.

Swallowing this hook, line and sinker, the batman reported this interesting piece of information to Montgomery with astonishment.

Now back to Pretoria. My *War Memoirs* had recently been published and had proved a far greater success than I had ever dreamed possible. Montgomery's own *Memoirs* were not written until many years later, but he had produced two factual accounts of the campaigns in which he had played so distinguished a part. They were called *El Alamein to the River Sangro* and *Normandy to the Baltic*, and have been mentioned in an earlier chapter.

During luncheon, the King turned to me and asked why I had not sent him a copy of my book. Almost blushing, I told him that I had not thought he would be interested and that I was very diffident about distributing my wares unasked. But as he wished to have the book, I would see to it that it was delivered to him the next day.

The Queen then said 'The King, I'm sure, would like you to autograph it for him, but,' she added with a smile, 'I suggest you don't inscribe it as your Chief did his book, which he recently sent the King.'

I politely inquired what had been written, and as far as I can recollect it ran as follows:

Your Majesty,
I am sure you will find this book intensely interesting.
Montgomery of Alamein.

How wonderful to have Montgomery's superb confidence in his own achievements!

I once related this story to him and his reply was simply: 'What's wrong in that? They were interesting, weren't they?'

ACKNOWLEDGEMENTS

To C. B. for reading the typescript and making various helpful suggestions and comments, to Horace Flather for his most useful advice and comments, and to Radford Jordan for the extremely able way in which he corrected the proofs. I should also like to thank my secretary, Elsa Estersson, for so laboriously typing the first manuscript from my almost unreadable handwriting.

F. W. DE G.

The author quotes in this book from the following copyright sources: *A Soldier's Story* by General Omar Bradley (publishers, Eyre & Spottiswoode Ltd., proprietors, Holt, Rinehart and Winston Inc.); *The Second World War* by Winston Churchill (Cassell & Co. Ltd.); *Lord Wavell* by Major-General R. J. Collins (Hodder & Stoughton Ltd.); *The Memoirs of Field-Marshal Montgomery* (Collins, Sons & Co. Ltd.); *Operation Victory* by Francis de Guingand (Hodder & Stoughton Ltd.); *The Sunday Times*. He gladly acknowledges his indebtedness for the permissions given.

A NOTE TO THE READER

If you have enjoyed this book enough to leave a review on **Amazon** and **Goodreads**, then we would be truly grateful.
Sapere Books

Sapere Books is an exciting new publisher of brilliant fiction and popular history.

To find out more about our latest releases and our monthly bargain books visit our website: **saperebooks.com**

Printed in Great Britain
by Amazon